Success with the Gentle Art of VERBAL SELF-DEFENSE

Also by Suzette Haden Elgin

THE GENTLE ART OF VERBAL SELF-DEFENSE

MORE ON THE GENTLE ART OF VERBAL SELF-DEFENSE

THE LAST WORD ON THE GENTLE ART OF VERBAL
SELF-DEFENSE

MASTERING THE GENTLE ART OF VERBAL
SELF-DEFENSE (audiocassette)

Success with
the Gentle Art of
VERBAL
SELF-DEFENSE

Suzette Haden Elgin, Ph.D.

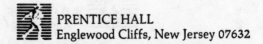

PRENTICE HALL
Englewood Cliffs, New Jersey 07632

Prentice-Hall International (UK) Limited, *London*
Prentice-Hall of Australia Pty. Limited, *Sydney*
Prentice-Hall Canada, Inc., *Toronto*
Prentice-Hall Hispanoamericana, S.A., *Mexico*
Prentice-Hall of India Private Limited, *New Delhi*
Prentice-Hall of Japan, Inc., *Tokyo*
Simon & Schuster Asia Pte. Ltd., *Singapore*
Editora Prentice-Hall do Brasil, Ltda., *Rio de Janeiro*

Library of Congress Cataloging-in-Publication Data

Elgin, Suzette Haden.
    Success with the gentle art of verbal self-defense / by Suzette
Haden Elgin.
        p. cm.
    Bibliography: p.
    Includes index.
    ISBN 0-13-688573-X. — ISBN 0-13-688581-0 (pbk.)
    1. Verbal self-defense 2. Business communication — Psychological
aspects. 3. Success in business. I. Title.
BF637.V47E434   1989
153.6—dc20   89-8388
                                                                   CIP

BOMC offers recordings and compact discs, cassettes
and records. For information and catalog write to
BOMR, Camp Hill, PA 17012.

PRENTICE HALL
BUSINESS & PROFESSIONAL DIVISION
A division of Simon & Schuster
Englewood Cliffs, New Jersey 07632

Printed in the United States of America

Preface

When I first began teaching at San Diego State University, I found myself both amazed and distressed by the vulnerability of my students to verbal abuse. SDSU is a large urban campus, and many of my students were adults and heads of families; nevertheless, they seemed to be almost defenseless against verbal attacks. I was a linguist, trained to observe patterns in languages and to describe them. It seemed to me that the most useful task I could perform in putting that training to use was to look at the language of verbal violence just as I would have looked at a language that had not yet been studied or written down. My goal was to make the grammar of English verbal abuse readily available to my students, and to others who might need it — so that verbal victims could learn to defend themselves, and verbal abusers could learn better ways of communicating.

Out of that project came my first book on the subject, *The Gentle Art of Verbal Self-Defense.* That book was a linguistic emergency handbook for dealing with one-on-one verbal confrontations. The response it drew made it clear that problems with verbal abuse, far from being confined to college students, were an epidemic at every level of our society. Two more books in the Gentle Art series explained the material to cover language interactions of other kinds — written language, public speaking, and listening skills. The third book introduced the concept of *syntonics,* a term taken from music theory and telegraphy, which I defined as "the science of language harmony." The book you are now reading takes the Gentle Art system and applies it specifically to the communication needs of professionals and executives. It adds advanced communication strategies to the system, along with several new syntonics techniques.

If you have read the earlier books you will find the terms and concepts used here familiar. If not, you will find an overview of the system included as an appendix of this book for your use as a quick and convenient reference source.

My grateful thanks go to Virginia Satir, to John Grinder, to George Miller, to Thomas Gordon, to Leonard Newmark, and to the many other scholars and researchers whose work laid the foundations on which mine is based. And thanks are due, as always, to my students, my clients, my readers, and my long-suffering household. Any mistakes or omissions are my fault, and mine alone.

If you have any questions about the subject of this book that are not answered, or if I can help you in any way with the problems that it addresses, please feel free to contact me directly.

Suzette Haden Elgin, Ph.D.
Ozark Center for Language Studies
PO Box 1137
Huntsville, AR 72740

How to Use
This Book

This book is intended to provide you with a complete program for the application of the *Gentle Art* system to your needs as an executive or professional. It contains the following:

1. Twelve chapters, presenting facts, concepts, and techniques.
2. Twelve Workout Sections, to help you gain full control of the information in the corresponding chapters.
3. A concise overview of the basic *Gentle Art* system, for reference and review.
4. An extensive list of references and recommended readings, to help you expand your information base and to supplement your reading in areas that are of particular interest to you.
5. A complete and thorough index, to give you convenient access to the book's contents.

The Workout Sections that follow each chapter have three major purposes:

1. To provide opportunities to practice techniques presented in the chapter.
2. To expand on and supplement the information presented in the chapter.
3. To provide resources that will enable you to tailor the book to your personal needs.

You will find a variety of different materials in the Workouts from which to choose those most appropriate for you. There are supplementary quotations ("Sight Bites") from many sources. There are recommendations for articles that are directly related to the chapter and would make valuable immediate reading. And there are numerous "pen and pencil" activities — as well as oral ones — designed to increase your skill and confidence with the material.

Above all — ENJOY the book.

Contents

5   Language and the Business/Professional Domain, 76

6   Malpractice of the Mouth, 95

7   Language and the Time Domain, 125

8   Language and the Public Relations Domain, 149

9   Semantic Modulation, 184

10 Language and the Personal Domain, 204

11 Lying, *229*

12 Conclusion: The Reality Bridge, *250*

Introduction

1

Language —
The Power Source
that Never Fails You

SCENARIO ONE **M**arian Steiner watched open-mouthed as John Martin came barreling through the room almost at a run, his face beet-red, his expensive jacket slung over his shoulder like an old sweatshirt, and clearly so furious he didn't even know the others were there. When he disappeared into his corner office with a thunderous slam of the door, Marian looked around and asked wonderingly, "What on *earth* was THAT all about?"

"*That,*" said the man next to her, "was about the fact that Paul has once again wiped the floor with him in a meeting. He can't stand it — he always acts like that afterward. You'll get used to it."

"Paul?" Marian was puzzled. "Paul Nelson? But John out*ranks* Paul Nelson!"

"*Sure* he does! And that's the *problem!* He's got twice the clout Paul has, and he makes twenty thousand a year more than Paul does. That's why it makes John so *mad* when Paul pulls off one of these coups. Our fearless leader will spend weeks getting a presentation ready, making sure it's perfect. And then he has to sit there while Nelson just *wings* it — but when the time comes to vote, the votes go to Paul. You can always tell when he's come out of one of those."

"Does it happen often?" Marian asked.

"As often as Paul wants," said her neighbor.

That was when she noticed the expressions on their faces. Every last one of them wore a grin, as if they'd just won a prize. Clearly, there wasn't much sympathy here for their "fearless leader's" plight.

Marian was baffled. She hadn't been here long, but she'd had time to learn that John Martin was an intelligent and capable man who knew the business inside and out and deserved his high salary. How could someone like Paul

Nelson give him so much trouble? And why did the others — all of them people who *liked* John Martin, she was absolutely sure — get such a kick out of their boss's distress?

Phony Power and Real Power

Marian Steiner is puzzled by this situation because she's young and inexperienced and she's never come across anything like it before. But most of us have learned that there are Paul Nelsons scattered around the landscapes of our lives. And we have seen them at work often enough to be able to fill in the details missing from the scenario above.

We know — without reading anything more — that John Martin is a man who does all the right things. He wears the right clothes. He drives the right car. He does the right kind of work. He has the right kind of office, with the right furniture inside and the right tasteful objects tastefully distributed around the room. He has the training, and the experience, and the title, and the perks, and the salary. AND HE OUGHT TO BE WINNING EVERY TIME.

We know all about Paul Nelson, too. We know how he can waltz in and wreck things, with what looks like effortless ease. All Paul Nelson has to do is say a few words, maybe smile that smile of his a couple of times, and John Martin's excellent work goes right down the drain. We've watched the Paul Nelsons, and — unless they happened to be on our team — we've often hated them. Because there seemed to be no way to explain what they do, no way to keep them from doing it, no way to learn how to do it ourselves, and no way to establish any control over their behavior.

What this familiar situation demonstrates is the difference between PHONY POWER and REAL POWER. Phony power is always temporary, and it always brings with it only temporary success. Phony power is always tied to something else you have — a weapon, or a title, or the trappings of wealth, or the protective influence of some other person. Phony power can be taken away from you any time somebody arrives with a bigger weapon, a more important title, more money, or a mentor with more clout than yours.

Phony power floats back and forth as the weights of circumstances shift from person to person. When phony power is all you have to rely on, you never know how long your turn at the top is going to be. You can get awfully nervous and stressed out that way. Always having to guard your flank. Always having to size up everyone around you, checking their strength against your own. Always having to put one more coat of polish on your armor. And never knowing what may be coming up behind you.

Real power is very different. It applies in all situations. It can't be taken away from you.

REAL POWER IS THE ABILITY TO GET PEOPLE TO DO WHAT YOU WANT BECAUSE THEY *PREFER* TO DO WHAT YOU WANT.

Real power is what we are seeing in action when we watch the Paul Nelsons of this world.

This is not news. But what may be very welcome news indeed is the fact that you can *have* real power if you want it. You can't get it in any of the usual ways. You can't buy it; you can't take it by force; you can't inherit it. But it's not something that just gets dropped on a few lucky people by a mysterious quirk of fate!

You *can* have real power, and the long-term success that comes with it. You can get it by reading this book and using the system explained in this book. You don't need a lot of fancy equipment. You don't need to spend hours with expensive "experts." You don't even need to fill out a form. All you need is the book, your own fine human brain, and a willingness to go beyond the *phony* power that is impressive when it's working, but that may fail you anytime — anywhere — and without warning.

Power Sources: Where Does It Come From?

Power does not come from out of nowhere. It has to have a *source*. If you try to run a manufacturing plant using power that has its source in a shallow river, you know you're taking a risk. ANY TIME, IF CIRCUMSTANCES ARE NOT JUST EXACTLY RIGHT, IT MAY FAIL YOU. When the weather is too hot, or the rain is too scarce, that river will dry up. If a man comes along with enough money to buy the land upriver, and he builds a dam between his plant and yours, that river will stop before it reaches you. If a gang of vandals decides to cut your intake pipes, that river will run right on by you. If a group of citizens gets together and convinces a judge that their right to the water outranks yours, that river might as well not be there, because you won't be allowed to use it. And you can't predict any of this, or any of a dozen other things that may put an abrupt end to the power you depend on.

All phony varieties of power are like that river: THEY DEPEND ON EXTERNAL SOURCES AT THE MERCY OF UNPREDICTABLE CIRCUMSTANCES. You need a power source that never dries up, that cannot be taken away from you because someone else has more money or more clout, and that cannot be spoiled by the unscrupulous or careless behavior of other people. And I am happy to be able to tell you that you *already* have exactly that kind of power source! You may not be aware that you have it — just as you might not be aware that a mighty underground river was flowing beneath your property — but it's *there*.

It belongs to you; it is internal to you; and it is subject to your control. All you have to do is develop it. It is yours by virtue of the fact that you are a native speaker of your language.

Let me give you just a few quick examples that clearly demonstrate the power of language:

☐ In 1964, experimenters chose 20 percent of the children in a west coast school at random, and told their teachers a fairy tale: that an IQ test had identified those children as exceptionally intelligent and sure to make exceptional gains in the following year. At the end of the year, the fairy tale had come true. All of these children *had* made striking gains; in some cases they had increased their IQ test scores by as much as twenty five points and they were all evaluated as superior to the other 80 percent of the students.

☐ In 1987, the company that makes AYDS diet products reported that their sales had plunged *30 percent* since the AIDS epidemic had taken over the headlines.

☐ After analyzing 70,000 reports of "near misses" and other blunders in American aviation since 1976, University of Colorado professor Phillip Tompkins reported that more than 60 percent resulted from VERBAL MISTAKES.

☐ In 1986, a study of 5,000 patients in the intensive care units of thirteen hospitals found that some ICUs saved up to three times as many lives as the others. The critical factor was not technology. IT WAS DOCTOR/ NURSE COMMUNICATION.

☐ In 1985, Peter Blanck and his associate researchers proved that California juries were twice as likely to convict defendants in criminal trials when judges knew of prior felony convictions, even though the law forbids judges to share that information with juries — and that the factor responsible for this difference was nothing more than the judges' TONE OF VOICE.

☐ In 1972, a group of researchers were able to get themselves admitted to twelve different American mental hospitals with the diagnosis of schizophrenia just by claiming to have heard voices saying the three words: "empty, hollow, thud." Once admitted, they behaved absolutely normally; nevertheless, they were held for an average of nineteen days and were treated for schizophrenia the entire time. On discharge their records said "schizophrenia in remission."

☐ The incident above had a followup that was just as startling. One prominent mental hospital challenged the researchers after their results were published, claiming that it could not possibly happen at their facility. Chief experimenter D. L. Rosenhan accepted the challenge. It was agreed that over the next three months he would send one or more pseudopatients to the hospital, and that all staff members would rate all patients admitted for the likelihood that they were pseudopatients. The total number of patients admitted was 193, and the staff rated forty-one of them as probable fakes — but in fact Rosenhan did not send even *one* pseudopatient during that period.

◻ In 1987 Carol Cohn, an anti-nuclear woman who was a visiting scholar at a major defense studies center, reported in the *Bulletin of the Atomic Scientists* that it made no difference how hard she tried to maintain her philosophical detachment. When she had to use the accepted "clean bomb" and "surgical strike" vocabulary she could not keep human lives as her reference point. To her great distress, she found that she "could go for days speaking about nuclear weapons, without once thinking about the people who would be incinerated by them."

As the examples above, and many more like them, clearly demonstrate, LANGUAGE IS THE ONLY SOURCE OF REAL POWER.

You have a language, of course. You may have more than one. But you have not been using that language with the kind of expert skill you are fully capable of. And I can tell you *why* you haven't. It's not because you "just aren't very good at it." Not at all! It's because you have been sold a bill of goods about language — a traditional sacred cow of a bill of goods.

You've been taught that people who use language with great skill — like Paul Nelson — are either "born with a silver tongue in their mouths" or have acquired their skill over the course of many long and costly years of intensive training with "experts." This is false.

You have been led to believe that your own language skills are ordinary at best, and that this is true of almost everyone, the exceptions being geniuses, people with doctorates in literature or foreign languages or linguistics, and people who (through blind luck) "have charisma." This is also false.

You have been persuaded that a whole set of myths about language and communication are true, and those myths are interfering with your use of your natural power source in exactly the same way that a dam or a slashed pipe will interfere with a system based on the power of flowing water. In order to take control of the power that is rightfully yours, you have to get rid of that interference. This book will tell you how to do that — at your own pace, at your own convenience, and in your own way.

In Scenario One, at the beginning of this chapter, executive John Martin is tearing himself to pieces — and providing most of his co-workers with much amusement — because HIS PERCEPTION OF THE SITUATION IS THAT HE IS HELPLESS AGAINST SOME SORT OF "MAGIC" THAT COLLEAGUE PAUL NELSON POSSESSES AND IS ABLE TO USE AGAINST HIM. That perception — that picture of reality — reduces John Martin to blind rage. It makes it impossible for him to think clearly or act effectively. It's eating away at the respect the others in his office have for him, and at his own self-respect. It stands between him and success, interfering with his ability to achieve his goals. He has bought into a reality in which Paul Nelson has power that he cannot understand or defend himself against ... and everything he says and does is going to reflect that reality. He takes it for granted that this picture of reality is the only one there is, and that everyone else is looking at the same picture he is. HE MAY BE VERY WRONG.

Let's look at another scenario — one that goes right to the heart of this problem, but on a smaller scale.

SCENARIO TWO   **F**rom the head of the conference table, John Martin smiled at Sharon Jamison and Eve Wong. The men on either side of the table, picking up the signals, paid close attention.

"Sharon," John said, "I know you're aware of the importance we're placing on the choice of a new slogan for the healthcare products line we're introducing next year."

"Oh, yes," Sharon said, nodding vigorous agreement. "I know that's going to be a major focus."

John smiled again; and then he said, "I wonder if you and Eve could put your heads together and work up two or three possible ideas .... emphasizing the six points that absolutely have to be carried by the slogan. If the two of you can free up the time, of course."

"Certainly we can!" Sharon assured him. "We'd be delighted. If you would just refresh my memory about the six points, John."

The men looked down at the table, their faces carefully bland, while John read the list and Sharon wrote down the six points.

And then John said, "Well — I know we can count on you two to do a terrific job with this! And we look forward to having your input. By ... oh, let's say, six weeks from today?"

"Certainly," Sharon said again. And Eve added, "No problem."

When Sharon and Eve left for lunch after the meeting, Sharon suggested that they go somewhere special.

"After all," she said, "this is an occasion! Finally — we're beginning to make a dent in the sexism around here! That assignment John Martin gave us is something that would *always* have gone to the men before."

"It does look like we're making progress, doesn't it?" Eve answered.

"Yes. It *does*. And now, if we put our heads together and turn out top-notch work, we'll be in a position to push for some major accounts."

"You're right," Eve agreed. "It *is* an occasion. Okay — I'm with you. Let's celebrate!"

Sharon and Eve are capable and competent, devoted to the firm, and good at their jobs. They are intelligent, sophisticated women. But they've made a major mistake here. AND THEIR PERCEPTION OF WHAT HAPPENED AT THE MEETING IS SO DIFFERENT FROM THE PERCEPTION OF THE MEN WHO WERE PRESENT THAT THEY MIGHT AS WELL HAVE GONE TO A DIFFERENT MEETING ALTOGETHER.

Let's compare the two versions of reality that apply to Scenario Two.

SHARON AND EVE'S PERCEPTION

John Martin, a man with a lot of power in the company, has made a point of singling them out in a meeting — in front of all the men. He has offered them a chance to do something creative for a change, something that he himself pointed out is a task of real importance to the firm. The two women noticed the way he glanced at the men on each side of the table to be sure he had their full attention before he spoke to Sharon — obviously, he wanted the men to be aware of the offer he was about to make, and he wanted them to see how the women responded to the offer. For John to give the women this particular task in public, when he could have just sent them a memo or called them into his office and told them privately — and to do that in front of the men who would ordinarily have expected to get the task themselves — means that he is making a *point* of the assignment. He's telling the men, "Look — these two women are capable of doing *excellent* work, and you're going to have to take them seriously from now on."

This is a breakthrough, and a striking change from the semi-clerical tasks that Sharon and Eve have had to make do with in the past. They are both very pleased indeed, and they plan to work late every night — and work weekends as well, if need be — to be sure they do such a good job that John doesn't regret giving them this chance.

THE MEN'S PERCEPTION

The men know that for the past six months John has been getting constant pressure from Sharon and Eve for more responsibility and more interesting work. They have been wondering how long he was going to put up with it. And now they've watched a demonstration of his skill in *dealing* with the problem. First: he had to tell Sharon and Eve what the six important points were; the women had no better sense than to admit right in front of everybody that they didn't *know* what they were, and to ask for a list and write it down on the spot. Second: he talked to Eve through Sharon, without ever speaking to her directly, and both Eve and Sharon cooperated in that. Third: he gave the women a six-week deadline for something that ordinarily takes no more than one week — and they didn't question that. The women have made it clear that they don't know what's going on, and they've done it publicly.

The fact that John did this in a meeting — instead of calling Sharon and Eve into his office, doing it there, and just passing on the information to the men over lunch — means that he's making a point of this. Next time the women claim they're given boring assignments because they're women, he wants to be able to say that he gave them a chance and they blew it ... and he wants to be able to count on the men to back him up. The women have been suckered — and they don't even know it.

CONSEQUENCES

For the next few weeks, everything that Sharon Jamison and Eve Wong do will be filtered through their perception that John Martin has singled them out for an important assignment and has done it publicly in order to demonstrate to the men that the days of sexism in their division are over. At the same time, everything the men do will be filtered through their perception that the women have made fools of themselves in public and are so blind to what happened that they think they've done something terrific. Every conversation between the women and the men, every interaction, will have these two separate and radically different realities behind it as a context. The longer it takes for Sharon and Eve to find out what has happened, the more work they will have put into making themselves even more ridiculous, and the less the men will respect them.

Later in this book we'll take a look at what happens to Sharon and Eve as the weeks go by — and how their perception of what happens differs from that of the men. We'll give careful attention to the language that makes it possible for a reality clash of this magnitude to occur and to go on so long. For now, let me just state the five basic points involved, to set the stage for later discussions.

□ Communication breakdowns at the executive/professional level almost always result from *reality gaps* — radical differences in the way people perceive situations.

□ Such breakdowns create gaps in *understanding*, across which every message transmitted is going to be badly distorted.

◻ This understanding gap is closely linked to yet another gap — the *power* gap that exists between individuals and groups when any one of them outranks the other. If the power gap exists, the understanding gap will be there as well, because they feed on each other.

◻ The greater the difference in power, the greater the potential for misunderstanding and communication breakdown becomes.

◻ The only efficient mechanism for building a bridge across reality gaps is LANGUAGE.

What You Can Expect to Gain from This Book

This book will make it possible for you to get in touch with language skills you did not know you had and perhaps thought you never would have. As you read *Success With the Gentle Art of Verbal Self-Defense*, and as you put the system presented here into practice, you can anticipate that you will:

◻ Learn to recognize inefficient and ineffective patterns of language behavior in your own speech — including both patterns of verbal abuse and "verbal victim" patterns — so that you can stop using them.

◻ Learn to recognize these same negative language behaviors in other people and to either defuse them or respond to them effectively.

◻ Learn to use patterns of language that will cause strong positive perceptions of you in other people, and to eliminate those patterns in your language behavior that are responsible for negative perceptions in others.

◻ Learn to interact with other people — both verbally and nonverbally — in a way that guarantees successful, efficient, and satisfying communication, as well as mutual understanding.

◻ Learn to eliminate from your language environment the verbal toxins that create hostility, tension, depression, and stress.

◻ Learn simple and quick methods for extending these benefits to your written language and your public speaking, including your interactions with the media.

◻ Learn how language *works*, so that you will understand language in the same way that you understand every other aspect of your professional life.

◻ Learn how to use language data to recognize the strategies being used by other people, including strategies intended to deceive or distract you. And you will learn how to use language to frame your own strategies in response to those data, in ways that greatly increase your chances of success.

◻ Learn how to use language data to predict the behavior of others in advance, allowing you ample lead time for preparation of your own plans — No more "winging it" or "playing it by ear."

☐ Learn how to use language so that those around you will do what you want them to do for just one reason — because they *prefer* to — rather than because they anticipate reward or punishment from you or others.

☐ Learn how to use language to redefine situations and circumstances, so that what might have appeared to be negative is reformulated as positive (or vice versa).

☐ Learn how to spot — quickly and easily — problems that are based upon drastically different perceptions of what is happening, and how to move forward successfully toward your goals in such situations.

☐ Learn a set of basic principles and techniques that can be used in any communication situation whatsoever — including situations of crisis — because once you understand the system you will be able to extend it yourself at will.

☐ Learn how to structure your language in such a way that you will always be perceived as believable and convincing; at the same time, you will learn how to spot lying and deception in the language of others.

☐ Learn techniques for eliminating stress in your professional life and your personal life, including the efficient management of your own space and time.

☐ Learn to take *control* of your language behavior and use language strategies deliberately, instead of relying on luck and intuition to get you by. And you will learn acceptable and noncoercive techniques for structuring the language behavior of others when that is appropriate.

☐ Learn how to bring about necessary change, even when you are facing substantial resistance, without creating an ongoing burden of hostility and resentment.

☐ Finally, your use of the *Gentle Art* system has a side effect that is a valuable bonus: it automatically improves the language behavior of *other people* who interact with you, even when they are completely unaware that the system exists or that you are using it.

At this point, as you review the list of benefits, I may be encountering resistance from *you*. You may be wondering how any one book could make it possible for you to achieve all of those results. That's sensible, and logical; it is exactly what you should be thinking. But I assure you, it *is* possible, and for a very good reason — a reason that will be explained in full as you read Chapter Two.

Workout — Chapter 1

1. Define *power*. Never mind what the dictionary says — what does the word mean to *you*? Write your definition down. And then surprise yourself —

have some of your friends, associates, family members, etc., give you *their* definition of the word to compare with your own.

2. Read the article by Carol Cohn titled "Slick'ems, Glick'ems, Christmas Trees, and Cookie Cutters: Nuclear Language and How We Learned to Pat the Bomb," in *Bulletin of the Atomic Scientists* for June 1987, pages 17-24. (If your library doesn't have it, the librarian can get it for you on Interlibrary Loan.) Whether you agree with Dr. Cohn's position on nuclear warfare is not relevant here. What makes this article important is its crystal-clear demonstration of the power language has to structure human thought *even in an individual who is actively struggling to resist.*

3. In a May 2, 1981, *TV Guide* article ("The Charisma Factor: Why Dan Rather May Be in Trouble") Gerald M. Goldhaber claimed that "the success of the show has far less to do with its informational content than with the charisma of the personalities who bring us the news." He defined charisma as "leadership derived through personality" and divided charismatic personalities into the Hero (like John F. Kennedy), the Antihero (like Jimmy Carter) and the Mystic (like Henry Kissinger.)

   Do you agree with Goldhaber's definition of charisma? How do you define "Personality"? Do you ever find yourself going along with a charismatic person on things you know you would reject if they came from another source? Which would you rather have — the power of charisma, or the power of money? Why?

4. Not long ago there was a series of unanticipated deaths in a Southern hospital — patients' hearts were stopping while they were anesthetized for surgery. An investigation traced the source to two anesthesiologists at the facility. They were waiting until just before patients were wheeled into the operating room to explain to them — as required by law — the substantial risks of anesthesia. The spate of deaths stopped when the hospital ordered them to provide their explanations well in advance of the operations.

   Is this another example of the power of language? Or did the investigation just alarm the anesthetists so much that they paid more attention to their work? (In which case: is *that* an example of the power of language?) Is there a parallel in your business or profession ... perhaps not one that means life or death, but one where you haven't considered the possible impact of routine information presented at a time of stress? Could you make a change in the timing of that information, or in the manner of presentation?

SIGHT BITES

1. "My personal view of power is that it's my job as chief executive officer to empower those around me."

   (Zane Barnes, CEO of Southwestern Bell, quoted in *Forbes Magazine* for May 30, 1988; page 122.)

2. "Funkhouser wants to overcome our love-hate relationship with the concept of power. In his view, power — the art of getting things done — is good. Control — the talent for dominating others — is bad."

   (From "Blueprints for a Better Business," by Don Wallace, in *Success* for November 1988; page 73. Funkhouser is author G. Ray Funkhouser.)

3. ". . . speech may not only reflect power differences in the world, it may also create them through a self-fulfilling prophecy."

   (From "Conversational Politics," by Mary Brown Parlee: in *Psychology Today* for May 1979; page 56.)

4. "How did Roosevelt hold together so many conflicting interests, opinions, personalities? Above all by a sublime self-confidence, the ultimate source of which no one could ever quite place."

   (Do you agree with this? It comes from the *Forbes* column titled "Other Comments," on page 24 of the August 22, 1988 issue.)

5. "I don't yet know the computer language LISP, the *lingua franca* programming language of artificial intelligence. . . . 'Learn LISP, Dan,' a person in the field urged me the other day. 'It will change your life.' That's what I'm afraid of."

   (From "The Imagination Extenders," by Daniel C. Dennett, in *Psychology Today* for December 1981; page 39.)

6. "[Ronald] Heifetz won't give you the usual blather about the personality traits of great leaders. He puts much more emphasis on the definition of leadership, in part because he understands the power of words. Label someone a leader — give him or her the leader's role — and a conscientious person tries to be or do what the label implies. That same label will likewise determine the expectations of the people in the group or organization being led. . . . To correct the problems, therefore, you must begin by offering a better definition . . . ."

   (From "Leadership Expert Ronald Heifetz," interviewed in *Inc.* for October 1988: page 37.)

2 Learning the Territory

Every human being, barring extraordinary physical and mental damage, is a native speaker of at least one human language. This is true even at severe levels of mental retardation, and it is independent of education. Whether you ever have a lesson in your language or not, you will begin speaking it at about eighteen months of age and have it essentially under control by the time you are five or six.

Your knowledge of your language is a special kind of knowledge — called *internalized* knowledge. It's not like your knowledge of economic theory or Latin nouns or art history or baseball scores. You know your language so well that you have it on automatic. You never have to stop and ask yourself, "Now, let me see ... how do you make a command in English?" Even if you were to go live in Spain for twelve years and speak no English in all that time, you would still be as fluent in English as ever. You don't have to review your knowledge of English periodically in order to continue using it. You have it INTERNALIZED, and nothing but a medical disaster can interfere with that situation.

However, although a nearly flawless internalized grammar of English was stored in your memory when you started elementary school, the educational system didn't consider that sufficient. On the contrary — it required you to take ten years or more of "language arts" and "English" courses. You not only were not taught to respect your internalized grammar, you probably were never told that you *had* one. And you learned a distorted respect for language skills as they are indicated by course grades and academic degrees. As a result, you now have no convenient way to gain access to the superb database that your internalized grammar could provide for you. It's as if you owned a library of thousands of books for which you had no index or card catalogue! You might know very well that you owned a particular book, and that it was in that library *somewhere*, but whether you could find it, and how quickly, would be a matter of blind luck. All that wealth of information is in there, and it all belongs to you — it's just not stored in a way that will let you use it properly.[1]

Fortunately, this situation can easily be changed. AND THAT IS WHY YOU CAN CONFIDENTLY EXPECT ALL THOSE BENEFITS ON PAGES 9-10 AS A RESULT OF READING THIS BOOK AND PUTTING ITS CONTENTS TO USE IN YOUR LIFE. I don't have to teach you enormous quantities of completely new information from scratch. Instead, I am going to put you in touch with information you already have, but for which you have no means of access. And I am going to show you how to organize that information and build on it, so that you get an abundant return on your investment of time and energy.

The *Gentle Art* system will enable you to accomplish three tasks that are critical to your success:

- ☐ It will put you in touch with your internalized store of knowledge about your language.
- ☐ It will let you build an index for that knowledge, so that you can use it as you were intended to use it — magnificently well.
- ☐ It will enable you to build on that internalized store of knowledge and to add new information, also indexed for ready access.

We will begin by taking a look at language from four different points of view: LANGUAGE AS SYSTEM; LANGUAGE AS TOXIC WASTE; LANGUAGE AS FEEDBACK LOOP; and LANGUAGE AS TRAFFIC. Each of these ways of examining language provides us with a different organizing framework — a different *metaphor*. The more metaphors you have for something, the more indexes it will have in your memory, with a direct payoff in greater understanding and ease of access.

Language as System

SCENARIO THREE   Thomas Lee frowned at the papers in his hand, very dissatisfied with what he saw there, and shook his head.

"Jack," he said disgustedly, "this just won't do. This is a complete FAILure. It's supposed to be a company newsletter ... I'VE seen better newsletters from the seventh graders at my kid's SCHOOL!"

"Well," Jack answered, "what did you *expect?*"

"What do you mean?"

"You wanted to save money by doing it in-house, Tom. Okay? We all tried to tell you. If you turn a newsletter over to people who've never taken a journalism class — never even had an English class since they were in high school — failure is what you're going to *get.* They don't understand grammar, they don't understand style, and they can't do the job."

Tom sighed heavily and dropped the sheets of paper into his wastebasket. "Okay, Jack," he said. "I guess we do need experts AFTER all. Find me a newsletter service — but try to find one that won't cost an ARM AND A LEG!"

Suppose you were a physician specializing in the treatment of various disorders and diseases of the blood, the specialty called *hematology.* Suppose that your training had included the following courses, and many more of the same kind: Blood Disorders in the Human Brain; Blood Disorders in the Human Liver; Blood Disorders in the Human Extremities, and so on. But *never*, in all the years of your training, had you ever been taught about the human body's *circulatory system*, for which all those chunks of specialized information are relevant. You might have heard a vague rumor that such a system existed. You might have suspected that surely such a system *must* exist. But no one ever suggested that it was important or that you should explore the matter further.

This is the way we are taught about our language. We take course after course, year after year, on the *pieces* of our language, but we never learn about the system into which the pieces fit. It happens that we *know* that system — it's part of our internalized knowledge. But we don't know that we know it. Educated adults, functioning successfully in their businesses and professions, will tell me they don't know any grammar, that they didn't understand grammar when they took it in school, and that they found it so confusing and so boring that they gave up any effort to "learn" it long ago. They *mean* what they say absolutely seriously — and it is compelling evidence of the way the truth has been kept from them.

Let's take a look at some of the things you know — but are probably not aware that you know — about your grammar. We'll start with an example that may surprise you.

Imagine, please, that you are looking at a wooden telephone pole with a dimension of thirty-three feet. It's doing what telephone poles ordinarily do: standing there, holding up the telephone wires through which your conversations travel. If I asked you to describe the size of that pole by completing the sentence below, what would you say?

"That telephone pole is thirty-three feet ...."

Now let's change the scene a bit. Imagine that a windstorm has come along and blown that telephone pole down. There it lies, flat on the ground. And I want you to describe the size of the pole again, as it lies there before your eyes, by completing the sentence below.

"That telephone pole is thirty-three feet ...."

Notice what happens? In the first case, you would have told me that the pole was thirty-three feet TALL or thirty-three feet HIGH. But when it was lying on the ground, you would have told me that it was thirty-three feet LONG. And if I were to try to do it the other way around, you would instantly — without having to go ask an expert or look the matter up in a book — tell me that I was flat out *wrong*. I agree with you. Absolutely. But the interesting question is: HOW DID YOU KNOW?

Consider the following rule:

When an object is at a right angle (or roughly a right angle) with respect to the horizon as it is seen by the speaker, it is described as being X units HIGH or TALL. When the same object is parallel with the horizon as seen by the speaker, it is described as being X units LONG.

Do you know that rule? Yes, you do. That rule, or something very like it, is the rule you used to complete the two sentences above. But were you aware that you knew it? Can you remember ever having read it or heard it? Not likely! But you *do* know it, nevertheless. And you make systematic use of it every time you have to make a choice between the words HIGH/TALL and the word LONG.

Here's another example of the same kind. Look at the sentences below, please, and put an asterisk by the ones that are unacceptable.[2]

a. We bought a small red car.
b. We bought a red small car.
c. We rented a large white stone house.
d. We rented a stone white large house.
e. The little yellow wooden chair is too expensive.
f. The yellow wooden little chair is too expensive.

Quite right; examples (b), (d), and (f) require an asterisk. But how did you know that?

One last example, this one from the sound system of English, and then we'll move on. Look at the list below, and put a check mark beside the items that could be used as the name of a candy bar in English.

They would have to be sequences that could be used to fill in the blank in the sentence, "Let me have a _____, please."

   a. Grible

   b. Ngaba

   c. Szchwally

   d. Tloosig

   e. Cheeb

And I ask you again, HOW DID YOU KNOW? None of the sequences is a "real" word of English. How did you know which ones *could* be an English word and which ones could not? What rule did you use when you rejected (b), (c), and (d)?

"Well, I just know, that's all!" won't wash. You cannot "just know" to reject items that you have never encountered before in your life. Your ability to make these judgments without hesitation is solid proof that you are using a *system*. A system in which you are an expert. And that you are applying the rules of that system for quality control. You know the parts of the system, with all their rules. You know how the parts and the rules fit together and interact. And you know the *metarules* — the rules that tell you such things as which rule to use when more than one possibility exists.

When someone like Jack Harrington — an educated man filling an important middle management position in a modern corporation — goes to a superior and explains that a job has been done badly because the people who did it have never taken any formal courses in the writing of their native language, it demonstrates the power of the traditional myths. The fact that his superior immediately accepted that explanation, along with the idea that people who haven't had such courses understand neither grammar nor style, makes it even more striking. Neither of these men, for all their training, education, and intelligence, is aware that every native speaker of a language has a flawless internalized grammar of that language to fall back on.

Remember our hypothetical physician back there, our hematologist, who had studied diseases and disorders of the blood that occur in the brain, and in the liver, and in the arms and legs — but not the system that related any one of those problems to the others? Such a doctor, faced with a patient whose difficulty involved blood and the kidneys, would not know how to help. Because that problem would never have appeared on his memorized list of medical rules.

THE MAJOR DIFFERENCE BETWEEN AN ARBITRARY LIST OF RULES AND A SET OF RULES THAT CONSTITUTES A SYSTEM IS THAT A SYSTEM CAN HANDLE SOMETHING NEW.

You have just proved that you have an internalized set of rules that constitutes the *system* for forming acceptable English words. If that were not true, you wouldn't be able to tell whether an *invented* English word such as "tloosig" met those criteria or not. And the same thing is true of the earlier examples. I could go on challenging you with new and different ones for days. Not only would I be unable to stump you, you would never even find yourself hesitating about your decisions. This is something you *really* know.

Your internalized grammar is a system that specifies what chunks of sound *are* English, what chunks of English can be combined with what other chunks, and the order in which they have to be assembled. It contains all the rules of English, including the *metarules* — the rules that provide you with necessary information *about* the other rules. AND YOU ARE AN EXPERT IN THAT SYSTEM, even if the highest grade you ever received in an English class was a D.

You use that system — your internalized grammar — to speak and write English, to understand and read English, to produce and interpret English body language, and to carry on English conversations. You can trust that system to carry you through in any language interaction whatsoever — whether it is one that you have specifically been taught to deal with or not.

LANGUAGE AS TOXIC WASTE

SCENARIO FOUR   **T**homas Lee stared at the man sitting across the desk from him; he took one very long, very loud, deep breath.

"You're KIDDING me!" he said. "I don't beLIEVE this!"

"Believe it," Jack told him. "It's true."

"WE spent nearly a THOUSAND DOLlars on this newsletter service, and the result is WORSE THAN WHAT WE GOT WHEN WE DID IT IN-HOUSE?"

"That's right, Tom. But I'd like to tell you what happened."

Tom leaned back in his chair, put both fists on the desk, and looked Jack Harrington right in the eye.

"What IS it with you?" he shouted. "WHY do you always screw up like this? WHY IS it that I can't give you EVen the SIMPLEST TASK and expect it to be DONE right, Jack? WHY IS that?"

"Tom, just let me tell you how —"

"Oh, CUT IT out!" Lee spat, contempt written plainly on his face. "Don't waste MY time with your stupid excuses! YOU'RE a TOTAL FAILure, Jack, you KNOW THAT? A TOTAL FAILure! Go on, get out of here . . . go ruin somebody ELSE'S day!"

If a speeding truck runs over you, you are going to get hurt. If someone points a loaded gun at you and pulls the trigger, you are going to be injured. If you fall off a cliff, you are definitely going to suffer harm. These dangers produce immediate and obvious damage about which there can be no question. No one would ever say to you, as you lay broken and bleeding in the street after that truck ran over you, "Oh, don't be ridiculous! You're just making a mountain out of a molehill, lying there like that! What's the matter — don't you have a sense of humor?"

But there are many other dangers for which the associated damage doesn't show up so immediately and unambiguously. Toxic waste, for example. If you have built your house on land where dangerous chemicals are buried, you're going to get hurt — but it may be a while before the damage is apparent. And you may have to go through a period when *you* know you've been harmed, but other people try to convince you that you're "neurotic" or "just imagining things," before all the facts are known and a diagnosis can be made.

The harm that language does tends to be like that done by toxic waste, rather than by speeding trucks or bullets. People rarely suffer serious injury as a result of contact with one word, or one sentence, or even one conversation. But long-term contact with verbal toxins can destroy both your physical and your emotional health.

If a stranger leans out of a window as you walk by on the sidewalk below and shouts insults at you, that's unpleasant; if someone you're fond of calls you names, that's worse. But when those are isolated incidents they are quickly forgotten. Real damage done by language happens when you face verbal abuse day after day, week after week, in situations you don't feel you can get away from.

When you go to your office every morning with your stomach in knots because you have to work with an executive vice president whose idea of management is to trim everything he says with a thick layer of sarcasm, that's long-term verbal abuse, and it's dangerous. The same thing is true when you face every Friday afternoon with dread because you have to spend it in a meeting where one powerful boor drones on and on endlessly, wasting everybody's valuable time and accomplishing nothing at all. When the thought of going home at night makes you half sick, because time spent at home is time spent in arguments and fights and emotional scenes, you are dealing with chronic verbal violence.

That kind of language is just like toxic waste — when your environment is contaminated by it, you are going to get hurt. It may take a while, depending on how tough you are and how intense the abuse is, but make no mistake — it will get you, eventually. When Jack Harrington, in Scenario Four, has to deal with Thomas Lee regularly, day after day, week after week, and listen to Lee's verbal abuse, he is headed for serious trouble. And so is the company that depends on him to be at his best. It's not trivial; it's not a matter of "etiquette." It's a matter of hard dollars and cents — and of *common* sense. If you let this kind of thing go on around you, you might just as well go out in the street and throw money away. It wouldn't cost you any more, and it would be a lot less painful.

In this book I am going to introduce you to the grammar of verbal abuse, so that you will recognize the nasty stuff early on and know what you are facing. And I am going to show you how to defend yourself against it.

Verbal self-defense, in the *Gentle Art* system, is not assertiveness. It's not smart cracks or counterattacks — both of which are just about as much use for putting an end to verbal violence as kerosene is for putting an end to fires. Let's define verbal self-defense properly, within this system.

VERBAL SELF-DEFENSE is language behavior that allows you to achieve three goals:

☐ You will establish a language environment in which verbal abuse almost never occurs.

☐ When you *do* encounter verbal abuse, you will know how to defuse the attack so that it cannot be completed.

☐ On those rare occasions when a verbal attack cannot be avoided, you will know how to overcome your opponent quickly, effectively, and honorably — with no loss of face for anyone involved.

The grammar of English verbal abuse, just like the grammar of English verbs, is part of your internalized knowledge about your language. Suppose someone says the following sentence to you:

1. "EVen YOU could pass THAT exam!"

Do you like that? Is it insulting? What does it mean? It certainly *looks* innocent enough, if you consider the individual words it contains.

But when you hear that sentence, you know immediately that the speaker intends you to understand two *other* sentences:

2. "The exam is trivially easy."
3. "You are basically incompetent and inferior."

How do you know that? None of those words appears in the verbal attack: "EVen YOU could pass THAT exam!" And I am absolutely certain that you have never heard or read the rule that would explain how you know that sentences (2) and (3) are part of the meaning of sentence (1). But you *do* know, because you know the grammar of your language, as a system, and you know how it works.

When you were five years old and one of the other kids said to you, "EVen YOU could climb THAT tree!" you knew what that meant. You already knew that rule. You knew that both you and the tree were under verbal attack. Unfortunately, you probably did not know how to protect yourself effectively, or how to make certain that the attack was not repeated.

Most of the training we get in our society for dealing with verbal attack is of just three kinds:

- ☐ We learn how to respond to verbal abuse with more verbal abuse of our own.
- ☐ We learn how to endure verbal abuse without complaint and without defending ourselves against it.
- ☐ We learn how to pass the pain caused by verbal abuse along to others by being verbally abusive ourselves.

Which of these tactics you choose in a given situation depends on how much power you have in that communication context. And all three of them are counterproductive. They don't lead to success; they only make matters worse.

When we come back to the verbal attack patterns of English in a later chapter, I will demonstrate to you that you can eliminate them from your language environment forever. Up to now you have been getting by on nothing but the rules that allow you to *recognize* verbal attacks and understand what they mean. I will show you how to add an additional set of rules for *responding* to attacks after you have recognized them.

LANGUAGE AS FEEDBACK LOOP

SCENARIO FIVE   **J**ohn Martin didn't waste any time on preliminaries. "Tom," he said, "we just can't have this kind of thing."

"What kind of thing?"

"Oh, come on, Tom — you know *exactly* what I mean! We can't have you throwing the book at people without even giving them a chance to tell you their side of the story."

Tom Lee laughed harshly. "Oh, *I* get it!" he snarled. "Jack's been in here crying on your shoulder the way he ALways—"

John cut him off abruptly. "No way, Tom," he said. "No, he hasn't. Jack hasn't said a word to me. The reason I know how you treated Jack is because everybody in the office could *hear* you bellowing at him . . . not because Jack ratted."

"And you're asking me to just ACCEPT his failure to carry out a piddly little job that MY KIDS COULD HAVE TAKEN CARE OF?"

"Tom," said John Martin, "I don't know anything about that. I haven't talked to Jack yet. But I will NOT accept YOUR failure to treat the REST of us DEcently!"

"Now YOU JUST WAIT ONE COTTONPICKING MINute, Martin!"

"No, YOU wait! YOU'RE DOING IT AGAIN!"

"DOING WHAT?"

"*BELLOWING!* AT THE TOP OF YOUR LUNGS! SO EVERYBODY IN THE DAMN COUNTY CAN HEAR EVERY WORD YOU *SAY!*"

"WELL, *SO ARE YOU!*"

Think of the last time you found yourself talking to someone who had a strong British accent, or a strong Southern accent. Remember how you developed an accent of your own that closely matched the one you were hearing?

Think of the last time you spent fifteen minutes talking with one of those people who says "like" or "okay" or "well" or "I mean," every few words. Remember how, to your horror, you heard yourself doing the same thing — and perhaps couldn't get rid of the habit for the rest of the day?

And think of the last time that you were involved in an argument that you *knew* was ridiculous, but in which it seemed that everything the other speaker said to you was so infuriating that you just could not let it pass — only to have what *you* said provoke yet one more outrageous and infuriating statement, *ad infinitum*? So that there was no way you could bring the argument to an end, and it went on and on?

Those experiences, and the interaction presented in Scenario Five, show language as a *feedback loop*, with at least one speaker at each end of the loop. John Martin would not ordinarily yell at others when he talks to them; he obviously had no intention of yelling at Tom Lee. But as the volume of Lee's voice rose, so did Martin's — without his being aware of what was happening — and soon *both* men were shouting. Like the British accent and the maddening "Like, well, you know," and the interminable series of confrontational statements in a stupid argument, the loudness of Lee's voice was contagious.

Consider how your air conditioning unit works. You set it for seventy-two degrees. It samples the air to find out what the temperature is and feeds that information into the loop. Whenever the temperature is higher than the seventy-two degrees target, the unit comes on and begins cooling the air. It goes round and round this loop until the target is reached, at which point it turns the cooling cycle off. That's a feedback loop, going only one direction, and it's the most efficient and cost-effective way to handle the process. It would be ridiculous to set the air conditioner to come on every three hours and run for twenty minutes, regardless of the temperature of the air. And it would be ridiculous to hook it up to a random number generator so that it would come on whenever the number "17" turned up and run until the number "11" was generated. It's equally ridiculous to go into language interactions with the idea that you'll say only certain pre-established (or random) things, regardless of what you may hear. Language doesn't work like that.

People do sometimes try to go into language interactions with their minds made up, having decided in advance what they will say. Perhaps this happens most often between parents and teenage children, when the weary parent only has to see the teenager's mouth open before saying, "Whatever it is, the answer is NO!" But even that is an example of a feedback loop. The only thing unusual about it is that the data the parent is using to adjust the response is data from the past and the hypothetical future, rather than the present. What is said is a response to things the parent has already heard the teenager say far too many times and is sure the teenager will say again. And that imaginary data is being fed back into the language system and responded to with a determined "NO." Still a feedback loop, although a pathetic and inadequate one.

It never happens that people choose an arbitrary sentence such as "Six people will fit into a telephone booth," and doggedly say only *that* in response to the speech of others. Nor do people ever say sentences entirely at random, as in this hypothetical "dialogue":

SPEAKER A: "Twenty-four dollars is too much money."
SPEAKER B: "It rains oftener on the railroad tracks."
SPEAKER A: "Yes, but the quality of mercy is not strained."
SPEAKER B: "Well, it takes *seven* people to change a lightbulb!"

Clearly, one of the rules by which we communicate says something roughly like "when a conversation is going on, each utterance must be based in some way on the utterances that come before it." There are also associated rules for breaking out of the loop without causing our conversational partners to decide we don't know how to talk. We learn to say things like "pardon me for changing the subject" as a way of demonstrating that we *know* the rule we intend to break.

The difference between the feedback loop in cooling systems and the linguistic feedback loop is that in language the feedback goes in both directions. I hear what you say, and I select what I will say on the basis of what I have heard. You listen to my response and you select what you will say on the basis of what *you* have heard. We maintain this interactive feedback loop for as long as we are carrying on the conversation, with the information being fed back at *both* ends of the loop. The more skillfully we do that, the more successful our communication is going to be.

The more data you are able to extract from the language you hear — the more information you are able to obtain from words and body language about what is actually meant — the better you will be able to choose a response that is effective and efficient. And the more skilled you are at this feedback process, the better you will be at saying things that obtain the responses you want in return.

If you are only listening to other people with half an ear, if you aren't observing their body language competently, you aren't getting enough feedback information. And without that information you can't construct effective responses — which means that the communication taking place will be much less satisfactory than it could be, and ought to be.

Should you care about that? Indeed you should, because YOUR SUCCESS DEPENDS ON IT.

Current books on business and management — THE PASSION FOR EXCELLENCE will do for an example — state very clearly what part language plays in your efforts toward success. You have to get out and *communicate* with everyone, at every level — customers and clients, colleagues and staff, suppliers, contractors, and administrators — *everyone* involved in your enterprise. These books tell you that you must talk well, that you must listen well, that you must build empathy and rapport and trust and mutual respect. They make an airtight case for the success of such methods over the traditional "it's a jungle out there and only the toughest and meanest survive!" methods.

BUT ALTHOUGH LANGUAGE IS THE ONLY TOOL AVAILABLE FOR TALKING AND LISTENING AND RAPPORT-BUILDING, THEY DON'T TELL YOU HOW TO *USE* LANGUAGE TO ACCOMPLISH THESE GOALS. They take it for granted that you have nothing to work with but gut feelings, vague hunches, and good guesses. And they recommend three mechanisms based only on intuition:

☐ Select people to be involved in your enterprises who are *already* highly skilled at communication, at building rapport, etc.

☐ Use these "natural" good communicators as models, putting them in strategic locations where they will serve as an inspiration to everyone around them.

☐ Allow the people around the good communicators some time to "catch" the ability that the good communicators had the blind luck to be born with, encouraging them in every way possible. And then, if they turn out to be immune, fire them.

This is a lot like throwing people into the water with one good swimmer as their model, in the hope that they'll learn to swim — and if they don't, letting them drown. It's based on the common belief that superb language skills can't be taught; that they are something you "either know or you don't"; that you have to either be born with such skills or "pick them up as you go along"; and that they are so mysterious that it's impossible to subject them to systematic analysis in the way that other skills are. These are serious errors, and it's time they were abandoned.

The most basic skill underlying successful communication is that of establishing and maintaining the interactive feedback loop — by talking, by listening, and by interpreting and generating body language. This book will teach you how to do all of those things and do them well, building upon your internalized knowledge base and your natural competence.

The interactive language feedback loop is easiest to produce and maintain — and works most effectively — when the people who are trying to communicate with each other can be said to be *syntonic*. This term comes from early music theory, and from telegraphy, where it is used to refer to two radio sets so well-tuned with respect to one another that they can be used for the effective and efficient transmission of information. Obviously, you can't set up a feedback loop between two radios — or two people — when they are trying to transmit on totally different frequencies. The system for getting in tune with people you are interacting with and using a shared channel for communication with them is called *syntonics*, defined in the *Gentle Art* framework as the science of language harmony.

LANGUAGE AS TRAFFIC

SCENARIO SIX   **J**ack Harrington sat at the cafeteria table, picking at his lunch, listening to his two colleagues, nodding now and then, and wishing he could figure out a way to get a word in edgewise.

"The NERVE of him!" the woman was saying. "Calling you a FAILure! I mean, everybody *heard* him, Jack ... and they haven't talked about anything else for three days! And then Martin called HIM in, and five minutes later the two of *them* were carrying on like hockey players! And you're not a failure at ALL — I mean—"

"Karen—"

"Wait just a minute, I want to make my point here."

And then they were both talking at once, the two of them, Karen and Fred. If it hadn't been *his* alleged failure that they were dissecting in public, he would almost have enjoyed watching them. Neither one had the remotest idea how to carry on a conversation. They didn't do conversations, they did *monologues*, and heaven help you if you needed to get anything across to either one of them in a hurry.

Jack went back to poking his macaroni salad with a fork, wondering whether he should make one more try at explaining how little difference it made to *him* that a turkey like Tom Lee had called him a failure, or just walk off and leave Karen and Fred to wear themselves out on their own....

By now you will be well aware that Jack Harrington is lacking in one crucial communication skill — that of getting his fair share of the turns in a conversation. You have seen him fail at that task twice: once in his altercation with the verbally abusive Tom Lee, and again in Scenario Six, where he is run over by two monologuists. His problem is a common one, sometimes found in people whose status makes its appearance a surprise — Britain's Margaret Thatcher is the most obvious example. Thatcher is a powerful and dominating woman who insists on running the show, but she is forever being interrupted. Not because people don't want to hear what she has to say, but because they think — due to the false signals she gives them — that she's through talking and ready to yield the floor. Jack does all right when he's involved in a placid exchange of utterances. But at the first sign of opposition he gives up, falls silent, and simply sits it out. This is why he's not going to go any higher than his current position as Assistant Manager for Marketing Development at Metamega Corporation. People know him to be an intelligent and capable man. But they also know that they can't count on him in the tight spots.

Language interactions, when properly done, are well-regulated systems of traffic. Just as you have rules in your internalized grammar that tell you what constitutes a possible word of English or a possible sentence of English, you have *traffic* rules that specify who gets to talk, for how long, and about what. Those rules, like most other rules, can be broken — but there are rules about that, too. No one would accept as an English conversation an episode in which three people all talked simultaneously for ten minutes, or one in which everyone had to observe five minutes of silence at the end of each sentence. We might accept such things as theater or as psychology experiments, but not as valid language interactions.

To get safely through the linguistic intersections, you need at least the following five skills:

- ☐ The ability to get a turn to speak and to hold on to it for as long as the rules allow
- ☐ The ability to propose a topic to be talked about, and to support and maintain that topic
- ☐ The ability to pass on the conversational turn to another person of your choice
- ☐ The ability to spot the signals that mean you have been selected as the next person to talk
- ☐ The ability to stop people who are determined to interfere in this process

You also need to know the metarules that specify how this system of traffic control works, so that you can plan several turns ahead and set up strategies for putting your skills to use.

This is not just a matter of "etiquette." Manners decree that anyone who hogs the floor is ignorant and rude, but we all know people who can speak at great length without anyone present feeling imposed upon. We know other people who can only say half a dozen words before we begin to feel that they've talked too long. Manners are all about what is "nice"; the traffic rules of your grammar have nothing to do with being nice. They have to do with the promotion of successful communication, and they are based not on courtesy but on linguistics. Your own real world experience proves this beyond all doubt. For example:

- ☐ If you think that it's your turn to talk, you're not going to be listening to what the other speaker is saying — and communication will fail.
- ☐ If it's your turn to talk and everyone's waiting for you to begin, but you've missed your cue, you won't be saying anything — and communication will fail.
- ☐ If you aren't able to set up your topic with sufficient strength to win and hold people's attention, they won't be able to listen — and communication will fail.

You do have all the skills necessary for maneuvering through the verbal traffic, but you may not be using them very well, and you may be at a loss for ways to improve the situation. That can be fixed — and this book will tell you how.

Now we are approaching the end of this chapter. And it is time for me to tell you that the prominent position of the word "failure" in each of the four short scenarios was no accident. If you go over the scenarios again, you will observe that although everyone involved is pronouncing the same word "failure," the speakers do not all *mean* the same thing when they make that sequence of English sounds.

Suppose that you and I were talking about planes, and the only meaning for "plane" in your internal grammar's dictionary was the one appropriate for air travel. We might talk at cross purposes for a long time, talking in increasing annoyance across the gap in our understanding. If I had a good deal of power over you, I might become so irritated by what I perceived as your stubborn refusal to make any sense that I would refuse to talk to you any longer. And you would go away from the interaction bewildered by what *you* perceived as my totally mysterious and baseless bad temper. If it did not occur to me that your grammar lacked the definition of "plane" as a carpentry tool — and there is no reason why that *should* occur to me — I might very well make a note somewhere that you are a stubborn and uncooperative person given to obstructing communication, and treat you that way thereafter. And you might never know why.

Differing understandings of the meaning of words like "plane" — words that refer to concrete and directly observable objects or living things — are the most trivial of reality gaps, and are easy to clear up. The primary barrier to bridging such gaps is the failure to suspect that a meaning difference exists. But when people have different meanings stored for words that refer to *abstractions* — things that cannot be directly observed — the situation is much more serious.

In our society today, radically varying meanings for certain key words cause severe communication breakdowns over and over again, leaving people baffled and frustrated and wondering what could have caused the resulting mess. Unless we have a way to construct bridges across these reality gaps, communication breakdowns will occur, and their consequences will be grave. The word "failure" is an excellent example of a troublesome word responsible for many a gap. In the next chapter, we will turn our attention to various meanings of "failure," and to methods for dealing with the amazing effects of that variety.

NOTES

1. The difference between the perfection of your internal grammar — which linguists refer to as your linguistic *competence* — and the way you put that grammar to use — your linguistic *performance* — is often striking.

Factors such as anxiety, illness, chemical substances, fear, drowsiness, and crosscultural contexts may interfere with your performance so drastically that you find it hard to believe in the existence of your flawless internal grammar. But the fact that, given time, you can always repair your own mistakes, proves that it is there and that it functions just as it is supposed to function.

2. Linguists customarily mark unacceptable sequences of language with an asterisk; when you read linguistic literature you will find that this is the standard practice.

Workout — Chapter 2

1. Read the article by Edward E. Jones titled "Interpreting Interpersonal Behavior: The Effects of Expectancies," in *Science* for October 3, 1986, pages 41-46. It begins with "Attempts to understand the personal characteristics of others, in interactions with them, are complicated by the fact that one tends to find what one expects" and goes on to review the major studies on self-fulfilling prophecies. In every case, the responsible factor is language as an interactive feedback loop.

2. MORE RULES YOU DIDN'T KNOW YOU KNEW....

In the example sentences below, those that are starred are not acceptable. Compare them with the others, and state the rule.

 a. He didn't lift a finger to help us.

*b. He lifted a finger to help us.

 c. I didn't turn a hair when I saw the total.

*d. I turned a hair when I saw the total.

 e. The terrified rabbit didn't move a muscle.

*f. The terrified rabbit moved a muscle.

 g. They didn't blink an eye at the outrageous proposal.

*h. They blinked an eye at the outrageous proposal.

And what additional piece of information does this pair give you?

 i. She refused to lift a finger to help us.

*j. She agreed to lift a finger to help us.

Here's another set of examples using idioms; what's the rule that blocks the starred ones?

   k. All the Scouts hit the sack early.

*l. The sack was hit early by all the Scouts.

  m. Martha cut off her nose to spite her face.

*n. Martha's nose was cut off by her to spite her face.

  o. The poor old dog kicked the bucket yesterday.

*p. The bucket was kicked yesterday by the poor old dog.

  q. Some of the managers grimly bit the bullet.

*r. The bullet was grimly bitten by some of the managers.

You'll notice, after you work with examples like these for a while, that *all* of them seem to be meaningless. If you clench your fist over and over again, the muscle cramps and it becomes difficult to continue; when you clench your brain, the same thing happens.

Here's one more rule for you to find, taken from the *sound* system of English this time. None of the sentences below is unacceptable, but speakers of this dialect seem to others to throw an "r" sound into their speech that "isn't really there." What is the rule that determines when they add that extra "r"?

  s. His IDEA seems sound to me.

  t. His IDEAR is ridiculous.

  u. CUBA lies off the coast of Florida.

  v. CUBAR is an island.

  w. The SOFA has one broken leg.

  x. We sat on the SOFAR and talked.

  y. They used to live in GENEVA.

  z. GENEVAR is a city in Switzerland.

3. In "The Power of a Name" (*Psychology Today*, October 1976) Mary G. Marcus reports on studies showing that "Americans who dislike their names do not feel as good about themselves as people who like theirs." She goes on to caution readers that "the impact of a person's name on his or her self-esteem and mental health is determined largely by how others *react* to a person with that name." Is this logical? Do you feel that you are affected by this invisible feedback system — that is, do you react to people on the basis of their names, with your reaction serving as input to your half of the feedback loop? Or are you able to ignore such things and base your reaction on *facts*? Do you think the psychologists are exaggerating?

    One more piece of information: the one factor that has most reliably predicted the winner of the contest for President of the United States has been *the length of the candidate's name.* (If this interests you, you'll find details in "The Presidential Name Game," by Dirk L. Schaeffer, on page 12 of the October 1984 issue of *Psychology Today*.)

4. ANOTHER INVISIBLE SYSTEM. . . . Speakers of English are often amazed by languages in which the word for *table* is feminine, the word for *bed* is masculine, and so on — they assume English is free of such things. But Jack Rosenthal tells us that when English speakers are given pairs of words and asked to assign gender to them they do so without any hesitation. Given "chicken soup/beef soup," for example, they immediately say the chicken soup is feminine and the beef soup is masculine; given "Ford/ Chevrolet" they say Ford is masculine and Chevrolet feminine. Try an experiment — assign this Hidden Gender for the pairs below. Then try to determine what you're basing your decisions on.

fork . . . spoon	cup . . . glass
salt . . . pepper	turkey . . . chicken
purple . . . pink	vanilla . . . chocolate
truck . . . car	lake . . . river
cricket . . . butterfly	Paris . . . New York

Did you run into any examples in which you were convinced that both members of the pair were masculine or both were feminine? Do you understand why you felt that way?

SIGHT BITES

1. "It's quite clear that if you treat people like idiots, they will behave like idiots."

   (Jerome Bruner, quoted in "Schooling Children in A Nasty Climate," in *Psychology Today* for January 1982; page 59.)

2. "...if even a small fraction of homeowners becomes persuaded that prices are about to topple, then they'll be right: prices will topple. . . . No one knows to what extent the consumer boom of recent years has been fed by people's belief that their houses were making them rich."

   (From "TRB From Washington: Blow Your House Down," in *The New Republic* for October 10, 1988; page 4.)

3. "*In Search of Excellence* . . . can be summed up in one sentence: Being a good human being is good business."

   (From "Surviving In Small Businesses," by Paul Hawken, in *Coevolution Quarterly* for Spring 1984; page 17.)

3 It's Only Semantics

How many times have you observed (or taken part in) an argument and remarked sagely at some point that the problem was "only" semantics? We all hear that — most of us have said it ourselves. But semantics is a very odd word to put after that variety of "only," the "only" that means "what follows here is rather insignificant." Semantics is *extremely* important. Your internal grammar has a number of interacting components, among which the semantic component is unquestionably the most powerful. In this chapter we are going to take a look at a technique for using your semantic expertise as part of your communication strategy, using the mechanism known as *the semantic feature*. We will begin with a scenario.

SCENARIO SEVEN   The expression on John's face was everything Sharon had been expecting. She looked down quickly at her hands, folded tightly in her lap... anything to avoid meeting his eyes, where his contempt was so obvious.

"I hope I didn't hear you correctly," he said icily. "I hope what you intended to say was that you and Eve aren't quite *finished* with the project I assigned to you — but you'll have it ready in time for the presentation this afternoon."

"No, John," Sharon said miserably. "There's nothing wrong with your hearing. I don't have anything to show you. Like I said before — every time Eve and I thought we could get started on it there was another crisis and we had to put it aside. I'm sorry."

"You did know that the material was critical for the meeting this afternoon?"

"Yes. We knew that," Sharon answered, still staring down at her hands. "We just failed to get it done in time, that's all. And we're both sick about it."

There was no sympathy on his face at all. She could see that it would be a waste of time to try to explain, because Martin was too disgusted to hear anything she might say. She told him one more time how sorry she was and left the room with as much dignity as she could manage, thankful that at least she hadn't cried.

Behind her, John Martin sat briefly rubbing his chin, his expression bland now, waiting to be sure she was gone. And then he picked up the phone and spoke to the secretary.

"Katy," he said, "put in a hurryup call for Josh Appleton and Tony Bellini; tell them to get up here, *fast.* Tell them we're ready for Plan B and we've only got three or four hours to work out the details. Thanks, Katy!"

Once again, these two people have been involved in a language interaction; once again, they are living in two very different realities. Almost nothing about their communication could be described as syntonic — they are on entirely different wavelengths. Let's take a look at the perceptions each one has of what has taken place.

SHARON'S PERCEPTION

John had given Sharon and Eve a special opportunity to demonstrate their competence, in a way that openly told the men in Advertising & Marketing they would have to treat the two women with more respect in future. The women had every intention of fulfilling that opportunity so well that no question could be raised as to whether it had been deserved. But then one crisis after another came along; and they found themselves hard pressed — even working many extra hours — just to carry out their regular duties and stay on top of everything they were obligated to do. It always seemed that there would be time to work on the slogans for the healthcare products in a day or two. But then, to their dismay, all the time was gone and the deadline was upon them, and they didn't have even rough notes ready to turn in.

Eve had refused to face John Martin at all, and had called in sick. She was already getting her résumé ready to look for another job and saw no reason to go through the ordeal. Sharon bitterly resented being left to face their boss by herself, but she knew she had to get it over with. She was not surprised when it went badly; she was only surprised that Martin didn't fire her on the spot.

Sharon knows how badly she and Eve have failed. She is ashamed and miserable, and she realizes that even if John is too charitable to fire her outright, there's no way that she can go on working with him or with the men who were bypassed for the assignment. The thought of having to leave Metamega and look for a position somewhere else is awful — she enjoys her job, and doesn't want to leave it — but she has no choice. The only question in her mind now is how to wind up the episode in a way that will enable her to get a decent reference despite her current disgrace.

JOHN'S PERCEPTION

John was willing to give Sharon and Eve the chance they had been demanding, and to do it openly. It was an experiment worth making, and one in which he made certain he could not lose. He offered the two women the assignment, but he didn't leave it at that. As insurance, he called in two of his best men and instructed them to do a few slogans for the new line themselves and be ready to argue for them — just in case.

John prides himself on being fair and open-minded. He had been 99 percent convinced in advance that Sharon and Eve would make a mess of the assignment and that it was far beyond their abilities. But if they had managed to get the job done, he would have been delighted, and he would have rewarded them with responsible assignments thereafter. If they had come to him after their division ran into the series of unexpected crises and told him frankly that they couldn't get the task done, he would have regretted the hassle, but he could have dealt with it. He would have understood, and he would have made a note to give them an alternative opportunity as soon as something suitable came along.

What they actually *did* — just letting the disaster happen, and leaving him, so far as they knew, high and dry — was inexcusable. If he had been so foolish as to rely on them, he would have been in serious trouble. But of course he had known better than to do that.

Still, John does not regret the experiment. On the contrary. From now on he will be able to assign the semi-clerical work to Sharon and Eve with a clear conscience. It will now be a matter of record that he has given them their chance — a very fair and public chance — and that they dropped the ball. He won't have to listen to any more nonsense about sexism after this — from either the women *or* the men — because the women have made his case for him. He is confident that they will now have a more accurate perception of their competence and will have the good sense to be satisfied with the excellent positions they hold in the firm and the very necessary work that they are doing. In John's opinion, the episode has come to a most satisfactory conclusion.

CONSEQUENCES

When Sharon and Eve hand in their resignations, John Martin is going to be astonished. In addition, he will conclude at once that they are leaving because their feelings are hurt, and that they are willing to sacrifice their jobs to punish both him and the corporation for offending them. This will be reflected in the references he gives them, and he will see to it that other references from Metamega convey the same message. These results — unpleasant and costly for everyone involved — clearly demonstrate an inconvenient truth: FALSE PERCEPTIONS HAVE REAL CONSEQUENCES.

The problem here is "only semantics" with a vengeance. If a meeting were held to discuss it, both sides would have a lot to say in defense of their actions. But nothing useful would be accomplished. There is a major reality gap here, with Sharon and Eve basing their words and their actions on one version of reality and John and the other men basing theirs on a quite different version. And a primary source of the breakdown is the word that turned up in all the scenarios in Chapter Two: the word FAILURE.

Introducing The Semantic Feature

Let's back up slightly now and introduce the concept of the *semantic feature*, using a very simple example. Consider the two words "mother" and "father": how do their meanings differ? Both words refer to physiological adults who are parents; both words refer to human beings. But one refers to a female and the other to a male. In Figure One this information is shown in the form of semantic features, with plus or minus values indicated.

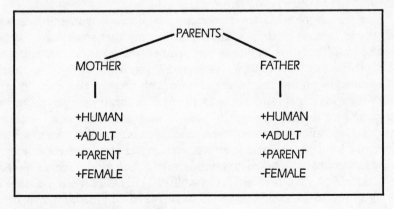

FIGURE 1. PARENTS

When you find yourself thinking that the features contain an error because they should read "plus or minus MALE" rather than "plus or minus FEMALE," your reaction points out dramatically the difference between language and logic. In logical terms it makes absolutely no difference whether "man" is defined as [+ MALE] or [- FEMALE]. They mean exactly the same thing, logically. In the real world, however, as proved by your reaction, the two are far from equivalent. Semantic features seem almost childishly simple — until one of them throws a phenomenon of this kind into sharp focus.

There are other semantic features besides [HUMAN], [ADULT], and [FEMALE] that the semantic component of your grammar knows quite well would be part of a *complete* definition. Many of them are summarized by the features shown; for example, you don't need a feature specifying that mothers and fathers have two arms and two legs, but no feathers, because those features are subfeatures of [+ HUMAN]. A semantic feature diagram like Figure One only needs to show the essential minimum.

Now let's apply the same technique to the word "failure." What does it mean? What is its semantic content?

We would all agree that "failure" has the semantic feature [minus CONCRETE]. That is, it's not a living thing or an object, but an abstraction. We would agree that it has the feature [+ NEGATIVE]; although failure is a major industry in America, nobody openly looks upon it as a good thing. We could use either [+ NEGATIVE] or [- POSITIVE] to express this fact. We could word a feature to express the semantic content "a goal not reached." On all these things, we would agree, and it would seem that we were all using the same word, with no possibility of misunderstanding.

But as we explored this question, we would hit upon the single semantic feature that is responsible for so many communication breakdowns, with so many unfortunate real world consequences attached to them. That feature is the feature [FINAL].

The reason John Martin is so surprised when Sharon and Eve resign their jobs is because for him a failure means only that something has been tried and hasn't worked, and that now it's necessary to try something else. This doesn't mean that "failure" ceases to be negative, but the negativeness is minor and has no shame attached. For both Sharon and Eve, however, "failure" is *very* final, and there is no option for trying anything new. Instead, failure means leaving the field in disgrace. (This is an extremely common difference between men and women in American society.) Everything John Martin and the two women did after the episode of the failed assignment was based upon this single feature difference — AND THE FACT THAT NONE OF THEM KNEW THE DIFFERENCE EXISTED.

If John had known, he would have called Sharon and Eve in and made it clear to them that he did not perceive their failure in this one episode as a catastrophe — and certainly not as anything worth quitting over. But he didn't know, and that didn't happen. Instead, he concluded that since they had "no reason to quit" the only possible explanation for their leaving was childish hurt feelings and anger.

If Sharon and Eve had known, the issue of leaving their jobs would never have come up. They would simply have chalked the failure up to experience and settled back to watch for an opportunity to try again, as John expected them to do.

This is what happens when you are dealing with "only semantics." But it doesn't have to happen. Not if you know that when the behavior of other people who share your language seems bizarre, or incomprehensible, or completely unlike your expectations, it's time to start searching for the key words that may be hiding a SEMANTIC FEATURE MISMATCH, and it's time to determine what that mismatch is.

In logical terms it's often possible to talk of features as being simply plus or minus, as in Figure One. In real world terms, however, it's not that simple. John Martin certainly realizes that with regard to the scheduled meeting Sharon and Eve's failure to have material ready *is* "final." In that limited sense, and to that limited degree. But it is far less final for him than it is for Sharon and Eve, just as it is far less *negative* for him than it is for them. One way to make this explicit is with a device like that shown in Figure Two, which is a rating scale for the *weight* of pluses and minuses on a given semantic feature.

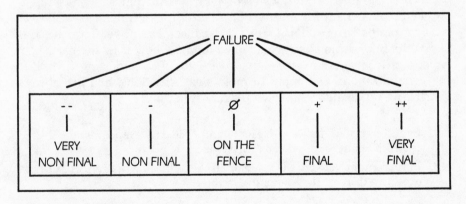

FIGURE 2. FAILURE

We could prepare another diagram of the same kind for the feature [NEGATIVE], as it applies to the word "failure." But notice your reaction to that idea. Like your reaction to describing a man as [+/- FEMALE], it is evidence that the semantic component of your internal grammar is fully operational and kicking in when you need it. You will immediately have thought, "Sure, we could do one of those for [NEGATIVE], but we don't need it! Because the degree of negativeness will always be the same as the degree of finalness. They will always *match*." And you are absolutely correct.

The system set up in Figure Two is very neat. It ranges over five values: from double minus (--) for "very nonfinal", through the noncommital fence-sitting null symbol (∅), to double plus (++) for "very final." That range will serve us adequately in this book. But it should always be remembered that it is only a convenience, and that for any fifty real people you would need more than five values.

Any time you need to discuss a failure with individuals for whom the finality of failure has the weight of *ten* pluses attached, you can predict that they will be far more upset about failing than persons for whom a double plus is sufficient. Any time you need to discuss a failure with someone for whom the value of FINAL for "failure" differs radically from your own, you will know in advance that communication will be difficult and explanations will be required. And you should prepare for the interaction with such differences firmly in mind.

Obviously, if you had access to printouts of the internal grammars of other people, where you could find diagrams like Figures One and Two for those people, it would be a great deal easier for you to understand their behavior and anticipate what they might say or do in an interaction. This is valuable information. Consider the obvious facts shown in Figure Three.

This diagram sets out the *stereotypical* information, showing a single plus before FINAL for the meaning of "failure" for an American executive, but five pluses before FINAL for the Japanese executive. To make full use of the information you would need to know how it fit the particular American or Japanese executive you were going to be dealing with. But the generalizations will apply to most such situations, and are always valuable as a baseline from which to work. They are:

☐ In an interaction between Japanese and American executives, the degree to which failure is considered FINAL will be significant.

☐ In such an interaction, the value of FINAL will be higher for the Japanese executive than for the American executive.

In *Inc.* for April 1986, Joel Kotkin and Yoriko Kishimoto state this emphatically, saying of Japanese managers: "It is actually *fear* that moves those managers. There is no tolerance for failure. The penalty for failure is out, finished. It's a powerful motivation." (This cultural difference demonstrates that the view of every failure as disastrous is not confined to women; most Japanese business people are male.)

It would be wonderful if somewhere there were a book — a sort of universal semantic directory — with diagrams like the one in Figure

Three for the executives and professionals of every ethnic and cultural group. So that before you went to negotiate grain prices with an Albanian executive you could check the book to find out what the most typical situation is. It would be wonderful if a similar book existed for the varying *professional* cultures, so that before architects went to negotiate contracts with neurosurgeons (and vice versa) everyone involved could find out how the two groups ordinarily differ in their judgments about the finality and negativeness of a failure. Books of the same kind for every sort of subgroup would be invaluable, but nothing of the kind exists.

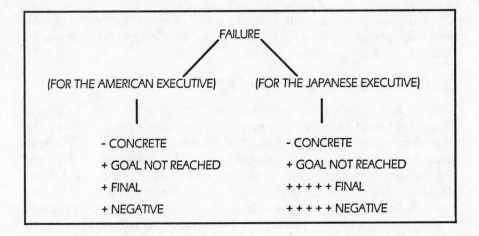

FIGURE 3. FAILURE

However, because of your linguistic competence you are fully equipped to use language to find out such information for yourself. You can then make a note of it for future reference, so that over the course of time you write your *own* universal semantic directory. I am sure I need not point out to you that it would be worth a vast sum of money.

Getting Semantic Information

Throughout this book I will be identifying words — like "failure" — that can reliably be recognized as reality gap words. You should learn them, and be prepared, whenever they come up in your interactions with others, to answer the following four questions.

☐ What semantic features matter for this word?
☐ Which of those features are likely to show a mismatch?

☐ Is the person I am interacting with on the plus or the minus side for the critical feature?

☐ Where on the scale from double minus to double plus will that person's choice for the critical feature fall?

If you do this routinely, and always record what you learn, you will soon have a powerful database of semantic information available to you.

There are three practical ways to carry out these steps. You can use information sources such as reference books, tapes and videos, and other media. You can ask people who are already familiar with the group or groups in question. And you can ask individuals directly.

Assume that we are still working with the word "failure," and that the person you are going to interact with is a middle-aged male American executive from Texas — that will do.

GETTING INFORMATION FROM MEDIA SOURCES

Go straight to the indexes, either at your library or on your computer. If you don't have access to a computer information service, chances are your library does.) What you want is a listing of titles from business magazines, news magazines, and such general publications as *Harpers* and *Atlantic Monthly*, containing words like "Texas, Texans, Dallas, Houston." A quick glance at the lists for even the past few years should give you several dozen to choose from. Read the articles you've chosen, looking for clues to how the typical Texan *reacts* to failure. How many of the articles you read will depend on how much time you have, how important the interaction with the live Texan is, and how long the association is likely to last.

If you were looking for examples dealing with Albanian executives or Laotian neurosurgeons, you would have to extend your search over a longer period of time, because there would not be as much material available as there is about Texans. But the process would be the same. If you had time to turn to full-length books as well as shorter pieces, and if the information was sufficiently important to you to make that investment worthwhile, that would be a next step. In some cases, such as the Japanese, you would have more resources available than you could possibly use; in others you might have to turn to university libraries and obscure scholarly journals. Always, you would be asking the same question and looking for its answer: "When a Texan fails, what does that Texan say and do?"

GETTING INFORMATION FROM OTHER PEOPLE

Ask them. Find yourself a Texan who is willing to discuss Texas with you — which will be easy. Frame your question in a way that will encourage the Texan to answer you in detail. For example:

> You know, I've always wondered . . . . when a Texan drills an oil well, and
> it turns up dry, and then does it again, and it turns up dry again . . . . and
> that keeps happening till all the money to drill oil wells is gone . . . how
> does he act? What is he likely to say? Do you know anybody that's hap-
> pened to?

Don't say "if a Texan" does such and such a thing; say "when a Texan"
does it. That's important. (In a later chapter we'll talk about why that
is true.)

If the Texan you're talking to doesn't seem helpful, say something
that will extract the information you need by inviting correction of your
errors, like this:

> You know, you're always hearing about Texans being different from other
> people. But I'm not at all sure I believe that. I'll bet you that when a Texan
> drills three oil wells in a row and they all come up dry, and he's got no
> more money to drill with, a Texan sits down by the last dry well and bawls
> just like anybody else.

Your strategy is to choose whatever you think is most unlikely, in order
to get a response something like this one:

> Sits down by the last dry well and *bawls*? A *Texan*? No way! What a *Texan*
> does is . . .

And then, once the information is being provided to you, be very sure
that you listen carefully.

GETTING INFORMATION FROM THE TEXAN HIMSELF

There are two ways to do this — the direct method and the indirect
method. The indirect method requires no further explanation; you proceed
with your Texan in the same way you would if you were trying to get
information from someone else, as in the preceding paragraphs. If you
want to use the direct method, however, you just explain. Like this:

> Bill, before we start negotiating this contract I'd like to be sure that we're
> going to be speaking the same language. For example, take a word like 'fail-
> ure.' What does that word mean to you?

If you are comfortable doing so, and your Texan is cooperative, you can
show him a few semantic feature diagrams, explain what you're after

and why, and ask him how his diagrams for "failure" would look. And then be prepared for him to ask you to return the favor.

Semantics, yes. But not "only" semantics. Semantics, properly used, gives you the information you need in order to predict much of what is going to happen well in advance, so that you have ample time to prepare your strategy. Semantics helps you avoid unpleasant surprises for which you are completely unprepared. Semantics helps you avoid wasting time talking from a position that isn't even in the same version of reality as that of the person you're dealing with. And the semantic feature technique is one of the fastest and least complicated available for going straight to the heart of a potential semantic conflict and setting matters to rights.

As we come to other words that are likely to create reality gaps, I'll point them out and discuss the application of the semantic feature technique to each one. In the meantime you might want to take another look at Scenarios Three through Six in Chapter Two, and decide what the semantic feature diagrams for "failure" (and the finalness of failure) would look like, for each of the individuals using that word or a related word and for the person or persons who heard them use it.

Stalking the Semantic Feature

It's easy for me to say, "Find out what semantic features other people attach to the word *X*." But it's not enough. For a linguist, it constitutes negligence, as it would if a physician told you to "find out what disease you are suffering from." It's no better than all those standard "listen carefully" platitudes I criticize. If I had no other choice, I would tell you that this was something you just have to pick up as you go along, using your common sense and intuition, and that with practice you would eventually figure it out — the way that teachers do, when asked what it means to say that a sentence is "awkward." Fortunately, I can be more helpful than that. There is an excellent technique you can use when you're searching for a semantic feature: you can make a list of *reality statements*.

It may be that the one-celled amoeba perceives reality directly, just as it is, with no filter between itself and what is "really" there. We will never know. We do know that humans can't function like that. The flood of information we must handle, every moment of our lives, is so overwhelming that if it weren't filtered it would soon drive us mad. We reduce that flood to a manageable trickle, and we process and organize what remains. The result is a reality composed of a set of simple statements like these:

- □ All beavers have tails.
- □ $70,000 is a large sum.
- □ The President of the United States lives in the White House.
- □ Sugar melts in water.
- □ Fire is hot.

And so on.

A culture — a human society, with all its snaps and buttons on — is formed whenever a group of people have many such reality statements in common. If all those shared statements could be listed, they would constitute a reality *consensus* for that culture. And this is just as true for the culture of a business or organization as it is for the culture of a nation or ethnic group.

A semantic feature is *shorthand* for at least one reality statement. A diagram showing the word "mother" with the feature [+FEMALE] attached is shorthand for the reality statement "All mothers are female." The feature notation is more efficient in terms of time and energy, the way contemporary numbers are more efficient than Roman numerals. Furthermore, finding features forces you to be specific. You can't waffle with a feature the way you can with a sentence. But it helps to work in both directions: to expand features into reality statements, and to reduce the reality statements to semantic features. Each serves as a check on the other, isolating flaws and making them apparent — as when you think you have found a feature but discover that it takes half a dozen reality statements to expand it. And the process of expanding and reducing, which is a kind of semantic translation, will help you fill in the gaps.

When you come upon a reality gap word like "failure," a word that attracts suspicion by turning up repeatedly in interactions you are dissatisfied with, begin the semantic feature analysis for yourself. Write the troublesome word on a sheet of paper. Beneath it, write down the semantic features that occur to you as part of its meaning for you personally. Give them their plus or minus values, as you perceive them. If the weight of a given feature is important to you, rank the value from double minus to double plus. For example, in defining the word "bird" there is no need to rank the feature [FEATHERED] for its weight in pluses or minuses; human beings do not suffer communication breakdowns over the issue of how feathered a bird happens to be. When you have listed the features that readily occur to you, stop; don't struggle to add more. Instead, convert those features to reality statements.

Now you have a rough draft of the meaning this reality gap word has for *you*. You have a tentative set of semantic features and a tentative set of reality statements. Because you are more accustomed to writing sentences than to writing features, it will be easier for you to find gaps if you work in that direction, using the following steps.

1. Look at your set of reality statements and decide whether you think it is complete and correct. If so, go to Step 5. If not, go to Step 2.
2. Do you see an immediate need to add other statements? If so, write them down.
3. Do you feel that you have two or more statements that should be a single statement instead? If so, revise the list and combine the two into one.
4. Do you see statements that are irrelevant to the context you are working with? For example, the statement "Human beings breathe oxygen" is not likely to be relevant unless you plan to do your negotiating at the bottom of an ocean or in some equally unusual environment. Eliminate those from the list.
5. When you are satisfied with the set of statements, go the other direction — translate them into semantic features.
6. Go back and forth between the two sets of data until you feel that the task is complete.

At the end of this process — which you will be able to do very quickly once you've worked through a few examples — you will have an organized and properly indexed representation of the word's meaning for you. Your goal is then to use communication, both verbal and nonverbal, to find out whether the other person's representation of the word's meaning differs from yours, and — if it does — to determine what the differences are and whether they matter in the context of your interaction with that person. You can ask questions like the following, INSERTING REALITY STATEMENTS FROM YOUR OWN LIST IN THE BLANKS:

☐ "Do you feel that . . . ?"
☐ "I wonder: do you agree that . . . ?"
☐ "It has often been said that . . . ; do you think that's accurate?"
☐ "Does the fact that ... cause you any concern?"

If the negotiation is critical — or simply as a way of building your semantic directory — take a copy of your own semantic diagram for the word with you, and fill in the differences on that sheet as you locate them. After the negotiation, fill in the other person's name, along with any other information necessary for indexing what you have learned, and file the sheet for future reference.

You will discover as you do this semantic investigating that within your own culture you run into a small set of variations on a single definition over and over again. You can then index the members of that set as, for example, FAILURE-1, FAILURE-2, FAILURE-3. Thereafter you will only need to write new names on the page as you run into people and learn which FAILURE is dominant in their picture of the world. Only with cultures other than your own will you keep running into new sets of features and new values.

Warning: The longer it takes you to pin down a particular feature, and the more reluctant you feel to bother, the more likely it is that getting at *that* feature really matters.

Semantics and Body Language

There are many books about nonverbal communication — popularly called "body language" — on the market today. Most of them, despite very interesting content and good intentions on the part of the authors, are either dangerously misleading or incomprehensibly technical. I am going to do my best to clarify the misunderstandings created by this situation as we go along. The three pieces of information about body language that you most urgently need to know right now are these:

☐ For American English at least 90 percent of all emotional information, and at least 65 percent of all information whatsoever, is carried not by your words but by the body language that goes with those words.

☐ The most powerful mechanism for body language is the voice: its quality, its tone, and the intonation it gives to words and parts of words.

☐ There is a grammar of body language, just as there is a grammar of words and sentences. You *know* that grammar, although you have probably never taken a course in it — but most of this knowledge is stored in your memory in a way that gives you no convenient or reliable access to it.

The best evidence for the power of body language and the power of the human voice comes from the drama departments of American colleges and universities, and is well known to every one of us. In every drama program, students are expected to be able to take one or two words — "You monster!" will do for an example — and say them in such a way that they express any and all of a long list of emotions: rage, love, terror, sexual desire, tenderness, admiration, and so on.

These students are not Richard Burton or Meryl Streep. They are just ordinary people, often very young and inexperienced people. The fact that they can do this task routinely and the fact that the other students watching them understand, without special instruction, which emotion is being expressed are proof positive that "the words you say" are not what matters most. Both speakers and listeners are working from their grammar of nonverbal communication; all they need is practice.

Here is the basic principle to remember:

ANY WORDS, BE THEY EVER SO FLAWLESS, CAN HAVE THEIR
MEANING CANCELLED BY BODY LANGUAGE — BUT NOT VICE
VERSA. THERE ARE *NO* WORDS CAPABLE OF CANCELLING THE
MEANING TRANSMITTED BY BODY LANGUAGE.

This is very important, and it applies to almost everyone, with the
exceptions being truly great actors, such as Richard Burton or Meryl
Streep. It's information that is critical to your success.

And this brings up two interesting questions: Why weren't you
taught this information in school, preferably elementary school? And why
do you so rarely read about it or encounter it in the nonprint media?

The answer is simple: The information is systematically, even
doggedly, suppressed. This is a conspiracy, yes, but it's a conspiracy in
which we all take part. It's not malicious, and it's not sinister. At worst,
it's laziness; at best, it's an attempt to protect ourselves.

Think about it. Think about the real world consequences of the
basic facts about body language. Think about the *inconvenience* they
represent in practice! Like the stunning facts in David Bodanis's *The Secret
House*, from which we learned about the sex lives of the millions of
dust mites that share even the cleanest of our beds with us — THESE
ARE THINGS IT WOULD BE PLEASANTER NOT TO KNOW.
Pleasanter — but not safer. What we have here is a massive cultural
conspiracy of neglect, an attempt to save ourselves trouble by ignoring
a set of burdensome facts into oblivion.

People are intrigued by the idea that if they learn to use some
particular set of body language elements (including an effective and
spellbinding voice) they will be able to manipulate other people and avoid
being manipulated *by* other people. They will buy all sorts of books and
tapes, go to all sorts of seminars and workshops, to acquire such
information. But they would be *appalled* by the logical and ethical
implications of this same idea, and that is why it is so rarely mentioned
in popular forums. I will be more than happy to state those implications
explicitly here, as follows:

BECAUSE YOUR NONVERBAL COMMUNICATION HAS POWERFUL
REAL-WORLD EFFECTS ON OTHER PEOPLE, EFFECTS THAT CAN
LITERALLY CANCEL THE WORDS YOU SAY, YOU MUST TAKE
RESPONSIBILITY FOR YOUR BODY LANGUAGE.

If your body language were nothing more than a collection of random
movements and noises over which you had no control except the
constraints of etiquette, it would be pointless to worry about it. But if

your body language is powerful — in the same way that cars and chainsaws and scalpels and antibiotics are powerful — it becomes yet one more thing with which you have to be *careful*. One more thing you should not use unless you know what you are doing. This is exceedingly inconvenient. As the physician told Greg Easterbrook in *Newsweek's* January 1987 lead article on modern medicine: "No way am I going to believe that makes a difference!"

We human beings want to believe that if we say The Right Words, we've done all that can be reasonably expected of us. Never mind how much this sounds like the standard party line for primitive magic — "Just get your incantations right and they'll always work!" — we still want to believe it. Because we know that it's relatively easy to improve our words. We can buy a good dictionary and a thesaurus. We can buy a computer program to increase and polish our vocabulary. We can take a quick course in usage and diction. But taking responsibility for getting our body language right doesn't sound easy — it sounds like a lot of hard work.

I'm sorry — these facts will not go away, and they must be dealt with. You can't *afford* to waste your words by using them with body language that cancels their meanings and substitutes other messages you hadn't planned to transmit. But things are not nearly as bad as you might think. Body language improvement sounds hard only because it is so unfamiliar. It isn't that hard to learn nonverbal communication skills, and the benefits of doing so will more than amply repay you for the time and energy you invest.

We will return to this subject frequently throughout the book. For now, just remember this: THE SEMANTIC CONTENT — THE MEANING — CONVEYED BY YOUR BODY LANGUAGE IS FAR MORE POWERFUL THAN THE MEANING CONVEYED BY YOUR WORDS.

Workout — Chapter 3

1. *Time Magazine* for August 22, 1988 had a long special section titled "The Republicans," written by Laurence I. Barrett. Barrett describes four separate occasions on which reporters asked George Bush if he felt betrayed and were told that that was the wrong word for the situation. Here they are:

   a. Bush was allowed to go on representing Taiwan in the U.N. while Kissinger and Nixon were making the secret deal with mainland China. Bush said, "No, I didn't feel betrayed . . . that's too strong a word."

b. Nixon repeatedly assured Bush during the Watergate mess that there was no coverup. Bush said, "I felt thoroughly disillusioned. . . . Betrayal is a word I don't particularly use, but this wasn't right, and I've so stated many times."

c. Bush was talking about how he felt after finding out that the White House tapes existed. "I can remember standing down here in this building when I heard about the White House tapes, and felt — betrayed means that somebody owes me something and thus — and I think it's broader than that."

d. Bush was asked if he felt betrayed when he learned of the secret arms sales to Iran. He said, "I don't think you ought to use the word betrayed, but that shouldn't have happened. . . . "

From his remarks, and the context, can you determine how George Bush defines the word "betray"? What semantic features does he attach to it, and how do you think he weights them? Would a semantic feature diagram for your own understanding of "betray" match his?

2. According to the medical literature, it's now scientifically possible for men to be pregnant (with delivery by caesarean section, of course.) How do we handle this new development semantically? Do we change the semantic features on "mother" — dropping [+FEMALE] because the mother's sexual gender no longer matters? Do we follow the "men first" practice in other areas of English grammar and change the feature to [-FEMALE]. (or [+MALE])? Or what?

3. In *Inc.* for May 1986 ("Introducing the 1986 *Inc.* 100," edited by Stephen D. Solomon), the following anecdote about Irwin Selinger's tenure at Squibb Corporation appeared: "A company officer criticized Selinger for flying coach, cautioning him that corporate executives flew first class." That's a reality statement for the Squibb corporate culture: Corporate executives fly first class. Can you list at least twenty such statements for your own business or organization?

4. Using semantic features and reality statements, make clear the differences in the meanings of the following words: *kill; murder; assassinate.* How about *slay — terminate?* Can you fit them into the set? Do all of these words mean "cause someone to die"? If so, why don't we say "Lee Harvey Oswald caused John F. Kennedy to die"? If you accidentally go off to your office with someone's prescription medication in your pocket, and they die when they miss the dose, did you cause that person to die? Did you kill — or slay, or murder, or assassinate, or terminate — the person?

5. For a detailed description of failure as perceived by someone who doesn't consider it part of a game in any way, read "After the Fall: Overcoming Failure," by Carole Hyatt and Linda Gottlieb, in the February 1987 issue of *Savvy Magazine*, pages 45-50 and page 79. It begins with this sentence: "No matter how many times people tell you that in the long run you will be stronger, in the short run there are few things worse than failing."

6. Here's another sentence about failure: "Failure to find does not constitute malpractice; failure to look almost always does." It comes from "Legal Rounds," edited by Gregory L. Henry, in *Emergency Medicine* for July 15, 1986. Is this the "failure" we've been looking at in this book, or something else entirely? What semantic features would you need to define it?

7. Many people have pointed out that in America today failure is a huge industry. When every single member of a class gets an A, we don't congratulate the instructor on a spectacular success, we accuse him or her of grade inflation. When a hospital's beds are empty, we don't congratulate the doctors and nurses on a job well done — the better the healthcare providers function in terms of keeping people well, the more the hospital will be criticized for "underutilization." Insurance is *based* on failure — you are told to buy it because you *will* get sick, you *will* have accidents, everything *will* break or burn down or blow away, and you *will* be in the wrong place at the wrong time. On my campus, whether a student was a "failure" depended on how much money the legislature appropriated in a given semester to fund "remedial" classes — the "failing" test score was adjusted each semester so that there would not be more "failures" than there were class slots. (Like the way we define "poor" by setting a poverty line.) Add this information to your database on the word "failure" — can you still define it?

SIGHT BITES

1. To find out what something means, find out what question it is the answer to.

2. "People can seriously misunderstand what it is they're not saying to each other."

    (From Jack Rosenthal's "On Language" column in the *New York Times Magazine* for July 15, 1984.)

3. "The common wisdom has long held that four out of five new businesses fail within five years. Once again, the common wisdom is wrong. . . . As for the companies that don't make it, Kirchoff is reluctant to call them failures, preferring the word 'exits' instead. Failure, he maintains, is an inaccurate and loaded term. . . ."

    (From the "Insider" column on page 22 of *Inc.* for July 1988; Kirchoff is Bruce Kirchoff, a professor of entrepreneurship at Babson College.)

4. "I was surprised by how much the corporate world was turned on to the human potential possibility if I called it 'wellness'."

    (Ken Dychtwald, quoted in "Redesigning America," by Curtis Hartman, in *Inc.* for June 1988; page 59.)

5. "The videotape catches many mannerisms and nuances. . . . There is the dance of the eyes, seen most clearly in one-on-one bargaining. The American

looks up, trying to establish direct eye contact, at which point the Japanese lowers his gaze, only to raise his eyes again when the American looks down at his notes. . . ."

(From John Pfeiffer's "Science of Business" column in *Science 85* for September 1985; page 81.)

6. "Technology exists to enable men to give birth. . . . The procedure would involve fertilizing a donated egg with sperm outside the body. The embryo would then be implanted into the mesentery of the bowel. A caesarean section would be required for delivery."

(From "The Professional Future of the Ob/Gyn Clinician," by Hugh R. K. Barber, in *The Female Patient* for September 1986; page 12.)

4 Language and the Game Domain

Introduction — Dividing Up The World

Something in the human brain loves branching tree structures and favors them for the organization of information. The sets and subsets of labels that result from such organization are called *taxonomies*. One of the earliest taxonomies is the one little children construct for animals. For most American children, it looks like this:

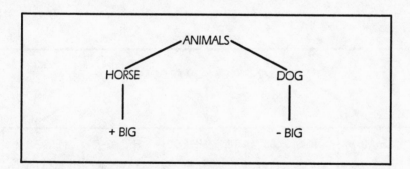

FIGURE 4. ANIMALS

This works well until the day the child encounters something the size of a large hog — too big to be a dog, too small to be a horse — at which point, the child has to do some restructuring. A typical solution is the addition of a third category marked [+ MIDDLE-SIZED].

Each time a new animal is observed, the child sorts it into one of the three categories on the basis of its size. This provides an index in

51

the memory and efficient access to the information. New categories and new features are added as they are needed, and eventually what you have is the elaborate memory storage area for ANIMALS in the adult brain. It would be much too elaborate to fit on this page, but the process by which it is set up is the same in the adult as it is in the child. And the adult faces the same problems the child does when an animal that won't fit readily into an existing category — for example, the kangaroo — is encountered.

If you set up a new category for every new thing you encounter, the result is not a taxonomy but a *list*, and that's not good. Lists are efficient only when they are kept to roughly ten items or less. The decision process that creates taxonomies is crucial to information storage. Asking yourself "What set does the kangaroo belong in, or does it have to have a set of its own?" and "What is it about the kangaroo that determines which set it goes into?" is what lets you attach associations to the "kangaroo" entry in your memory so that you can find it again later on. Anything that you can organize into a taxonomy will be easier to remember and use than either a random batch of data or a list.

The way most people think about language interactions — and the power relationships and arrangements that are established by language interactions — is better than random, but not much better than a list. We can improve this situation by setting up a taxonomy at this point. We'll use the relatively neutral word "domain" as our general label, and divide the world of language/power domains into five basic categories, as shown in Figure Five.

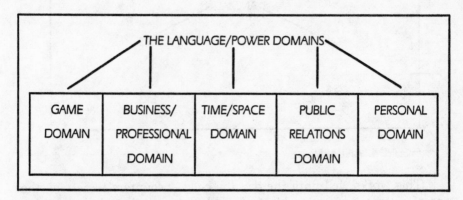

THE LANGUAGE/POWER DOMAINS

GAME DOMAIN	BUSINESS/ PROFESSIONAL DOMAIN	TIME/SPACE DOMAIN	PUBLIC RELATIONS DOMAIN	PERSONAL DOMAIN

FIGURE 5. THE LANGUAGE/POWER DOMAINS

It is the nature of taxonomies in the real world that they make false claims; Figure Five is no exception. Drawn this way, it makes the claim that each of the five domains has an *equal* importance in the life of every individual. This is clearly false, like giving most semantic features only plus or minus as their value. How *much* importance any one of the domains has will vary from person to person, from situation to situation, and over the course of time. But we can use this rough index as a basis from which to work, in the same way that we use the equally rough scale of weights from double minus to double plus for semantic features. We can then make adjustments in the basic index, as they are needed, for specific real world situations.

The Game Domain

The game domain has greater importance in mainstream American society today than any of the other four domains. Gameplaying is so all-pervasive that for many individuals — and especially for dominant adult males — it would be more accurate to set up one of the two taxonomies illustrated in Figures 6 and 7.

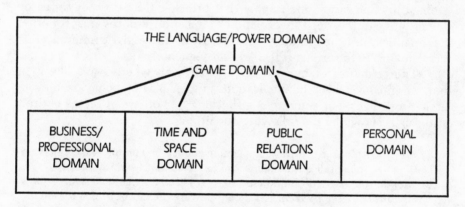

FIGURE 6. THE LANGUAGE/POWER DOMAINS

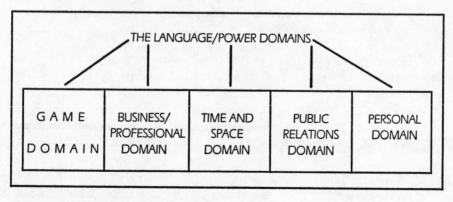

FIGURE 7. THE LANGUAGE/POWER DOMAINS

Because dominant adult males by no means constitute the entire population, or even the largest segment of the population, the most basic diagram is the one shown in Figure 5. But dominant adult males do control most of the power in America today, and all of us have to spend large amounts of time *interacting* with dominant adult males. This makes it necessary to keep Figures 6 and 7 conveniently filed where we can get at them quickly and easily.

For the vast majority of adult American males, the following principle holds:

ANYTHING THAT INVOLVES NEGOTIATION IS ASSIGNED TO THE *GAME* DOMAIN UNTIL THE NEGOTIATION IS COMPLETED.

In other words, most American men today define anything that involves negotiation as a game, at least temporarily, and they switch to gameplaying behavior for the duration of the negotiation. American women, by and large, don't apply that principle. Nor do they agree on the meaning of the word "negotiation." Similar differences exist for other nationalities and other ethnic groups. This leads to massive communication breakdowns, with serious real world consequences.

The structure of our society is such that, whether we like it or not, we *must* consider the implications of gameplaying behavior in every area of our lives. For some this is shocking; for others, it seems entirely natural, as shown by the following quotation:

> A friend's teenage son was complaining about a boy on his basketball team who habitually called him names and beat him up. His mother asked, "Then why do you play with him?" He looked at her in disbelief and said, "Because he's *on my team*," as though it were the most obvious reason in the world. Women don't understand this peculiar idea that you can hate someone and still work with him.
>
> Janice Larouche, quoted in "Trouble Spots," by Nancy Arnott, *Executive Female*, May/June 1988.

However we may feel about this, it has to be reckoned with if we are to achieve our goals. Let's take a look at a scenario that illustrates this problem.

SCENARIO EIGHT   **S**haron Jamison knew exactly what her brother-in-law was going to do — she recognized the courtroom stance. "Will," she began, "there's no point in trying to change my mind. I—"

Will Clayton cut her off abruptly and stood there ticking off the points on his fingers, one at a time. "It's clear to me," he said gravely, "that: (a) you love your job, you're good at it, and you don't want to leave; (b) the reason you *are* leaving is because you think you've done something your boss would be justified in firing you for; and (c) you think it's better to resign than to be fired. I have no quarrel with points (a) and (c), Sharon. But point (b), now! Point (b) is seriously flawed."

"But, Will—"

"No, I mean it!" he said. "So John Martin asked you and Eve to write a few slogans, and you two had so much other work to do that you didn't get them done in time. So what? What's the big deal?"

"Will," Sharon answered, "you don't understand. Those slogans were part of a crucial presentation for a new client. John had to go into that meeting with the most important part of the sell missing, because Eve and I blew it. *That* is a big deal."

"I don't believe it."

"It's true!"

"Come on, Sharon! This was the first time Martin ever turned anything like that over to you, right? Well... no *way* would he just let that float, hoping you'd come through! He'll have had somebody else working on it too — just in case. And he will have gone into his meeting with every last thing he needed. What *else* are you supposed to have done?"

"He trusted us," she said slowly, distracted, wondering if it could possibly be true that Martin had had backup people on the slogans without telling her and Eve. Could he have done something as sneaky and dishonest as that? Surely not! "None of the men thought we could do it," she went on, "and John Martin ignored them. He took a chance on us, and we let him down. He'll never forgive us for that, Will. And he's right."

The young attorney made a rude noise at her. "Wrong!" he said. "Listen, Sharon ... what happened is very simple. You and Eve kept insisting you could carry the ball, and Martin finally decided to throw it to you. That's fair. And you dropped it. That's too bad. But it was just one *play,* Sharon — it wasn't the whole *game.*"

Now Sharon was angry, and she made that very clear. "It wasn't a game at *all* !" she told him sharply. "I am not talking about *games* ! This was serious business — *is* serious business! You're talking about a big contract. You're talking about our *jobs.* And I'm sure John Martin has sense enough to understand that, even if you don't!"

Will stared at her, obviously bewildered. "I was only trying to help," he said. "What did I say to get you so upset?"

GAME VERSUS NON-GAME

What upset Sharon in this scenario was hearing her brother-in-law talk about her problem as if it were a *game*. For Sharon, the phrase would be "as if it were *only* a game." When she thinks about games she thinks of "Ring Around the Rosy" and "Trivial Pursuit." And for her the relevant semantic features on "game" are roughly as shown in Figure 8.

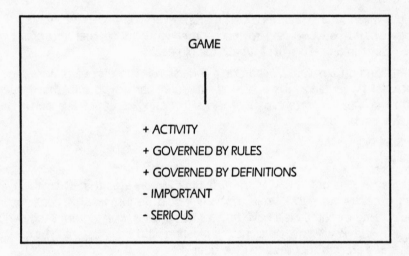

GAME

+ ACTIVITY

+ GOVERNED BY RULES

+ GOVERNED BY DEFINITIONS

- IMPORTANT

- SERIOUS

FIGURE 8. GAME

For her brother-in-law, on the other hand — and for almost all American men — games are very serious and very important. So serious and important that a grown man will be extremely well paid and highly respected for playing them well. When Will thinks of games, he thinks of baseball and basketball and football — especially football. For him, the features IMPORTANT and SERIOUS in Figure 8 have a plus in front of them, not a minus.

This matters. People who understand "game" the way Will does take it for granted that *all* adults worthy of respect perceive the world that way. When such people interact with people like Sharon and Eve, both groups misunderstand what's going on around them, and the consequences are always unpleasant.

Will Clayton (and John Martin) look upon Sharon and Eve's failure as the failure of a single *play* rather than as the loss of the whole game. This is why, for them, the failure is not final and not a reason to resign. This is why John, who feels that the women are resigning with no good reason, concludes that their resignations must be based on their emotions alone.

There are lots of plays in a game, and lots of games in a season. As Will said, "What's the big deal?" And Will would agree with John that Sharon and Eve's major mistake was not their failure to get the slogans done but their failure to warn him — something that *might* actually have put the entire game at risk if he hadn't had the foresight to provide backups. If you're on a team playing Saturday morning, and you realize on Thursday that you won't be able to make it, you go tell the coach — so that a replacement can be lined up. You don't just do nothing until midnight Friday night, hoping a miracle will occur, and *then* tell the coach.

In mainstream America today, no matter what your field is, no matter what activity you are involved in, you can't function successfully in an interaction unless you have the answers to the following questions:

☐ Are we playing a game?

Guidelines. If the situation is a negotiation of any kind, and if the participants are dominant adult males, the answer is yes. If the situation is not negotiable — for example, if it is a matter of life and death — the answer is no. If the participants are women, or children of any age, the answer is no.

☐ If the answer is yes, what game are we playing?

Guidelines. Most of the time, it's football. If not football, another team sport, such as baseball or basketball. Next most likely is the game of chess (especially if the participants are military personnel), followed by poker and tennis. The answer to this question will tell you the limits of the field, the governing definitions of terms, and the rules of play.

☐ If the answer is no, what are we doing instead and who's in charge?

Guidelines. The answer to this question is not predictable, but there are some likely categories.

— *Genuine emergencies,* when someone is literally risking life or limb, and WHEN IT'S NOT BEING DONE DELIBERATELY. Examples: major surgery; auto and plane crashes; major fires and floods and natural disasters; battles. In all such situations, it is expected that a professional of some kind will be in charge. Note that the requirement for the feature [-DELIBERATE] rules out such activities as professional sports, despite their danger.

— Any situation related to *romantic love.* For many people (and especially for women) no such situation can be a game. It is unfortunate that in such situations there is often *nobody* in charge.

— Situations in the *academic environment,* where teams are rare and individual performance is the highest goal. Often some sort of committee is in charge.

— *Idiosyncratic* — and sometimes startling — *situations.* For example, an individual might arbitrarily decide that *nothing* involving his cat, or his bass boat, or his art collection, or the President of the United States, can be a game. In these cases, whoever has the most power at the time will be in charge.

The only reliable tool for getting past these general guidelines to specific answers is LANGUAGE.

In any interaction you need to know what the word "game" means to the other people involved. You need to know whether it means the same thing to them that it means to you. If it does, you can relax and move on to other matters, knowing that what happens is going to make sense to you even if it doesn't go exactly as you want it to go. If the values of [SERIOUS] and [IMPORTANT] for "game" are double minuses for the other person, and pluses or double pluses for you, you need to know that immediately, because the potential for serious misunderstanding is so great.

Consider what it would be like to go out onto a field to play football, with twenty-one other people on the field, if you couldn't be sure that all of them knew that's why they were there. When everybody knows, you can be reasonably sure what will happen when you throw the ball, where other people will go, and what — from a limited set of possibilities — they will do. But if some people are there to do calisthenics, and some are there to play tennis, and some have no *idea* why they're there, ANYTHING CAN HAPPEN! That's not SAFE. People are going to get hurt. The game is going to go badly. Time will be wasted, and goals will not be made. This is no way to do anything important.

How do you find out whether the others involved in the interaction have the same semantic values for "game" that you have? The same way you would find out if they spoke English: talk *game* to them. Do it openly and blatantly, and pay attention to their responses. For example, say something like this, and watch for reactions.

> "I think our strategy on this first play should be pretty conservative — I don't think we should try for a touchdown this soon."

or

> "Now if this first play doesn't work out, we ought to have a couple of choices about which way we're going to run on the next one, and who's going to carry the ball."

If the people you're talking to stiffen and look insulted or annoyed, that's a clue. If they suggest that this is serious business and the sports metaphor isn't appropriate, that's a clue. If they try to talk *game* back at you and they make serious errors in choosing the vocabulary, that's a clue.

Alternatively, you can go after the information directly and just *ask* for it, wording your questions in the way that is most appropriate for your situation. Which brings us to a point at which I want to call "time out" and present another useful taxonomy — the set of language behavior patterns called "the Satir Modes."

Recognizing and Responding to the Satir Modes

Virginia Satir, a famous family therapist, discovered that when people are involved in confrontations or noncasual language interactions, their language behavior tends to fall into one of five consistent modes. She gave them the following names: BLAMING; PLACATING; COMPUTING; DISTRACTING; and LEVELING. The greater the stress people are under, the more likely they are to select the Satir Mode they're most comfortable with and to have difficulty communicating in the other modes.

The usefulness of this information is not limited to therapy. Knowing the Satir Modes well — being able to recognize them when others use them, and being able to frame *your* speech in the Satir Mode most effective for the situation — is a powerful technique for taking control of your own language behavior.

You'll find it easy to recognize the Satir Modes once they have been described to you. They are already part of your internal grammar, but they're stored in your memory without any useful index labels. Here's a quick description of each one, so that you can tack the labels on for future use.

Blaming. People who use Blamer Mode are openly hostile and belligerent. They use lots of "I/you" words, and words like "every, always, never, nobody, nothing." They make accusations and threats; they give direct and abrupt orders. Their body language is threatening; they shake their fingers and their fists at people; they loom over people; they frown and scowl and peer at others. They speak too loudly, or they spit out their words between their teeth, or they hiss at you. They put an unusual number of strong, emphatic stresses on words and parts of words in their sentences. This is a typical Blaming utterance: "WHY don't you EVer consider what anybody ELSE in the firm might want? You ALways have to do EVerything YOUR way!"

Placating. People who use Placater Mode also use "I/you" words and unusual, strong stresses a great deal. But instead of appearing belligerent and overbearing, they appear desperately anxious to avoid giving offense. They plead and cajole and wheedle; they praise excessively; they hedge even the smallest request heavily. Their body language, Satir said, will remind you of a cocker spaniel puppy. A typical Placating utterance is: "Oh, YOU know how I AM! WHATEVER everybody ELSE wants to do is okay with ME!"

Computing.   People using Computer Mode avoid "I/you" words and do everything they can to restrict their language to generalizations and abstractions rather than the personal. They try for the most emotionless and neutral communication possible. Their body language is minimal — a flat tone of voice, very little movement, a single noncommital facial expression. This is a typical Computing utterance: "There is undoubtedly a good reason for this delay. No sensible person would be alarmed."

Distracting.   People in Distracter Mode appear to be totally disorganized, if not panicked. They cycle rapidly through the other modes ... a sentence or two of Blaming, then a switch to Computing, back to Blaming, on to Placating ... and so on. As the word patterns cycle, the body language cycles too, and the effect is — as the label suggests — distracting. Here is a Distracter talking:

> One would think that some planning would be done prior to an urgent meeting. There is no excuse for failure to plan. And I am *not* going to put UP with this kind of garbage, wasting my TIME like this! But what do *I* know? Shoot, I'll bet these people had some kind of emergency that kept them FROM doing any planning... And so on.

Leveling.   The language behavior of the person in Leveler Mode is recognized by the *absence* of the word and body language patterns characteristic of the other Satir Modes. It is the "diagnosis of exclusion." There is no *typical* Leveler utterance. Leveling will always be the simple truth, in that particular context, to the extent that the Leveler *knows* the truth. The Leveler who can't stand the sight of you will say, "I can't stand the sight of you," and the body language will be appropriate for those words.

Warning: Since Leveling can always include the same *words* as those used in any other Satir Mode, it's important not to be confused by the words themselves. Compare the two sentences below:

> BLAMING: "WHY are you LEAVing so EARly?" (Frown on face; fists clenched at sides.)

> LEVELING: "Why are you leaving so early?" (Expression of neutral concern; relaxed posture.)

Remember that language is a feedback loop. Suppose Person *X* opens a language interaction in a given Satir Mode. For Person *Y* to respond in the same Satir Mode is FEEDING THE LOOP BEGUN BY PERSON

X. When you feed any such loop, by matching the Satir Mode you have recognized, the results are predictable. As follows:

- ☐ BLAMING at someone who is BLAMING creates a confrontation — a scene, a row. Always.
- ☐ PLACATING at someone who is PLACATING creates an undignified delay.
- ☐ COMPUTING at someone who is COMPUTING creates a dignified delay.
- ☐ DISTRACTING at someone who is DISTRACTING is panic feeding panic — it creates more panic.
- ☐ LEVELING at someone who is LEVELING is the simple truth going in both directions.

Based on these outcomes, and on the syntonics metaprinciple — ANYTHING YOU FEED WILL GROW — here are the rules for responding to the Satir Modes.

RULE ONE:

When an escalation of the Satir Mode coming at you is something you want, match that mode. Otherwise, choose some other mode.

RULE TWO:

When you don't know which Satir Mode to choose, go to Computer Mode and maintain it until you have enough information to make a reasoned choice.

There are three *types* of Satir Mode choices. All represent communication strategies at some level, in the simplistic sense that the speakers are of course choosing to talk in the way they believe will work best for them at that point. But the reasons *behind* the choices are very different. Let's look at the set.

First. There is the choice triggered by severe stress and crisis, as when a person becomes locked into a preferred mode at the scene of an auto accident or in an emergency room. This choice is made below the level of conscious awareness, and seems to be basically a survival mechanism.

Second. There is the choice made either consciously or unconsciously, but *naively*, often with a resulting mismatch between internal knowledge and feelings and their external expression, as follows:

People who feel insecure and powerless choose Blamer Mode, because they are convinced that nobody will do what they want unless they throw their weight around. The inner message is I HAVE NO POWER; the outer message is I HAVE *ALL* THE POWER.

People who care desperately, whose greatest fear is that others will become angry with them, choose the "*I* don't care — whatever YOU want is okay with ME!" language of Placater Mode. The inner message is I CARE SO TERRIBLY; the outer message is I DON'T CARE AT ALL.

People who are alarmed by the *intensity* of their emotions choose Computer Mode in an attempt to hide them. The inner message is I HAVE TOO MANY EMOTIONS AND THEY ARE TOO POWERFUL; the outer message is I HAVE NO EMOTIONS.

People who choose Distracter Mode have no idea *what* message they want to express. They cycle through the various modes at random, motivated only by panic. The inner message is HELP — I DON'T HAVE ANYTHING TO SAY! The outer message is HELP — I HAVE TO SAY *EVERY*THING!

People who choose Leveler Mode are the exception. All three of their communication channels — inner feelings, words, and body language — *match*. (This self-syntonic state is often referred to as *congruence*.)

Third. There is the third type of Satir Mode choice — the systematic skilled choice made by someone who understands the modes and how they are best used. When you select your own Satir Mode as a STRATEGIC RESPONSE to someone else's, using the rules given above, that is a systematic skilled choice.

I cannot emphasize too strongly the necessity for knowing which of these kinds of Satir Mode choice you are observing. You need to know whether a suggestion that you should make all the decisions is coming from a Leveler or a Placater. You need to know whether someone's open attempt to display power is the phony display of the Blamer or reflects a Leveler's honest conviction. The success of your actions depends upon your having such information.

Fortunately, it is always available to you, using the third syntonics metaprinciple: WATCH FOR MISMATCH. The clash between the words and the body language of the speaker, as well as the way the intonation differs from normal stress patterns, will always give you the necessary clues. The Satir Mode taxonomy provides you with the necessary categories and their identifying characteristics, so that you can swiftly classify language behavior *as you are observing it*. — And so that you can tailor your response to it — on the spot — for maximum effectiveness.

You will have seen other taxonomies of this kind, dividing people into categories based on their unpleasant behavior. For example, there is the very successful book, tape course, and seminar series by Dr. Robert M. Bramson, *Coping With Difficult People*. There's a major difference between most such systems and the Satir Modes: the Satir Mode a person chooses is a function of the *situation*, not a label for the personality, and will shift accordingly. Nobody "is" a Blamer, or a Placater, or a Leveler. Rather, people consistently choose a particular Satir Mode for a particular role or situation in their lives.

BACK TO THE GAME

Now we can return to the topic of asking where other people draw the line between what is a game and what isn't, and how serious or important they consider games to be. In Leveler Mode you just explain what you want to know, like this:

> "You know, some people look at the strategy for negotiating a contract like this as if it were a football game or a game of chess. Other people don't like that, because it seems as if it's not taking the whole thing seriously enough. It will make matters easier if we start by saying which of those two groups we belong to, so let's do that first."

But you may not be comfortable doing that. It may seem too open and too likely to be taken advantage of. In that case you might prefer to make the same statement in Computer Mode, like this:

> "There are various ways to think about the strategy for negotiating a contract such as this one. Many people look at it much as they would look at a football game or a game of chess. Others object to that on the ground that it fails to show sufficient respect for the seriousness of the situation. When two such widely different ways of looking at things are so common, it would undoubtedly be useful to determine in advance which view is held by each person present."

Notice that both of these utterances SAY THE SAME THING, in terms of the *facts* conveyed. But emotionally they are very different, and they will not produce identical responses from those who hear them. The advantage of Leveling is that it gets things done very *fast* — all the information is right out in the open, ready to be acted upon. Computing is not as efficient — which is why a primary strategic use for Computer Mode is the introduction of dignified delay into language interactions. On the other hand, Computing is more neutral, and does not completely remove the barriers between the speaker and the others present.

People are more likely to respond to the Leveling version with "That's the stupidest idea I ever heard!" or "I'm not about to tell you that!" than to the Computing version; Computing may therefore be your preference.

What matters is not that you choose any one Satir Mode rather than another. What matters is that when you use a Satir Mode it is because you have *made* a choice, with full awareness of what you are doing.

It will be obvious to you that you don't want to frame your query about someone's GAME versus NON-GAME orientation in Blamer or Placater Mode, and that Distracter Mode can be ruled out on a blanket basis. But it's worthwhile to examine typical Blamer/Placater versions, so that you will recognize them coming at you. Here they are.

> BLAMING: "SOME people think of a contract negotiation like this one the way they think of a FOOTball game, or a CHESS game — and some people DON'T. To make this WORK, I have to know which kind of person YOU are, and you have to know what MY position is. I'm NOT going to put up with any WAFFling aROUND, EITHer!"

> PLACATING: "Now I KNOW you're going to think this is a stupid idea, and I REALLY respect your JUDGment about these things — and if you feel like you can't take the time, I won't inSIST — but I just don't feel seCURE unless we all know WHO at this table thinks about contract negotiations like this one the way they think about a game of FOOTball, or CHESS, and who DOESn't. Either WAY is okay with ME, of course — I don't care! But if it wouldn't be too much of an intrusion, I would REALLY like to just get that straight before we start, oKAY?"

Team Versus Non-Team

We've talked about the need to determine where people draw the line between GAME and NON-GAME and how much value they assign to the features SERIOUS and IMPORTANT when they refer to games. There is another important distinction that has to be made, using the techniques presented above. You need the answer to the following question: When the other person in the interaction thinks of games, which concept is dominant: TEAM games or NON-TEAM games?

People whose gameplaying is based upon games like baseball and football — the usual case for American males — will behave differently from people whose gameplaying is based on singles tennis or golf. For example, instead of playing the positions assigned to them, they may keep trying to pitch in and help those playing *other* positions, creating tremendous confusion and much hostility and misunderstanding all around. Strategies are very different when a game pits one individual against another than when teams are involved. People who grow up without involvement in team sports are at a disadvantage in our society; all too often they are like a man trying to play football by the rules of tennis, or a woman who assumes that the point of football is for *one* of the twenty-two people on the field to pile up more touchdown points than anyone-else.

The game of chess falls squarely in the middle. It does consist of one player facing another player, one on one. But each player has a "team" at his or her disposal — a team of chess pieces. (Learning to play chess can sometimes help people with very strong NON-TEAM preferences modify their gameplaying behavior so that it does not clash so drastically with that of TEAM people.)

You can predict in advance that people with NON-TEAM orientations who are involved in your TEAM projects will wreak havoc, despite the fact that they are genuinely doing their best. (In fact, the harder they try, the more damage they will do.) You can also predict that they will be hurt and baffled and angry when their dedicated efforts are not appreciated by others. No one, in my experience, challenges any of these statements.

However, I run into genuine astonishment at the idea that these NON-TEAM people *really* do not understand what you mean by "team player." I want to emphasize this, therefore. Trust me: they are not pretending. They are not being deliberately uncooperative. They just do not speak your language, nor do you speak theirs. If you want them to be able to function on your team,. you're going to have to provide some training.

If your projects are NON-TEAM ones, you can be equally certain of the harm that will result from the vigorous efforts of a TEAM person to function alongside you. On both sides of the fence, it's very difficult to *believe* that the opposite point of view exists in otherwise intelligent and competent people, much less to understand it.

One effective way to dispel semantic fog is to take an unusual vantage point and work from there — stepping outside the forest so that you can see the trees. Allow me to demonstrate.

Think back, please, to your years in elementary or secondary school. Did your class get together at the beginning of the year and select one student — let's call that student Tracy — who was to get the *A*s? Did you then all work together to make sure Tracy had every possible opportunity to get *A*s? If you were taking a test, and Tracy began to cough, did your class demand "time out" until the coughing spell was over, so that Tracy's progress would not be interfered with?

Suppose some other student — call her Sarah — found herself piling up so many correct answers and good papers that she was very close to getting an *A* ... did Sarah carefully miss a few questions to make certain she would remain a *B* student and stay out of Tracy's path? Or if Sarah seemed unable or unwilling to take that action herself, was Tracy able to count on the rest of you to take care of the problem? And were you all in agreement that deliberate actions of that kind were in no way cheating, or unfair, or dishonest?

I'm sure that what I've just described sounds like Alice in Wonderland's forest, with *demented* trees. You will be thinking that you've never read such nonsense ... that American classrooms are not *like* that ... that they are strictly an "every man or woman for him- or herself" environment.

And that is precisely the reaction I wanted to provoke. BECAUSE THE WAY YOU FELT AS YOU READ MY DESCRIPTION OF THE HYPOTHETICAL CLASSROOM — WHERE TRACY WAS THE STAR AND THE REST OF THE STUDENTS WORKED TOGETHER TO PRESERVE TRACY'S STAR STATUS — IS THE WAY *OTHER* PEOPLE FEEL WHEN THEIR *TEAM* VERSUS *NON-TEAM* ORIENTATION CLASHES WITH THAT AROUND THEM. From their point of view, nothing anybody does makes any sense, and everybody else is *nuts*.

And that is the critical cue you need. Watch for body language — listen for words — be on the alert for actions — telling you that the other person involved thinks your behavior simply does not make sense. You are looking for information that says, perhaps not very clearly or coherently, but unmistakably: "YOU ARE NOT PLAYING BY THE SET OF RULES I AM PLAYING BY."

When you find yourself in this situation — two players on the same field, apparently playing different games (or one of the two playing no game at all) — there's no point in going on until the confusion has been straightened out. It's a total waste of time and energy. Stop the play — call a Time Out — and say something like this, keeping intonation and other body language neutral:

> "I think it would be helpful if you'd tell me your understanding of the strategy we're following here. What are the steps in that strategy, as you understand them?"

If your suspicions were correct, one of three things will happen.

1. The response will be, "I don't know what the strategy is — I don't think there *is* a strategy!" This is someone who not only doesn't share your game plan but doesn't even know what game it *is*. It's as if you were playing football with someone who doesn't know how to play or is so unskilled at it that the game hasn't yet been recognized.

2. The response will be a careful outline of a strategy radically at odds with your own. This is someone who may be perfectly capable of understanding what you're doing, but who has taken it for granted that you're playing some other game. It's as if you were playing football with someone who is playing tennis or soccer or poker, and assumes you're doing the same.

3. The response will be an accurate outline of your strategy, followed by "but I don't agree with it." It's as if you were playing football with someone who knows how to play, and is aware that that's what you're doing — but who doesn't approve of your choice of game, or has objections to your choice of plays.

Once you have this information, there's hope. Now you can explain the source of the confusion, to everyone's benefit, carefully choosing the appropriate Satir Mode. You don't say "What's the MATTER with you, ANyway? If you can't even understand what's going ON, why didn't you send somebody that DOES? Don't you have any consideration at all for other PEOPLE?" That's Blaming. Don't say "Would you mind VERY MUCH if I tried to explain to you why things aren't going well? I DON'T mean to be offensive — I REALLY DON'T. I just want everything to be all RIGHT, and it won't take very long, I PROMise." That's Placating. And don't panic and go into Distracter Mode. Use Leveler or Computer Mode, consistently, and state your case.

Miller's Law and Perceptual Filters

In a 1980 interview with *Psychology Today*, psychologist George Miller said something so important to human communication theory and practice that I call it Miller's Law. He said:

> In order to understand what another person is saying, you must assume that it is true, and try to imagine what it could be true *of*.

This is most emphatically not what happens in a large percentage of language interactions. In fact, much of the time what you will see is the *opposite* of Miller's Law in action, with people assuming that what the other person has said could not possibly be true and trying to imagine what could be *wrong* with that person that would lead them to say anything so ridiculous.

Let's look once more at the section of Scenario 8 where Will Clayton is discussing John Martin's behavior toward his sister-in-law.

> WILL: "This was the first time Martin ever turned anything like that over to you, right? Well... no *way* would he just let that float, hoping you'd come through! He'll have had somebody else working on it, too — just in case. ..."

Hearing this, Sharon Jamison wonders if John "could have done something as sneaky and dishonest" as what Will suggests and concludes that it's not possible. We can be sure this would have come as a surprise to Will Clayton. If Sharon had stated her feelings aloud the dialogue would have gone like this:

> SHARON: "I do not believe for even one minute that John would have done anything as sneaky and dishonest as that! He may have flaws, Will, but he is *not* a liar!"

WILL: "Huh? That's not lying, Sharon, that's good business! That's the way the game is played!"

SHARON: "If he told me I had the job, and there was really somebody else doing it, he lied to me. A child could understand *that*, Will."

WILL: "Well, you'd better talk to a child, then, because I *don't* understand it!"

Let's consider what would have happened if Will Clayton had applied Miller's Law. If — instead of throwing up his hands in despair over Sharon's bizarre ethics and walking away — he had said this to himself: "Now let's assume, just for the purposes of finding out what's going on here, that what she says is true. What could it be true *of*? What kind of reality would it have to be, for that to be true?"

If Will gave that some serious thought he would realize that it's true for *students*. No teacher would ask one student to write the class play and at the same time — without telling the first student — ask some other student to write an alternative play that could be put on if the first student failed at the task. For the teacher to have said "Sharon, I've chosen you to write the class play!", while knowing very well that someone else was going to be given the same task secretly, would be LYING. It would be a sneaky and dishonest and outrageous thing to do. Contrast this, please, with football games, where pretending that you have the ball when you really don't is not only not lying but is something to be encouraged and rewarded.

Like Sharon, Will has been a student; he knows that reality well. Once he realizes that Sharon is interpreting everything in terms of the classroom, WITH EVERYTHING SHE KNOWS ABOUT THE CLASS-ROOM ENVIRONMENT ACTING AS A PERCEPTUAL FILTER FOR HER, he can use his own shared experience of that environment as a basis for their communication. This will eliminate much of the potential misunderstanding, saving time and effort and energy.

RULE ONE: WHEN YOU FIND YOURSELF INVOLVED IN AN INTERACTION THAT ISN'T GOING WELL, APPLY MILLER'S LAW.

Do this even when you think you already know what the problem is, just in case you're wrong. For all you know, your own perceptual filters are distorting your understanding of the situation. Assume — not accept, just assume! — that what the other person is saying is true. Ask yourself: WHAT COULD IT BE TRUE *OF*?

Often the answer will immediately come to you — it could be true of a football game, of a tennis match, of a classroom, of a courtroom, or of any one of hundreds of other situations that you know well. And knowing that single piece of information — what it could be true of — means that once again you will be able to anticipate the other person's words and actions. Suddenly those words and actions will make sense to you, and you will know how to respond to them. The rule is:

RULE TWO: REFORMULATE THE SITUATION IN TERMS OF THE PERCEPTUAL FILTER BEING USED BY THE OTHER PERSON.

For example: When the other person is behaving as a student would behave in an academic situation, you know what roles are available to you. In classrooms you will find students, teachers, and the occasional visitor — and the teacher is in charge. Your next move will now be obvious: reformulate what you do and say so that you fill the role of teacher. Other *students* might say what Will said to Sharon and walk off in a huff; when Will does that Sharon will perceive him as she would another student. The *teacher* would not do that. The teacher would be patient and firm and tolerant and helpful; the teacher would explain; the teacher would *teach*. — Like this:

> "Sharon, business rules are not the same as the rules you learned in school. If John Martin asked someone besides you and Eve to work up some slo- gans for the meeting, without telling you, it was for the best of reasons. He knew you wouldn't do your best work if you didn't think he trusted you to do the job yourself — to give you a fair chance, he had to let you think you were on your own. But he knew that his first obligation was not to you but to the firm, and it was his *duty* to make certain that the firm would not suffer if you failed to carry out the task."

Patient. Firm. Tolerant. Helpful. And teacherly.

In a business situation, a speech like that would be boring, or insulting, or both. But because Will is talking to Sharon, who is functioning in this situation according to the rules of the classroom, it is exactly the right thing to say.

Warning. It's crucial for Will to make the speech above in LEVELER MODE. He absolutely must not talk like this:

> "SHARon, honey, business rules aren't the SAME as the rules you learned in SCHOOL! If John Martin asked someone besides you and Eve to work up some slogans for the meeting, without telling you, it was for the BEST of REASons!.."

And so on, with a smirk on his face, and a tone of voice commonly used by those who enjoy teasing children.

If you're not sure about the difference between the two styles, read the matching sections aloud. In the second version, give extra emphasis — like the emphasis on the first syllable of "nightmare" — to the words and parts of words written in capital letters. If possible, read the two versions into a tape recorder and then play them back and listen to the results. This should clear up any haziness you may feel.

The Man/Woman Problem

If you are a woman, you need to know that when you are involved in any situation perceived as a game, FAILURE TO WIN ON ANY GIVEN PLAY IS NOT WHAT MATTERS. What matters is failure to *follow through*. In mainstream male gameplaying, there are three ways to follow through:

1. You can complete the play yourself.
2. You can find someone else who can be trusted to complete the play and turn it over to that person.
3. You can go to the individual who assigned the play to you (or an authorized representative of that individual) and explain that you won't be able to complete the play after all. You do this *as soon as you know what the situation is*, to allow plenty of time for finding your replacement.

No shame is associated with any of those choices. The first one is the best choice, most of the time. The second choice is perfectly acceptable — just remember that you remain responsible for the play, and if you turn it over to the wrong person the fault will be yours. Choose carefully, and make sure that you give instructions to the person chosen to report to you immediately if there is any problem.

The third choice is the hardest for a woman to make, but when it is done promptly and frankly, without a lot of excuses and attempts to put the blame elsewhere, there's nothing at all wrong with it.

The choice that is ALL wrong is the choice Sharon and Eve made — continuing to behave as if they could complete the play long after they knew it was hopeless. That is *never* acceptable.

If you are a man, what you must remember is that it's not fair to assume that a woman will be familiar with the list of approved ways to follow through. Men learn it when they are children, and they can safely take it for granted that other adult men will know it. Women do *not* learn it, most of the time. Your role is to explain it, without hostility or sarcasm or sexist trappings. That's fair. If you were racing against a woman runner, you would object if her starting position was a hundred yards farther back than yours — because that's not fair. A woman who doesn't know the follow-through list faces precisely that sort of handicap, and everyone involved will suffer negative consequences if it isn't fixed. Since you're the one who *does* know, do what you can to fix it.

One more thing ... you may have read Betty Lehan Harrigan's fine book, *Games Mother Never Taught You: Corporate Gamesmanship for Women*. It's a valuable book for *both* genders. It provides you with useful information about the perceptions of the other sex. But every now and then it makes a claim that the games and gameplaying behavior of men are childish nonsense. Lehan Harrigan is Leveling — expressing her own honest perception of the truth — and is to be respected for doing so. But her claims are dangerous, because they set up a distorting perceptual filter.

When women interact with males whose behavior can accurately be described as childish nonsense, those males are ordinarily small male children over whom the women have a considerable amount of power, as in the environment of the nursery and the kindergarten. If you are a woman who perceives the adult males you interact with as small powerless children, that perception will be reflected in your body language and in your behavior — and you cannot possibly function successfully in your interactions with those men. You are likely to get hurt badly in the process.

However childish the gameplaying behavior of adult males may seem to you, they are *not* small children. And they have power that no small child will ever have. The validity of your perception (or of Lehan Harrigan's perception) is irrelevant in the real world, with real adult males. If they know you think of them as small boys playing silly games — and if that's how you feel, I assure you they *will* know, because your body language will betray you no matter how carefully you watch your words — and they will go out of their way to make you regret it. Consider your own reaction when you know that *you* are being viewed as a small and foolish child. It works both ways.

Workout — Chapter 4

1. During *time out,* gameplaying behavior goes on hold, and entirely different rules apply until the game begins again. One of the most valuable things you can know about another person is what constitutes time out for him or for her. But before you can work up a strategy for finding out how *others* perceive time out, you need to know your own definition for the term. What does it mean to you? What has to happen in a game before you feel that time out should be called or cancelled? For example, is it correct to say that for you, time out can be called only when it's *literally* a matter of life or death? (Any time you have this item of information about another person, make a note of it, and put it where you can easily find it again.)

2. *MD* for March 1986 (page 25) cites a report from Jimmy Breslin about a conversation he had with a young male criminal. The young man complained that the police aren't *fair*, because they arrest you for things done in the past. "If they catch you while you're doing it," he said, "that's one thing; but three months ago — that's bullshit." What does *fair* mean for this man? What are the critical semantic features? How does your own definition compare with his?

3. Try an experiment. Define — carefully and thoroughly — the word *negotiation*. Then get a member of the opposite sex to do the same, and compare the two.

4. For a *flawless* detailed portrait of a person locked into Blamer Mode, read "Ghost Story," by Joshua Hyatt, on pages 78-88 of the July 1988 issue of *Inc.* magazine. Here are two typical utterances from the piece (two of the milder ones!): " 'When are you going to learn to do the right thing, Briggs?' he'd bellow. 'And what are you doing standing around?' " " 'You idiot!' Mr. Doherty blasted. 'Who is going to pay $3.50 for a tie? You must be absolutely crazy!' " (This piece — like most reports of real speech — gives the reader very little information about intonation.) IF YOU SUSPECT THAT YOU TEND TO RELY TOO MUCH ON BLAMING MODE, BUT YOU'RE NOT SURE, THIS ARTICLE IS A MUST — IT WILL SETTLE THE QUESTION FOR YOU.

5. Here are three hostility-provoking utterances routinely faced by health care providers, followed by two answers each: one typical answer, certain to feed the hostility loop, and one answer in Computer Mode.

   a. "WHY IS it that EVERY TIME I COME here you keep me waiting for TWO HOURS?"

   ☐ "You're not the ONly patient we HAVE, THAT'S why!"

   ☐ "Waiting is very difficult when people are anxious and uncomfortable."

   b. "HOW can you POSSibly ask me for MONey at a TIME LIKE THIS, when my WIFE is in AGONy?"

   ☐ "There are rules I have to FOLLow, Mr. Jones — I'm just DOING MY job!"

   ☐ "When people know that someone they love is in pain, it's very hard for them to think about money."

   c. "YOU PEOPLE don't care about healing — ALL YOU CARE ABOUT is your FEE!"

   ☐ "I RESENT that, Mrs. Jones — we do the BEST WE CAN around here! And your attitude is NOT going to make things any BETTer!"

   ☐ "The idea that doctors and nurses are more interested in money than they are in their patients' welfare is very common, unfortunately."

   In your own business or profession, there is undoubtedly a similar set of hostile utterances that you or your staff hear over and over again.

Make a list of them, and write Computer Mode responses to them, for future use.

6. Investigate your own Satir Mode patterns — keep track of which mode you ordinarily select in which stressful situation. Do the same thing for people you frequently interact with. And record all the information in a file for your future reference — it's extremely valuable.

7. Sometimes a taxonomy can be fun, as well as instructive. For example, there's the taxonomy constructed by John Flowers and Bernard Schwart, two Southern California psychologists. It includes "Reverse Paranoids, who suffer from the belief that they are following or persecuting someone," "Inverse Paranoids, who feel that they are not good enough to be followed or persecuted by anyone," "Cataclonics, the 'Typhoid Marys' of stress, who carry it but are unaffected by it after you have caught it" and are "happy and mellow only when they are creating a problem," and "Sufferers from Pre-Traumatic Stress Syndrome, who are anxious because of the knowledge that since nothing traumatic has happened to them yet, something is sure to happen soon." (Reported by Berkeley Rice in *Psychology Today* for July 1982, pages 25-6.)

What do you think? Is this just frivolity and wordplay — just a couple of weary professionals letting off steam? How difficult would it be to get an article published about one of the disorders in that taxonomy, treating it absolutely seriously? Can you add any more members to the set of categories?

8. "Talking to farmers in Sedalia, Mo., Quayle floundered when he tried to explain his opposition to a major farm bill. Asked his view of a complex local agricultural issue, he replied with a joke: 'Whatever you guys want, I'm for it.' " (From a "A Quick Lesson in Major-League Politics," by Laurence I. Barrett, in *Time* for September 5, 1988; page 17.) Is Dan Quayle's remark in Placater Mode or Leveler Mode? How can you tell?

SIGHT BITES

1. "Most men prefer exercise to communication."

   (From "The Male Stress Syndrome," in the July 1987 issue of *Pest Control Technology*; page 44.)

2. "[*Oliver North*] lifted the ball out of the committee's hands, substituted his own, and pitched to his heart's content.."

   (From "On the Hill: Curtain Call," by Henry Fairlie, in *The New Republic* for September 8, 1987; page 17.)

3. ". . .the world leader who sees the international scene as a global gridiron can, with the best intentions, speak of the last minute of the last quarter of a war."

(From "Light Refractions: The Great Muddling Metaphor," by Thomas H. Middleton, in *Saturday Review* for June 14, 1975; page 59.)

4. "Folks, I'm going to tell you the playing field is never level. . . .Too many of us grew up in a world where we owned the bat, the ball, the stadium, both teams and the lights."

(H. Ross Perot, quoted in "H. Ross Perot on Restoring the Nation's Edge," in the *Los Angeles Times* for December 14, 1986; from a talk Perot gave before the Economic Club of Detroit.)

5. "Entrepreneurial businesses stumble onto something, get a big boost out of it, and grow significantly. Then, as soon as they think they're rounding third base, someone always seems to move home plate."

(From "What Goes Up. . ." by David L. Birch, in *Inc.* for July 1988; page 25.)

6. "We found that lack of confidence and low self-esteem are characteristic of managers who bark orders and refuse to discuss the issues involved, of couples who constantly shout and scream at each other and of parents who rely on harsh discipline. These hard tactics result from the self-defeating assumption that others will not listen unless they are treated roughly."

(From "The Language of Persuasion," by David Kipnis and Stuart Schmidt, in *Psychology Today* for April 1985; page 46.)

7. "To many people, communication is now thought of as a performance art. It's like a tennis match in which all you do is serve. At cocktail parties, you see people waiting for verbal on-ramps to score points."

(Richard Byrne, quoted in "Conversation Interruptus: Critical Skill or Just Plain Rudeness?" by Beth Ann Krier, in the *Los Angeles Times* for December 14, 1986.)

8. "Almost from its inception, industry has utilized women, sometimes on a scale so vast that females comprise the preponderance of employees, sometimes on a basis so small that the contingent is statistically negligible. In either case, women have been included in the workforce — what they have been excluded from is the *game* of business: the pursuit of profit and power."

(From "Why Corporations Are Teaching Men to Think Like Women . . . And Other Secret Game Plans That You May Not Have Been Briefed On," by Betty L. Harragan, in the June 1977 issue of *Ms.*; page 62.)

9. "No matter how skilled a player you are in business, at some point you're going to find yourself on defense. Your opponent could be: an upset boss, an angry customer, a rival negotiator, or even a news reporter seeking an inflammatory quote from your company.

Remember what the coaches say: 'You can't score on defense. Get the ball.' Your strategy for scoring from a defensive position is to turn or blunt the attack and mount your own offensive."

(From "Scoring on Defense: Tactics to Defeat the Hostile Questioner," by Roger Ailes, in his communications column for the December 1988 issue of *Success*; page 14.)

5 The Business Professional Domain

SCENARIO NINE　　The men around the table were not at ease. Wary, they sat upright in their chairs, instead of leaning back relaxed as was their usual habit. Their eyes were wary, too, glancing sideways at the client who was the reason for the hasty meeting, and then straight ahead, carefully blank, at nothing at all.

The client's name was Edward Kleeg, and he was absolutely furious. Nobody liked Kleeg, even when he was in a *good* mood. He was clumsy and coarse; he was given to telling lengthy bad jokes (often off-color jokes); he liked to tell long rambling anecdotes about his personal life and seemed unaware that they were excruciatingly boring. It was fortunate that he had inherited money and had sense enough to hire good people to look after his affairs; if he'd had to actually earn the money himself he would have starved. Kleeg was a flaming pain in the neck under the best of circumstances, and these were emphatically *not* the best of circumstances; his anger at Metamega Corporation was entirely justified. True, Metamega couldn't have foreseen the paper shortage that was holding up his product, but there was no excuse for not having warned Kleeg. Because nobody had wanted to deal with him, they'd been two weeks later giving him the word than they should have been.

In a case like this, you turned the matter over to Paul Nelson and you tried to stay well back out of the line of fire. They were just there to watch Paul Nelson perform.

". . . stupid inCOMpetence!" Kleeg was yelling, at the top of his lungs. "If I could get my hands on the idiot responsible for this MESS, I'd TEAR HIS DAMN HEAD off!"

Nelson chuckled, and leaned back in this chair with his hands clasped behind his head. "That'd be a great feeling, wouldn't it?" he asked.

76

"*Damn right* I" Kleeg bellowed. "You people have put both feet in it THIS time! And I have had it up to *HERE*" — he slammed both of his fists into his chest — "with you!" And then he roared into a seemingly endless tirade, specifying in precise and obscene detail the errors Metamega had made and the way those errors should be punished. Through it all, Paul Nelson just sat there, showing no distress or irritation of any kind, listening to Kleeg's abuse, saying only "mmmmm . . ." and "mmmmhmmm . . ." and — mystifyingly — "Gotcha!" over and over and over. Until gradually, little by little, Edward Kleeg began to wind down; until, with Nelson's last "mmmmhmmmm" he subsided, out of breath.

Paul sat up then, and he leaned forward toward Kleeg with his elbows on the table. "Mr. Kleeg," he said solemnly, holding Kleeg's eyes with his own, "what really impresses me is the *grasp* you have of this situation. You are totally in touch with the problem — warts, cracks. bumps, rough edges, and all. And that makes me feel confident that we can smooth this over."

"I guess I do get a little carried away," said the obstreperous client, his voice now pitched at a normal volume.

"You do," Paul agreed amiably. "You get all bent out of shape."

Edward Kleeg sighed, and looked embarrassed. "I'm sorry," he said — to the amazement of the spectators. They hadn't been aware that the words "I'm sorry" were in Kleeg's vocabulary.

Paul grinned at him. "Don't be," he said. "We *did* put both feet in it, just like you said. We should have let you know sooner that there was going to be slippage in the delivery cycle. But mistakes get *made*, Mr. Kleeg, even in the best of businesses. We put our backs into our work here — we mean for everything to go as smooth as silk. But sometimes we fall short of our goals. *This* time, for example. We'd like a chance to make it up to you."

"Well . . ." The man was frowning, obviously thinking hard. "How do I know you'll handle it any better next time?"

Paul chewed on his lower lip and frowned too: he leaned back in his chair again, kicking way back so that it was balanced precariously on two legs. The others hated it when he did that. For one thing, it was inappropriate for a business environment. For another, you couldn't keep your mind on anything except wondering when Nelson was going to crash to the floor. They were not surprised when Kleeg's eyes wandered.

"You *don't* know, Mr. Kleeg," Paul said bluntly. "You *can't know*. But what's your gut feeling?"

"Mmmmm?" Kleeg's eyes were on the teetering chair.

Nelson straightened up, the chair legs hit the floor with a thud, and the other man jumped, startled back to full attention. "*What's your gut feeling?*" Nelson repeated, more sharply this time.

"Well . . ." Ed Kleeg smiled at him. "I'll give you another chance, I guess. Hell . . . anybody could get careless *once*."

And Paul smiled back. "Sure they could," he said comfortably. "But you've got us on our toes now, Mr. Kleeg. *Trust* me. Everything's going to be all right."

For the people at Metamega, the most annoying thing about Paul Nelson's language behavior is the seeming *effortlessness* with which he keeps winning. Watching him is like watching magic tricks — they know that what they're seeing must involve skill, not magic; but no matter how hard they try, they can't figure out how it's done.

In this chapter, we're going to take a close look at just *one* part of Nelson's language behavior, and we're going to learn that technique, as he uses it.

Recognizing and Responding to the Sensory Modes

Every human being, in order to function in this world, has to process a constant flood of information from the external and internal environments. This isn't simple; it involves at least the following four steps:

1. You have to decide what information you're going to pay attention to.
2. You have to divide that portion into two subparts: (a) information to be noted and discarded; and (b) information to be stored for future access.
3. You have to organize and index the information you want to keep, for transfer to long-term memory.
4. You have to make the transfer, and do it successfully.

At the same time, while you're dealing with all of this, you have to *respond* to much information that you have no intention of keeping, using your short-term (working) memory — and carry on your functions in the external world.

You accomplish these formidable tasks by using your *sensory systems.* There are more than a dozen of these, but we will restrict our discussion to those that are most familiar: SIGHT, HEARING, and TOUCH (with an occasional reference to TASTE and SMELL.)

We all know people who understand and remember best when they can look at a picture or a diagram or a film. We know others who have to *hear* information if they are to do their best work. We know people who need to get their information "hands on" — people who struggle when they have to read or listen, but who can take things apart and put them back together with awe-inspiring ease. The sensory system that allows you to function most satisfactorily will be your preferred — and sometimes your dominant — sensory system. And this preference will be reflected in your language, as your preferred Sensory Mode. Like this:

SIGHT

"I see what you mean."
"It looks pretty good to me."
"He's the apple of his father's eye."

HEARING:

"I hear you loud and clear."
"It sounds fine to me."
"That's music to my ears."

TOUCH:

"I get it."
"It feels right to me."
"She has all the figures at her fingertips."

English also has utterances from the systems of taste and smell (which should perhaps be considered as a single system rather than two separate ones). For example:

"It was so close I could almost taste it!"
"It leaves a nasty taste in my mouth."
"What a sweet deal that is!"
"I can almost smell money when I drive through here."
"I smell a rat."
"This whole deal stinks."

However, taste and smell appear to be very rare as preferred Sensory Modes and often are useful only for saying something negative. We don't know why this is true. There are other languages — Japanese is a good example — that have much larger taste and smell vocabularies than English does, with many terms that have *positive* meanings. It may be that taste and smell occur more frequently as preferred Sensory Modes in such languages.

Under ordinary circumstances people can shift from one Sensory Mode to another with little difficulty. But when they are tense, when they are under stress, when negotiation and confrontation are going on, there's a drastic change: THEY TEND TO BECOME LOCKED IN TO THEIR PREFERRED SENSORY MODE. The greater the stress, the tighter the lock. And this restriction in their language behavior — which they are not conscious of — works in both directions. They not only have trouble expressing themselves in other Sensory Modes, they also have trouble *understanding* any mode except the one they prefer.

Think about how you would feel if you went to a business meeting and you were the only speaker of American English there — if everyone else spoke Cockney, for example, or a Scottish dialect. You would be able to follow what was going on, after a fashion, but it would be hard work. You would be tense and cross and in a bad humor before it was over. This is essentially the situation for someone locked into a particular Sensory Mode because of stress. Certainly they can manage language in other Modes, but it's a strain that interferes with their performance.

You're probably not able to switch from one dialect of English to another at will, as a way of making speakers of those dialects more comfortable and capable in their interactions with you. But you *can* learn to switch from one Sensory Mode to another, consciously and deliberately, to achieve the same goals. The technique involved is simple, easily remembered, and can be put to immediate practical use. You won't have any difficulty recognizing the Sensory Modes others use, because the vocabulary of each of the modes is stored in your internal grammar. Once you know which mode you're hearing, you have only two rules to follow:

RULE ONE:

Match the Mode coming at you.

RULE TWO:

If you can't follow Rule One, use no Sensory Mode vocabulary at all.

For example, by Rule One:

> FRED: "How bad does the situation look to you?"
>
> ANNA: "I don't see it as very serious."
>
> FRED: "Are you sure you have a clear picture of the problem?"
>
> ANNA: "Crystal clear — and it looks manageable."

And by Rule Two:

> FRED: "How bad does the situation look to you?"
>
> ANNA: "I don't think it's very serious."

FRED: "Are you sure you have a clear picture of the problem?"

ANNA: "I'm sure — and I'm convinced that it's manageable."

In the first example dialogue, Anna has recognized Fred's speech as Sight Mode and has responded with Sight Mode vocabulary — matching the Sensory Mode she hears. The effect of such mode matching is to build trust and rapport.[1] The listener thinks, "Here's a person who speaks my language — someone who perceives the world the way *I* do!" And Anna is applying Miller's Law. She is assuming that it is *true* that the sensory system of sight is the best one for carrying on this interaction and adopting it herself, as a way of finding out what it is true *of*. Each time she matches a Sensory Mode, making it easy for Fred to understand and process her language, she is feeding that language loop, helping it grow.

Two of the metaprinciples of *Gentle Art* syntonics are illustrated clearly in this technique. They are:

METAPRINCIPLE ONE:
ANYTHING YOU FEED WILL GROW

METAPRINCIPLE TWO:
ANYTHING YOU STARVE WILL FESTER OR DIE.

We know these metaprinciples well, and we apply them systematically when we are trying to produce better people or animals or plants. It's difficult to understand why we behave as if we were ignorant of them when we are trying to produce better communication.

In the second example, Anna is not matching Fred's mode, but she is being very careful not to *clash* with it. This is the *neutral* response. It doesn't do as much for the interaction as mode matching, but it's far better than *mis*match. For example:

FRED: "How bad does the situation look to you?"

ANNA: "I don't feel that it's very serious."

FRED: "But you don't have a clear picture of the problem."

ANNA: "Of course I do! I've kept in close touch with all of the factors involved."

FRED: "I don't see how you could have enough information to do that."

ANNA: "There's no reason for you to take that attitude, Fred!"

That's sensory mode mismatch. Anna is responding to each of Fred's sight mode utterances with something from the vocabulary of touch. And because Fred is under stress, he is growing more and more uneasy about her understanding of the situation with every line they exchange.

You can't change the fact that when people are involved in business and professional interactions their language behavior will be altered, sometimes drastically, by tension and stress. But you don't have to go into such situations unprepared — these language phenomena are to a large degree *predictable*. Your advance knowledge of these facts gives you a significant advantage, and your skill in using the techniques for dealing with them increases that advantage substantially.

With this new information in mind, let's go back now and re-examine the scenario at the beginning of this chapter.

The furious client, Mr. Kleeg, opens with a loud and vivid physical description of what he would do if he could get his hands on the person responsible: he would tear that person's head off. And Paul Nelson responds with, "That'd be a great feeling, wouldn't it?" This is his first strategic linguistic move, and he never deviates from this strategy. Here are more examples from the scenario:

KLEEG:

"You people have put both feet in it . . . "

"I have had it up to here . . . "

"I get a little carried away . . . "

"How do I know you'll handle it any better . . . "

"Anybody could get careless once . . . "

NELSON:

"Gotcha!"

" . . . the grasp you have of this situation . . . "

" . . . totally in touch with the problem — warts, cracks, bumps, rough edges, and all."

"And that makes me feel confident that we can smooth this over."

"You get all bent out of shape."

" . . . there was going to be slippage . . . "

" . . . mistakes get made . . . "

" . . . put our backs into our work . . . "

" . . . we mean everything to go as smooth as silk . . . "

"But what's your gut feeling?"

" . . . you've got us on our toes . . . "

Now you will have no difficulty spotting what Paul Nelson is doing and understanding that no magic is involved. As Paul observes Mr. Kleeg's body language and listens to his words, he notes an unmistakable preference for Touch Mode — and he immediately *matches* it, both verbally and nonverbally. Every possible word is put into Touch Mode (including the otherwise odd "Gotcha!"). And Paul generates a flood of body language that would provoke negative reactions in anyone who preferred Sight or Hearing Mode, but which reassures Mr. Kleeg that Paul is his kind of person and should be trusted. If Paul had sat rigid and upright in his chair, maintaining an expression of neutral courtesy, he would have been speaking a language that was not Ed Kleeg's language; he did not make that mistake. Instead, he delibertely tuned himself *to* Ed Kleeg, so that the two of them would be as syntonic as possible, both verbally and nonverbally.

In this example, of course, Paul Nelson had dealt with Ed Kleeg many times before and was already aware of the man's Touch Mode preference. But he would have behaved precisely the same way if it had been his first encounter with Kleeg.

This technique is easy to do. So easy that people typically complain that it couldn't possibly work, on the principle of no pain, no gain. I would like to point out to you that it's something you can try for free, without filling out any forms or installing any new equipment. If it doesn't work, you can stop doing it as easily as you started. My personal experience, and that of thousands of other people, is that the results will astonish you, repaying your minimal investment of time and energy many times over. It is the simplest of all the *Gentle Art* syntonics techniques, and is the *perfect* such technique, because (a) it cannot go wrong, (b) it has no exceptions, and (c) it serves as the foundation for all the other techniques in the system. When you are comfortable with Sensory Mode matching, you will find that all the other techniques are easy for you to understand, to remember, and to put into practice.

You're certain to find that at least one of the Sensory Modes makes you feel awkward and clumsy and uncomfortable when you use it. If you prefer Sight Mode, you will feel strange using Touch Mode, and vice versa. BUT THIS IS THE POINT. When you use a Sensory Mode that isn't natural for you, you find it distracting and frustrating. The more tense the situation is, the more distracting and frustrating the nonpreferred Sensory Mode will be for you. And that is the mode which you should *practice* using, for that very reason — so that when you need to use it to match the language of another person, it will *not* be so burdensome for you and you will be able to make the switch.

The Touch Dominance Problem

There are already so many "disorders" and "disabilities" that nobody should add a new one without being absolutely certain that it is needed. For that reason, I've waited a long time to introduce this one. But I have spent more than a decade observing closely the problems that people face in our culture when their preferred Sensory Mode is touch and when that preference is so strong that mode-lock is triggered even by minor stress. The problems are so severe, and the consequences so serious, that I consider it necessary to say that for the native speaker of English this preference constitutes a handicap deserving its own label. I call it "Touch Dominance" (and will use the abbreviation "TD" where appropriate).

We live in a society that has strong negative attitudes about touching. From the time our children can crawl, they hear a barrage of "Don't touch!" and "Keep your hands to yourself!" commands. Many parents are almost incapable of touching their children to express affection once the children are past the toddler stage. The recent wave of scandals about sexual abuse of children has made it taboo to touch anyone else's children, even when you interact with them all day long. We appear to be incapable of separating touching from its role in sexual relations, in physical violence, and in breaking things. Touch is a function of the body far more obviously than seeing and hearing are. But by the time we are two or three years old we know that much having to do with the body is considered at least unsuitable for any situation except total privacy, and at worst downright nasty.

Imagine what it must be like to be a child with a strong preference for touch as the best way to process and express information about the environment. Think how many times a day such children are going to discover that what is most natural and effective for them in interacting with their world provokes anger or ridicule, and may be totally forbidden! We don't take children whose preferred Sensory Mode is sight and insist that they go through life with their eyes shut or with a blindfold on; we would call that cruel and irrational. But we impose precisely that kind of handicap on TD children.

Such children are *always* in trouble, and rarely understand why. By the time they are adults, they usually have one of a long series of labels attached to them. If the labels come from professionals, they will include "remedial, slow learner, learning-disabled, withdrawn, uncooperative, hostile, antisocial, borderline personality, neurotic," and whatever is trendy. If the labels have been attached by family and associates, they will be less elegant terms such as "stupid" and "bad" and "pain in the neck." Whatever the label, it means "somebody who is troublesome to have around."

I don't mean to suggest that these labels are meaningless, or that there are no individuals for whom they are accurate. But again and again I have been asked to work with individuals so described, only to learn very quickly that the real problem was Touch Dominance.

This sort of confusion is tragic, and a great waste of resources. What to do about it is a subject beyond the scope of this book. But it's important for you to know that the problem *exists*. So that when your first impression of someone is that you are perceiving stupidity or sullen hostility or anything else from the label list, you will stop for a minute and ask yourself: IS THIS REALLY ONLY TOUCH DOMINANCE?

If it is, matching that person's Touch Mode vocabulary will work wonders. What you say will be better understood; what is said to you will be easier to understand. You'll be amazed at how much the person seems to *improve* socially, and how quickly. If it isn't Touch Dominance, mode matching won't help, but little time or energy will have been spent finding that out. It is *always* worth making the effort to find out.

Many incidents that are perceived as sexual harassment happen when TD individuals' attempts at communication — often clumsy and inarticulate, since they are accustomed to rejection and have come to expect it — provoke a negative reaction. This creates stress and tension, locking them into Touch Mode. The tighter the mode-lock is, the less appropriate their language is likely to be, which causes even more negative reactions. Which creates more stress and tension, feeding the loop, and it goes round and round and round, with terrible results.

Perhaps the worst feature of Touch Dominance is that people who suffer from it are helpless to explain what's wrong. It's a tremendous relief for them to know what the problem is and to have something they can say when they need to explain. Not because they can use the label as an excuse for behavior that our society frowns upon, but because they can use it as an *explanation*. And because it can replace other labels, assigned to them in error, that are so much worse.

Faced with someone you think may be a TD person, the rules to follow are:

RULE ONE:

Match the person's Touch Mode language every time you can.

RULE TWO:

Use as much Touch Mode language yourself as you can: don't confine it just to your responses.

RULE THREE:

Use as little language from Sensory Modes other than Touch as possible. (Don't say "Look . . ." or "Listen . . ." or "See here . ." or "Can't you see . . ." or anything of that kind.)

RULE FOUR:

When you have no Touch Mode language available, use language that includes no sensory vocabulary at all.

RULE FIVE:

Keep it firmly in mind that for this person touching is only communication, so that you won't misinterpret it.

RULE SIX:

If you don't object to physical contact with the person, touch and allow touching. If you do object, DO NOT TRY TO FAKE IT, EVER. THE TOUCH DOMINANT PERSON WILL KNOW YOU ARE LYING. Just say, in Leveler Mode, "I'd feel better if you wouldn't touch me." Or "I'm sorry if I seem unfriendly. I'm just one of those people who doesn't like to be touched.

RULE SEVEN:

Don't forget that the intonation of the voice is part of *body* language, not part of the words spoken.

The Ethical Problem

When I explain techniques for using Satir Modes and Sensory Modes in my seminars and workshops, I can always be certain in advance that someone will rise to protest. Typically, these people say that the techniques are manipulative, and that they do not approve of — and would never stoop to use — verbal manipulation. Their opinion of Paul Nelson's language behavior would be unequivocal: it's at best unethical, and very probably immoral ... one of those "There oughta be a law!" phenomena. This matter has to be addressed.

The problem with classifying any variety of language behavior as manipulation is that to do so assumes the existence of a variety of non-manipulative neutral language behavior to contrast it with. But there is *no such thing*. The idea that neutral language behavior exists is a myth; it feeds and supports our treasured image of ourselves as Nice People.

All language is manipulative; all language is attempted persuasion. Any time you talk, you are attempting to persuade the others present to listen to what you have to say, rather than talking themselves; you are taking and holding the floor. When you talk, you want to be listened to, believed, respected, appreciated, accepted, agreed with. No matter how much you may wish to be neutral in your communication, you cannot *not* manipulate. AS SPEAKER, YOU ARE CONTROLLING THE CONVERSATIONAL SPACE, WHETHER YOU LIKE THAT IDEA OR NOT. And you cannot escape by refusing to talk, either; unilateral silence is one of the most manipulative forms of language, and one of the most negative.

Since you cannot choose between manipulative and nonmanipulative communication, your only choice — unless you are willing and able to withdraw totally from all human interaction — is the choice between skilled manipulation and unskilled manipulation. It is my firm opinion that since you *must* manipulate others with your language, it's best for you to know what you are doing and do it with skill. The ethical questions then become questions of (a) your motivations and (b) the potential for abuse.

It would be useful to return to the concept of gameplaying at this point, to provide a context. What is "fair" and "honest" in a game is not the same thing that it is in a non-game. We do not say that the football player who only pretends to have the ball is cheating or lying. The players in the scenario are Paul Nelson and Edward Kleeg; the others present are spectators. Certainly a game is being played, and it will repay analysis.

The Three Gameplaying Strategies

There are only three valid gameplaying strategies in mainstream American society. They are:

- ☐ PLAYING TO WIN.
- ☐ PLAYING TO PLAY WELL.
- ☐ REFUSING TO PLAY — WHILE STILL SURVIVING.

Each of these primary strategies has a number of substrategies. Playing to play well is the most neutral of the three and is the strategy of least risk. Playing to *win* may involve playing very badly (deliberately, as part of a larger game plan); playing to play well never does. Refusal to play is always dangerous and is of two basic types: refusal to play the game in question and refusal to play any game at all.

Ed Kleeg, the furious client who knows he has been shabbily treated by Metamega Corporation, is clearly playing to win. But what about Paul Nelson? In this scenario, Nelson *does* win, in that Kleeg forgets all about his intention to punish Metamega by taking his business elsewhere. BUT NELSON IS NOT PLAYING THE GAME KLEEG IS PLAYING.

Kleeg cares about the outcome of the game in business terms and in terms of the power relationships between his firm and Metamega — in terms of *football*, essentially. He is on the field as Edward Kleeg, of Kleeg Associates, Inc., and for him the negotiation is a business transaction.

Paul Nelson, by contrast, has no interest at all in the struggle between Kleeg Associates and Metamega. He has no interest in the business aspects of the negotiation, either corporate or personal. He doesn't care about getting ahead, or being part of the team, or achieving financial security or a promotion. He is refusing to participate in that game. But he has obviously won *some* game: the question is, what game *is* it? And this brings us back once again to ethics. Because the game Paul is playing is the real world equivalent of a game of chess, and he is using the people he interacts with as pieces on his gameboard. He is interested only in moving them around, using them to show off his skill and their helplessness against him.

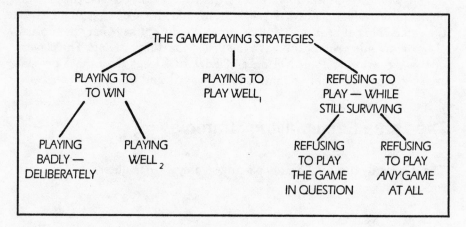

FIGURE 9. THE GAMEPLAYING STRATEGIES

It's very important to realize that this is a METAgame — a game at a different level of play. Nelson would have enjoyed the scenario even more if someone else had been chosen to represent Metamega. This would have allowed him to use his techniques to manipulate *both* sides, playing them against one another for his own amusement, and to further his own goals.

Is this wrong? Is it immoral? Is it unfair, or dishonest? IT DEPENDS ON WHAT GAME YOU HAPPEN TO BE PLAYING. Let's consider a few of the pieces of relevant data.

1. Ed Kleeg is unaware that he has been used as a gamepiece by Paul Nelson and is perfectly happy with the outcome of the negotiation.

2. Metamega Corporation still has its client, and the client is happy.

3. Kleeg Associates has lost no money that cannot be made up under the new conditions promised by Nelson and will not have to go through the hazards of changing a business alliance, learning the ropes of a new business relationship, etc.

4. The other men present during the scenario are in precisely the same condition they were before it — they risked nothing, took no part in the negotiation, and enjoyed watching the action.

5. Nelson has not been given a prize, or a bonus, or a medal, or any other form of "ill-gotten gain" — he's just had fun.

To sum up, from Nelson's point of view, and from the point of view of a large portion of American society: NOBODY GOT HURT; NOBODY WAS EVEN IN ANY DANGER, AT ANY TIME; THEREFORE, NO WRONG HAS BEEN DONE. This is not unethical, or immoral — it's good clean fun.

You don't have to agree with that position. You may well feel that for Nelson to use Kleeg as he did — as an *object* — was degrading dehumanizing, and wicked to the core. You may feel that for Kleeg to come out of this ignorant of what has happened to him *is* harm done, and harm that continues. You may feel that for Nelson to do this kind of thing, while the other men at Metamega watch and admire — and remain as ignorant as Kleeg — is a kind of corruption. There are plenty of arguments in your favor.

If you and I were talking face to face, and we had plenty of time, we might be able to resolve this in some way satisfactory to both of us. But it's not like that, and this is the real world. In terms of your success in the real world, what matters is not whether you think Nelson's behavior is good or bad. What matters is that you know the Paul Nelsons are out there, and how they view the world, and what tactics they use. So that if you find *yourself* in Ed Kleeg's position, what happened to him cannot happen to you. And so that — if by chance it's too late for that, and you have already served as gamepiece for a Paul Nelson somewhere — you will now understand what happened and be better able to keep it from happening again.

In a situation like this, there are two things you need to remember and three things you need to find out.

TO REMEMBER:

☐ The only weapon that Nelson is using is the weapon of *language*.

☐ Language is the only defense against him.

TO FIND OUT:

☐ Is Nelson's game at the top of the gameplaying tree? That is, is there someone else, for whom the game Nelson is playing is only a part of yet *another* game?

- ☐ If so, does Nelson *know* that?
- ☐ If he does, why is he participating?

Games within games within games! Yes, indeed. And far too many people are out on the field wandering around, unaware that the games exist, endangering both themselves and everybody else.

ABOUT LISTENING

Although listening is a critical component of your language skills, it gets little attention. I have reviewed dozens of books and tapes and other materials on listening, looking for something that I could recommend wholeheartedly, to no avail. All the materials I have seen fall into the following classifications:

- ☐ Scholarly and highly technical materials, of great value in informational terms but awkward and time-consuming reading for the nonspecialist
- ☐ Inspirational materials that tell you how important it is to listen carefully and respectfully but offer no information about how that is to be done
- ☐ Materials allegedly about listening but actually about taking good notes.

None of this meets the needs of the busy executive or professional, much less the general public.

Fortunately, listening is an *automatic* skill, in the sense that your brain will take care of it for you if you simply refrain from interfering with the process. It requires an active effort on your part only if you have to break the bad habits of many years. For example, none of the following, carried on while you are supposed to be filling the listener role, constitute LISTENING:

- ☐ Rehearsing or thinking about what you are going to say when it's your turn to talk
- ☐ Thinking about how badly the speaker is handling the topic and how much better someone else (or you yourself) could do it
- ☐ Thinking about extraneous matters such as whether you are overparked, what you will do after you leave, how you are going to handle tomorrow's crisis, whether you remembered to turn off your computer, how much you dislike the speaker personally, etc.
- ☐ Hanging on the speaker's every word, but only with the goal of being certain to grab the turn the instant a pause occurs
- ☐ Doing your best to write down every single word the speaker says

While any of these activities are going on you may very well be hearing the speaker, but you are not listening.

Many people, particularly busy people, have had that list of nonlistening habits for so long that they are almost *incapable* of listening — if they had a listening gland, it would be atrophied from disuse. The results can be bizarre. For example: I was once sent to a cardiologist, who decided that I needed an arteriogram. I told him I was convinced that my chest pain was due not to my heart but to my postpolio spine. He talked about his hypothesis: I talked about mine. In time, the arteriogram was done; as I had expected, it was normal. When I went to his office for the standard followup visit, he told me solemnly that my heart was fine, but that he had discovered the reason for the chest pain. It was, he announced, due to my postpolio spine. This man is a native speaker of English, and he had indeed sat across the desk facing in my direction while I talked to him — but he was not listening.

Mistakes of this kind, whatever your field, are bad for your image and can lead to unpleasant altercations. You cannot apply Miller's Law to anyone's language if you do not listen. You cannot use the techniques for recognizing and responding to the Satir Modes and the Sensory Modes if you do not listen. Hearing alone, or half-hearted intermittent listening, will not give you enough information to achieve good communication. Only *syntonic* listening, in which you are tuned to the speaker with full attention, will enable you to process the language coming at you successfully and construct an effective response. So: how do you go about learning to listen syntonically? How do you break your bad listening habits?

You do it by *practice*. And you don't practice on living human beings. You have available to you an ideal practice partner for this process: your television set. Choose a program that features one person talking at length — a television minister, a lecturer, a speaker on a public affairs program. If you have access to the televised proceedings of Congress, you will find more speeches going on there than you could possibly need.

Sit down and give the speaker your full attention. Do not take notes; do not read while you "listen"; just pay attention. Try assuming that what you are hearing is true, and then try to imagine what it could be true *of*. Every time you notice that your attention has wandered, drag it forcibly back again and return it to the speaker. You may have to do this every sentence or two at first, and how much time goes by before you can listen with a respectable degree of skill will depend on how rotten a listener you are when you start. But the time will come when you can listen to a speaker with full attention for roughly half an hour. And that's long enough. No speaker is entitled to ask for your full attention for longer than that. At that point, you are ready to begin practicing on human beings who are present while they speak to you.

One final note: in reading Scenario Nine you will have noticed that Paul Nelson did not interrupt Ed Kleeg's tirade even once. That may or may not mean that Nelson was listening to Kleeg. In either case, however, it was a skilled move on Nelson's part. The most efficient way to communicate with adults who are having a verbal temper tantrum is to be still and let them exhaust themselves. Make a sound now and then to let them know that you are still there and that you are listening at least minimally, and let them wind down. THEY WILL NOT LISTEN TO YOU UNTIL THIS HAS TAKEN PLACE — which means that anything you say to them before they've run out of steam is a waste of your valuable time and energy. It's frustrating to sit through an adult tantrum, but it's much quicker in the long run than interfering with the tantrum — because each time you try to stop the barrage of words you will feed the speaker's anger and escalate the situation, often to such an extent that he (or she) feels obliged to start over again. The alternating sequence of the speaker's attempts to talk you into the ground and your attempts to interrupt constitutes a tantrum loop. Such loops lead to endless delay. Let it all go by — then talk.

Now, before we go on to the next Language/Power Domain, it's necessary for us to stop and look at something important: the phenomenon I call Malpractice Of The Mouth.

NOTES

1. John Grinder and Richard Bandler, founders of the system called Neuro-Linguistic Programming, observed Virginia Satir matching the Sensory Modes of her clients in therapy sessions, and were impressed by the results. They make extensive use of the mode-matching technique in NLP, where preferred Sensory Modes are called "primary representational systems." Earlier discussions of the concept are found in the work of Edward T. Hall and Carl Jung.

Workout — Chapter 5

1. In Scenario Nine, Paul Nelson is functioning primarily in Leveler Mode (with a large *Phony* Leveling component, of course). Rewrite his dialogue in Computer Mode, and compare the two. Do you think the revision would be as effective as the original? What are the *strategic* differences between the two versions? Which would you be more comfortable using yourself?

2. Determine your own preferred Sensory Mode. Pay attention to the sensory language you use, watching for a clear pattern. What kinds of sensory sensory language do you usually *avoid*? Is that because you find them awkward and unnatural or because you have been taught to avoid them?

Ask yourself: when you have to learn something, and it's extremely important for you to learn it quickly and remember it well, what kind of input do you prefer? Written material, diagrams and charts, audiotapes, videotapes, demonstrations . . . . something else?

Suppose I told you to close your eyes and to imagine, as vividly as possible, that you were at the beach — and then I said, "Quick! Tell me what you're most aware of!" What would you say? Try it, and find out. Try the same experiment for other places that you know well enough to form clear imaginary profiles of them.

Ask other people to help you with this project if you feel comfortable doing so; they may be able to tell you almost immediately that you prefer a particular mode, or that there is some mode that they almost never hear you use.

Once you are certain of your preference, make an effort to practice using the *other* two major modes.

3. A primary strategy in Japanese conversation is wording questions in such a way that no one will ever have to say NO — without in any way jeopardizing the goals of the interaction. Try to do this in English for a day or two. What changes do you have to make in your language behavior? What reactions do you notice in other people when you use this strategy?

4. Look at some written materials in your field — proposals, reports, prospectuses, solicitations, briefs, etc. Do you see any Sensory Mode language patterns? Try rewriting them in other Sensory Modes, or with no sensory language at all, or with language intended to cover as many modes as possible. Compare the various versions to determine which seems most effective. If you were going to send out an appeal for funds by direct mail, to a large general audience, what kind of sensory language strategy would you follow?

5. Read the article titled "The Abilene Paradox: The Management of Agreement," by Jerry B. Harvey, in ORGANIZATIONAL DYNAMICS for Summer 1974, for an excellent presentation of the communication breakdowns that can occur when everyone is *trying* to cooperate with everyone else. The name of the paradox comes from the author's memory of a blistering hot Texas day when he and his family left a comfortable house and a pleasant situation to go "do" Abilene, because everyone thought — incorrectly — that everyone *else* wanted to do that, and nobody wanted to spoil the others' plans.

SIGHT BITES

1. "Much of the confusion that arises in the course of bargaining is the result of one party missing the meaning of the other's words — usually because the first party's mind is occupied rehearsing what he or she will say when his or her turn comes. Successful negotiators generally do more listening than talking."

"The most critical time to keep quiet is when there is nothing more to be said."

(From "The Art of Negotiation," in *The Royal Bank Letter* (Royal Bank of Canada) for July/August 1986; page 3.)

2. "So why the appeal of fax? ... because people are better at getting the picture if they can see it on paper. Any technology that makes getting the picture easier as well as faster will be with us for a long time to come."

(From "Managing Technology: Fax Finding," by Cary Lu, in INC. for November 1988: page 159.

What is your reaction to the idea that fax lets you "get" the picture? Does the quotation above hold only for people who prefer Sight Mode, or is Cary Lu missing something?

3. "A hand-lettered, oversized envelope inscribed with magic markers and pasted-over with Polaroid photos of the product inside is much more likely to get attention. Better yet, send free samples of your product."

(From "Seize the Moment," by Ken Hakuta, in *Success* for December 1988; page 51.)

How does this quotation tie into what you now know about Sensory Modes? Can you incorporate the concept into your own professional life?

6

Malpractice
of the Mouth
and Verbal Violence

Introduction

When little children do harm with their language, we make allowances for their lack of experience. When adults who are physically or mentally impaired do harm with their language, we make allowances for their lack of competence. We make similar allowances for adults who are simply ignorant. In all such cases we do everything we can, consistent with the individual's capacities, to discourage the offensive language behavior, but we try to be tolerant. We assume that if the person's circumstances were different the language would be different as well. This is rational — even admirable.

But when verbal violence is committed by educated and competent adults in positions of responsibility, allowances should *not* be made. The grammar of verbal violence is part of their internal grammar. They are skilled in its use, just as they are skilled in any other aspect of their language. And when the adult is an executive or professional, such language behavior constitutes Malpractice of the Mouth.[1]

If you think of verbal abuse as strings of curses and obscenities and epithets and threats and ethnic slurs — with the peak of sophistication represented by something like "Drop dead, you stupid ass!" — your set of semantic features for verbal abuse will include [+ PRIMITIVE] and [+ CRUDE]. You may feel that no professional who exhibited such behavior could last long enough *as* a professional to require attention. That image of verbal abuse is the traditional one, carefully supported by our society and our media. It's the image we learn as we grow up. But it's badly distorted.

People who yell curses and obscenities and all the rest of that ugly list do so as part of a pattern of *physical*, not *verbal*, abuse. They use words precisely as they use their fists, and for the same reasons. Genuine verbal abuse is something quite different. Something very sophisticated, and entirely consistent with education and intelligence and skill. Something far more dangerous, and far more widespread, than the neanderthalian behavior — rare in executives and professionals — that you had in mind. In this chapter we will take up one of the most common forms of verbal abuse: the verbal attack patterns of English, which are the major vehicle for Malpractice of the Mouth.

Recognizing and Responding to the Verbal Attack Patterns

In this section I'll be discussing a set of example sentences that illustrate verbal attack patterns. I recommend that you read the examples aloud, giving extra emphasis to all the words or parts of words that are in capital letters. If it's possible for you to tape the examples and then play them back, that's even better. These patterns are not the full set for English, but they will provide you with a solid foundation for recognition and response; when you encounter others you will know exactly how to proceed. We'll begin with one of the most basic attacks and its common variants.

Attack Pattern 1. (The speaker is a physician.)

"If you REALLY cared about your health, YOU'D stick to your DIet!"

(or)

"If you really CARED about your health, YOU'D stick to your DIet!"

This pattern has two parts: (1) the presupposed attack, headed by "If you REALLY"; and (2) the *bait*, which follows. The bait can be almost anything. For example:

"If you REALLY cared about your health, YOU wouldn't SMOKE three packs of cigarettes a day!"

"If you REALLY cared about your health, YOU wouldn't SPEND all your time watching television!"

The bait is the part intended to get the verbal victim's attention — the part that contains open insults and is designed to provoke anger and cause pain. What the attacker expects (and wants) is a dialogue like this one.

PHYSICIAN: "If you REALLY wanted to get well, YOU wouldn't SMOKE three packs of cigarettes a day!"

PATIENT: "I *don't*. I do NOT smoke three packs a day! I am a very careful and moderate smoker."

PHYSICIAN: "I see. Why *is* that? Why do you think you should be careful? Is it because you know you're ruining your health?"

PATIENT: "I am NOT ruining my health! That's all a lot of propaganda!"

PHYSICIAN: "Oh? Then why NOT smoke three packs a day? Why stop at only two and a half?"

PATIENT: "Listen — I DO NOT SMOKE two and a half packs of cigarettes a day!"

(And so on, with NO dignity for the patient.)

You learn to understand and use this pattern as a child ("If you REALLY loved me, YOU'D buy me a POny like all the OTHER kids have got!"), and it follows you everywhere you go for the rest of your life. Like this . . .

"If you REALLY wanted to make the team . . ."

"If you REALLY wanted to graduate . . ."

"If you were REALLY interested in getting a job . . ."

"If you really WANTED a promotion . . ."

"If you really CARED about our position in the community . . ."

"If you REALLY understood this nation's economy . . ."

And each of those "if you really" sequences will be followed by an openly insulting and hurtful chunk of bait that the verbal attacker fully expects you to grab, swallow. and run with. Including such all-purpose blind stabs as " . . . you wouldn't BE the way you are!" and " . . . you wouldn't DO the things you do!"

Taking the bait is all wrong, however, unless you happen to be rooting for the verbal abuser. The part of this attack that should get your attention is not the bait — no matter how infuriating and how outrageous it may be — but the *presupposed* attack that follows "If you really."

The word *presupposition* is defined in a variety of different ways, depending on the scholar doing the defining and the field in which the scholar works. Always, it refers to something assumed — "presupposed" means "supposed in advance." In the *Gentle Art* system it is defined like this:

A PRESUPPOSITION IS ANYTHING THAT A NATIVE SPEAKER OF A LANGUAGE KNOWS IS PART OF THE MEANING OF A SEQUENCE

OF THAT LANGUAGE, EVEN IF IT DOESN'T APPEAR ON THE SUR-
FACE OF THE SEQUENCE.

Consider the sentence, "EVen JOHN could close THAT deal!" Hear
the presuppositions? As a native speaker of English, you know that
sentence presupposes two additional sentences, neither of which appears
anywhere on the surface:

1. "The deal doesn't amount to much."
2. "John doesn't amount to much, either."

People who are not fluent speakers of English are unaware that
the sentence is insulting to both John and the deal in question. How
could they know? I repeat — because this is one of those situations where
people are too close to the forest to see the trees — there's not a single
negative word about either John or the deal *in* that sentence. Nevertheless,
because you are a native speaker you hear those negative presuppositions
loud and clear.

Think once again about Attack Pattern 1. It begins with "If you
REALLY wanted *X*" or "If You really WANTed *X*" What does that
presuppose? Right! The presupposition is that YOU DON'T REALLY
WANT *X*, whatever *X* may be. And when you take the bait and let that
presupposition go by, you are making two mistakes:

1. You are giving the attacker exactly what he or she wants and expects.
2. You are admitting the truth of the presupposed attack by default.

Don't do that. Respond directly to the presupposed attack instead,
as in the examples below.

PHYSICIAN: "If you REALLY wanted to get well, YOU wouldn't SMOKE
three packs of cigarettes a day!"

PATIENT: "When did you start thinking that I don't want to get well?"

EXECUTIVE: "If you REALLY cared anything about our sales, YOU
wouldn't TAKE a vacation!"

SALES MANAGER: "When did you start thinking that I don't care anything
about our sales?"

The reason for beginning questions with "When did you start
thinking that *X* . . ." instead of "Why do you think that *X* . . ." or "What
makes you think that *X* . . ." is once again the presuppositions involved.
"When did you start thinking that *X*?" presupposes only "At some time
you started thinking that *X*." Since the verbal attacker has just *said X*,

there's nothing confrontational about your question — it is a neutral utterance. A question that begins with "Why do you . . . " or "What makes you . . . " presupposes "You have a *reason* for thinking that what you say is true, and I want to know what that reason is." You can be quite certain that if you hand a verbal abuser an invitation like that it will be accepted. Like this:

EXECUTIVE: "If you REALLY wanted this project to succeed, YOU'D quit coming in LATE!"

MANAGER: "What makes you think I don't want the project to succeed?"

EXECUTIVE: "Are you getting hard of *hearing*? I TOLD you — the way you come DRAGGING IN HERE LATE every morning makes me think so!"

"When" questions don't have that effect. Instead, one of two things will usually happen. Your attacker will be so astonished at your refusal of the bait that he or she will simply drop the whole thing. Or your question will be answered with a specific incident — such as "When you came in yesterday morning at eleven, and you KNEW the meeting started at ten o'clock!", and then you'll know what the attack is *about*. It's always much better to have a specific charge like that to deal with — a single specific incident in the real world — than a vague general accusation with no details provided.

Alternatively, if you're pressed for time or you don't want to continue the discussion, you can respond with a firm "Of COURSE I want this project to succeed!" "Of COURSE I want to get well!" "Of COURSE I want the promotion!" Followed by a swift and total change of subject, without a pause during which your attacker can say, "Then why DO you (smoke three packs of cigarettes a day?) (always come in late?)", etc. DO NOT PAUSE BETWEEN SENTENCES, EVEN FOR A MOMENT; DO NOT MAKE ANY EYE CONTACT WITH YOUR ATTACKER. Look right through him or her and say something like this: "Of COURSE I want this project to succeed! Now, when I was driving in this morning I saw something that gave me an idea. How would you feel about . . ."

Notice what you are doing when you use these responses, whether you choose the question or the statement.

□ You are ignoring the bait — which has the advantage of surprise and which short-circuits the loop your attacker has planned.

□ You are responding directly to the presupposed attack instead of letting it pass unchallenged — equally surprising.

□ You are transmitting a metamessage: "DON'T TRY THAT WITH ME — IT WON'T WORK. I WON'T PLAY THAT GAME WITH YOU."

This strategy, which is the one you use with *all* verbal attacks, is a vast improvement over wasting your time and energy in a ridiculous row, and it demonstrates very clearly that you flatly refuse to be a verbal victim for the abuser in question.

Now, let's look at the two variations on Attack Pattern 1.

Attack Pattern 1A.   (The speaker is a minister.)

> "If your family REALLY mattered to you, YOU wouldn't WANT to gamble!"

Notice how strange it is that just "you gamble" can serve as bait all by itself in this attack. And we could make it even stranger, because almost any sequence will serve. Consider "If your family REALLY mattered to you, YOU wouldn't WANT to play golf!" Or "If your family REALLY mattered to you, YOU wouldn't WANT a Pulitzer Prize!" The power of this pattern is so overwhelming that its negative quality taints all the rest of the sentence and turns *whatever* you "want" into something bad.

The first section of Pattern 1A — "If your family REALLY mattered to you" — presupposes that your family *doesn't* really matter, as in the corresponding section of Pattern 1. But there's an additional presupposed attack tucked into the bait: the claim that you can control your desires by will power alone.

This claim is nonsense. All of us are capable of refraining from doing things we feel we should not do, by using our will power. But we can't voluntarily keep from *wanting* to do them! The example above means, "The mere fact that you WANT to gamble *proves* that your family doesn't really matter to you," and that is a truly vicious statement.

Now you have a choice. The example contains two presupposed attacks, and you can respond to either one of them. If you decide on the "If you REALLY" attack, you proceed as with Attack Pattern 1, asking "When did you start thinking that my family doesn't matter to me?" or stating firmly, "Of *course* my family matters to me!" If you choose the second one, the dialogue will go like this:

> MINISTER: "If your family REALLY mattered to you, YOU wouldn't WANT to gamble!"
>
> YOU: "The idea that people can control their desires by will power alone is very interesting." (Or "is absolutely fascinating" or "is something you run into once in a while.")

Notice that this response is in Computer Mode. It ignores the personal attack and moves straight to the abstract situation. (The "you" in "something you run into once in a while" is not a real "you"; it's the

American English equivalent of the British "something one runs into once in a while.") This is an excellent idea, especially when the alternative is a row over an emotionally charged issue. Now the *attacker* must make a choice: either (1) to follow you into an abstract discussion of whether people can or cannot control their desires by will power alone; or (2) to revise the first attack and launch a new one. It isn't possible for the minister to simply sail on into the row as if you had countered that your gambling was your own business, or had nothing to do with your feelings about your family.

Attack Pattern 1B.   (The speaker is a banker.)

"A man who REALLY wanted a loan wouldn't COME to the bank dressed like a thug!"

Compare this with the same attack using Pattern 1:

"If you REALLY wanted a loan, YOU wouldn't COME to the bank dressed like a thug!"

The first difference between the two versions is in the Satir Modes used. "If you REALLY..." is in Blamer Mode, while "A man who REALLY..." is in Computer Mode. This choice on the part of your attacker is a way of adding as a sort of linguistic frill: "I'm so dignified and important that I don't STOOP to diRECT attacks!" But that doesn't keep you from knowing you are the target.

The second difference is that there is an additional presupposition here that is not an attack, but that is logically dictated by the structure of the sentence. It goes like this: "If there were a man who really wanted a loan, it would be true of that man that he wouldn't come into the bank dressed like a thug." You can take advantage of the presence of this built-in item and respond by simply agreeing with *it.* Say, "You're absolutely right." Your attacker may then want to back up one step and ask, "If you agree with me on that, why ARE you dressed like a thug?" — but you can head that off easily. Do not pause after stating your agreement. Do not allow your attacker to make eye contact. Switch straight to Computer Mode and tackle the abstract issue, as in this dialogue.

BANKER: "A man who REALLY wanted a loan wouldn't COME to the bank dressed like a thug!"

YOU: "You're absolutely right. Many people place a great deal of emphasis on how others dress. The question of what is appropriate for a given situation is an intricate one." (And so on, being very careful never to say "I" or "you." Don't hesitate to throw in a "Studies show that . . . " or two.)

One danger associated with this attack pattern is that the victim will respond as if it *were* Pattern 1, with results like this:

BANKER: "A man who REALLY wanted a loan wouldn't COME to the bank dressed like a thug!"

CUSTOMER: "Hey . . . I'm NOT dressed like a thug! I'LL have you know, this pair of slacks cost me nearly a hundred BUCKS!"

BANKER: (Icily.) "Well . . . I wasn't aware that we were discussing YOU, Mr. Jones. But since you've brought it UP . . ."

That's a sucker punch; don't let it happen to you.

Attack Pattern 2.   (The speaker is an engineer.)

"EVEN if that prototype DOES collapse, I'LL never say you stressed it all wrong!"

In this example, "You stressed the prototype all wrong" is the bait and "that prototype will collapse" is the presupposed attack. You are expected to leap right in with a "Whadda YOU MEAN, I stressed it all wrong? I did NOT!", so that the attacker can spend twenty minutes of your time arguing about that in tedious detail. Don't provide that opportunity. It's a waste of your time, and it gives the attacker far more than he or she is entitled to get. This pattern also has a presupposition (signalled by the heavily stressed "I'LL") that goes like this: "I'm very unique and special and wonderful and superior to all other people who might find themselves in this situation." Just respond to *that* sequence, saying "I wish everyone had your good judgment," and leave the attacker with jaw hanging and a frustrated power itch.

There is one exception to this strategy. If — and only if — the attacker is in a state of genuine fear or severe distress, use the "When did you start thinking that *X*..." response instead. Suppose that you are a surgeon, and a patient in obvious distress says to you, "EVEN if I DO die on the operating table, MY family would never sue you!" In that case, you do not compliment the patient on his good judgment. You say, "When did you start thinking that you're going to die on the operating table?"

Attack Pattern 3.   (The speaker is a stock broker.)

"Even a WOMan could manage THAT portfolio!"

This pattern (which has been mentioned briefly before) is a mystery to non-native speakers of English. It revolves around the word "even," but nothing you can find in a dictionary will explain the phenomenon.

It gets still more mysterious — notice the sentence "A WOMan could manage THAT portfolio!" It means the same thing; but "even" is still in there, in the same way that the word "you" is still in "Sell your stocks." It's not there in the surface structure of the sentence, but it's there in the presuppositions. Fortunately, native speakers of English understand the meaning of Pattern 3 even (there's that word again!) if they are helpless to explain it.

The presupposed attack(s) and the bait are not as tidily separated as in the earlier patterns, but your internal grammar will provide you with the correct analysis. Both the woman and the portfolio are under attack, and we don't have enough information to determine which of the attacks is the bait. The *victim* would know, however, on the basis of the situation, and would take the bait by responding with one (or both) of these utterances:

> "There's NOTHING WRONG with this portfolio! It's an EXcellent portfolio!"
>
> "Women make very GOOD financial managers, and there's NOTHING WRONG with being a woman!"

Responses like these are what the verbal attacker wants, and will allow him or her to tie the victim up for a quarter hour of undignified verbal struggle.

Pattern 3 presupposes that whatever fills in the blank in "Even a(n) ... " is inferior and second-rate. Don't take the bait. Respond directly to that presupposition instead. Like this:

> "The idea that women are somehow inferior and second-rate is a very common one — but I am astonished to hear it from you."

Or you can say, "The idea that women are somehow inferior and second-rate is a very common one; I'm sorry to hear that you feel that way."

It's not unusual for this pattern to be used by people who have convinced themselves that they have the best of intentions, like the teacher who tells the third graders that "Even the SECOND-graders can pass THIS test." To the child who speaks English, this is not helpful. The automobile salesperson who says, "Even an ELderly person can drive THIS car!" will claim that the intention was only to reassure the senior citizen. That's possible — but there's no way to be sure that the person who hears this pattern won't take it as the verbal abuse it almost always is.

ATTACK PATTERN INTONATION

This is a suitable place to clarify something extremely important. It would be easy to get the impression that verbal attack patterns are identified by the *words* they contain. This isn't true. Compare the two sentences that follow. One of them is an example of Attack Pattern 4; the other contains *exactly* the same words, but it's not an attack at all.

Attack Pattern 4. (The speaker is an architect's relative.)

> "WHY do you keep building the SAME BORING BUILDing OVER and OVER and OVER again?"

> versus —

> "Why do you keep building the same boring building over and over and over again?"

Do you hear the difference? If you're not sure, read the two examples aloud, giving strong emphasis to the words and parts of words written in capital letters. LISTEN CAREFULLY. And try this simpler pair . . .

> "WHY did you SAY that?"

> versus —

> "Why did you say that?"

In all such pairs, the verbal attack is the sentence in which multiple strong stresses give the words an abnormal intonation — an abnormal melody. The other sentence in the pair may be rude. It may be none of the questioner's business. BUT IT IS NOT AN ATTACK. It's a neutral request for information, from someone who *is* interested in knowing the answer. The most typical situation is one in which the non-attack version of the utterance comes from someone talking in Leveler Mode — in which case, you are free to Level right back. Just *say* "It's none of your business." But be aware that no attack was intended.

Verbal stress — strong emphasis on some portion of an utterance — is part of *body* language. Listeners perceive it as slightly higher pitch and louder volume than the unstressed parts of the utterance have, and as slightly slower. It requires more muscular effort and more tension in the vocal tract than the unstressed elements require. For English — in which 90 percent of the emotional information, and more than half of *all* information, is carried by body language — this is very important. THE MOST RELIABLE CLUE YOU HAVE TO VERBAL ABUSE IS YOUR RECOGNITION OF ABNORMAL STRESS PATTERNS IN AN UTTERANCE. No matter *what* words you hear, abnormal stress signals you to be wary.[2]

Any question that begins with the word "why" presupposes something like this: "YOU HAVE A REASON FOR X, AND I REQUEST THAT YOU TELL ME WHAT THAT REASON IS." When the word "why" carries *heavy stress*, however, there is an additional presupposition: "AND I KNOW IN ADVANCE THAT YOUR REASON IS NOT ACCEPTABLE!" The heavy stress makes the question an attack and a direct challenge. And there is an effective way to handle it, called the Boring Baroque Response. Like this:

> RELATIVE: "WHY do you keep building the SAME OLD BORING BUILD-ings OVER and OVER and OVER again?"

> ARCHITECT: "Well, I think it must be because I had such a good time doing that little office building over on 4th street. I did that one in April of 1963, remember? That was the year that . . . . No. Wait a minute. It wasn't 1963, it was 1964. I'm sure of that, because it was in 1964 that Jimmy won the tennis tournament. Or, no . . . no, maybe it *was* 1963! Because . . ." (And so, interminably on.)

Your strategy here is straightforward.

◻ You do not intend to take the bait and fight about whether your buildings are boring or not.

◻ You do intend to respond to the presupposition that you have a reason and that your attacker has is entitled to know what it is.

◻ You intend to demonstrate — IN SPADES — that playing this game with you is going to be excruciatingly boring and unpleasant, and that the attacker would be well advised to go play it with someone else.

By answering in this way you have taken control of the exchange away from your attacker completely.

This technique of answering someone into exhaustion is the single best possible way to deal with a chronic verbal abuser. Suppose you have one person in your group who is constantly attacking people with these vicious "WHY" questions. "WHY do you always..." and "WHY don't you ever..." and the like. Your best move is to introduce the Boring Baroque Response, as widely as possible. When such questions are answered IN FULL AND AT INTERMINABLE LENGTH, with a straight face and a neutral demeanor, the verbal abuser learns that asking them is never going to be any fun and either gives up the nasty habit or takes it elsewhere.

The Boring Baroque Response is also the best possible way to deal with another group of attack patterns — the ones illustrated by these examples:

Attack Pattern 5.
"DON'T you EVen CARE about world HUNGER?"

Attack Pattern 6.
"HOW could you POSSibly SAY something so AWful?"

Attack Pattern 7.
"You could at LEAST have the decency to exPLAIN!"

Faced with any of these patterns, or anything like them, behave as if they were serious questions or claims and answer them as interminably as you can.

- ☐ "Of COURSE I care! Why, I remember a time when the statistics indicated that . . ."
- ☐ "I think the reason I say such awful things is because once when I was about fourteen years old . . ."
- ☐ "I'd be happy to explain. Once, in 1939 — or maybe it was 1940 — or maybe it *was* 1939, because that was the year that . . ."

Go on and on and on, until it's obvious to you that your attacker regrets choosing you as a victim.

As always, if the person who attacked you is someone in great pain or fear, and their state of acute crisis has triggered the attack, switch to a "When did you start thinking that X . . . ?" response.

There are also special circumstances in which you will want to deal with a "WHY" question by making its presupposition false on the spot. Suppose you are a doctor whose patient says, "WHY don't you ever LISten to me when I try to TELL you my SYMPtoms?" Or suppose you are a teacher, and your student says, "WHY don't you ever give me a chance to exPLAIN why my paper is late?" Unless you have rock-solid evidence that the attacker could not possibly be in the right, *stop*. And make the presupposition that you never listen (or never give the person a chance to explain) false. For example:

- ☐ "All right. Tell me which symptom is bothering you most right now."
- ☐ "All right. Explain to me why this paper is late."

And then, sit down and listen. With your full attention. When you have heard the speaker out, either discuss the issue raised at that point or promise to do so at the first possible opportunity — and keep your promise. Say, "I wish I could stay and discuss that with you right now, but I can't. But I'll be back this afternoon and we'll talk about it then." Or, "But if you'll come to my office hours Tuesday morning we can talk about it then." — Whatever fits your situation.

Occasionally you will run into a verbal abuser who is a native speaker of English but insists that he or she can't be held responsible for verbal attacks because "I can't HEAR those stress patterns — *I* don't even know they're THERE." You can determine very quickly whether the claim of tone-deafness is true or not. Just say this:

"EVen YOU should be able to hear THIS pattern!"

If, as has always happened in my experience, the verbal abuser reacts angrily to that sentence, the claim is false.

Attack Pattern 8. (The speaker is a hospital administrator.)

"EVeryone underSTANDS why you can't get along with any of your COLLeagues, Miss Jones."

This attack relies on human frailty, and signals a fishing expedition. Because you are a human being, you are almost certain to have at least one unpleasant personal secret. It may be something of major significance, or it may be trivial. Whatever it is, however silly or serious others might find it, it looms large to *you* and you don't want it to be public knowledge. The verbal abuser who uses the "EVeryone underSTANDS" pattern is counting on that, and is counting on you to react by thinking, "Oh, NO — THEY'VE FOUND OUT!" and blurting out an apology or explanation. Like this:

ADMINISTRATOR: "EVeryone underSTANDS why you can't get along with your COLLeagues, Miss Jones!"

MISS JONES: "Look . . . I KNOW I shouldn't keep taking time off because of this knee — I know it makes it hard on everybody. But if you people could just give me a *little more time ...*"

This is a mistake. The chances are good that until Jones began talking the administrator was unaware of the knee problem. Now she knows, and Jones has handed her the information on a platter, under conditions that are anything but favorable. This should not happen. Instead, the dialogue should go like this:

ADMINISTRATOR: "EVeryone underSTANDS why you can't get along with your COLLeagues, Miss Jones!"

MISS JONES: "Well, I want you to know that I appreciate their support."

Now the administrator is in an awkward position. Now it appears that if there really *is* a problem, everyone knows it except her. She could say, "I meant, everyone understands except *me!*" or "I don't understand anything, actually — I was just fishing!" But if she had that kind of courage, she wouldn't have tried this shabby tactic in the first place.

Throughout the exchange, it's crucially important for your body language — and especially the intonation of your voice — to remain calm, neutral, and controlled. If any of your responses sound sarcastic or insolent, as they will if you include too many strong stresses on words or parts of words, they will be perceived as *counter*attacks and they will fail.

The bait in this example is "You can't get along with your colleagues." The attacker expects you either to take that bait and begin protesting that you do NOT have problems getting along with your colleagues, or to blurt out your secret as in the first dialogue above. Don't do either of those things.

Notice that three elements in the Attack Pattern 8 example are emphasized by strong stress. This intonation will tell you that you're under verbal attack, no matter how many kind and caring words may be thrown in to distract you. The fact that an attack has "darling" tacked on at one end and "honey" tacked on at the other will not confuse you if you are listening for the stress patterns.

It's normal for English sentences to have one word containing a strong stress, usually just before or at the end of the sentence; if this stress is marked at all in print, it will be underlined. It's normal for them to contain what is called *contrastive* stress, as in "It wasn't twenty dollars, it was THIRty dollars!", and "Ellen DIDn't call that in, she MAILED it." It's normal for two or more strong stresses to turn up in questions when someone isn't sure they heard correctly, as in "She said the PRESIDENT CALLED?" And it's normal to hear strong stresses in emergency situations, as in "LOOK OUT! It's on FIRE!", or in news bulletins such as "HEY! I WON the SWEEPstakes!" Your internal grammar contains a checklist of the environments in which several strong stresses in a single sentence are normal, and it includes all of these. Otherwise, this rule holds:

WHEN YOU HEAR TWO OR MORE STRONG STRESSES IN ANY ONE SENTENCE IN THE SPEECH OF AN ADULT, COME TO FULL ALERT.

This is not being neurotic, or paranoid. It's evidence that you are linguistically competent.

Attack Pattern 9.   (The speaker is a dentist.)

"YOU'RE not the ONly patient I HAVE, you know!"

This pattern is so easy to deal with that it's hard to understand why it is so widely used. The only possible explanation is that it *works*. That is, people fall for it. They respond with "WHAT do you mean by THAT?", which gives the attacker permission to provide a list of their faults and flaws. Or they go into Placater Mode and respond like this:

PATIENT: "Oh, Dr. Everett, I KNOW that! Oh, dear — have I been behaving like I thought I was your ONLY PATIENT? I assure you, I didn't MEAN to! I'm so sorry — I KNOW how BUSY you are, and I KNOW that you have HUNDreds of people counting on you and wanting your time. And . . ."

This is absurd. All that the attack logically presupposes is "I HAVE OTHER PATIENTS;" the bait is composed entirely of the intonation and the context. There is only one appropriate response to any attack of this kind, and that response is cheerful agreement. "I couldn't agree with you more." "You're absolutely right." — Something of that kind. The chances of the presupposed item being false are near zero; just agree with it, and leave the attacker trying to figure out what to do next.

The same thing is true for Attack Pattern 10, which is a not very subtle attempt in Computer Mode that goes like this:

"SOME managers would FIRE an employee who couldn't meet his SALES quotas!"

As with Pattern 9, the chances that this is not true for some managers, somewhere, are almost nonexistent, and the proper response is, "I'm sure that's true."

A BASIC STRATEGY TO REMEMBER: Any time a verbal attack presupposes some innocuous statement that is 99 percent certain to be true in the real world, your best move is probably to ignore everything else and agree with that statement. Always, this accomplishes four useful things:

- ☐ It surprises the attacker.
- ☐ It short-circuits the verbal Violence loop planned for you.
- ☐ It transmits the message that you refuse to play the attacker's game.
- ☐ It obliges the attacker to make a new move if he or she wants to continue on the offensive.

We have now looked at ten English verbal attack patterns. There are others, but the set is small; my guess is that there could not be more than fifty and that twenty-five is a more likely total. When you run into what you think might be a new pattern, the first thing to do is to try rewording it. Put it into different styles and different Satir Modes. How many ways could you say roughly the same thing? Most of the time, this rewording exercise will demonstrate that it's not a new attack but a variation on a pattern you already know.

You will be able to recognize verbal attacks, no matter what their wording, in three ways:

- ☐ By the abnormal emphatic stresses they contain — by their distinctive intonation

□ By the rest of the nonverbal communication that accompanies them

□ By the context — the situation in which they occur — and the information you have about the people involved in the situation

Faced with any verbal attack, familiar or unfamiliar, your first step is to divide it into presupposed attack(s) and bait. Sometimes the division will be very clear, as in Pattern 1; sometimes the two elements will be scrambled and interwoven. But your internal grammar will always be able to identify the parts. And once you know what they are, you follow three simple rules.

RULE ONE:

Ignore the bait, no matter how outrageous.

RULE TWO:

Respond directly to one of the presuppositions.

RULE THREE:

No matter what you do, transmit the metamessage: "DON'T TRY THAT WITH ME — IT WON'T WORK. I WON'T PLAY THAT GAME."

Verbal attack patterns function in communication as *action chains*. An action chain is a behavior sequence with distinct parts in a distinct order, which — if interrupted — usually has to be started all over again if it is to be completed. (A handshake is an example of a *non*verbal action chain.) For the verbal attacker, this action chain has three steps:

1. The attacker begins the action chain by using one of the verbal attack patterns.
2. The intended victim takes the bait and responds to it directly.
3. There is a volley of verbal abuse from both parties, until one is exhausted.

Interrupting this sequence, like interrupting a handshake, makes it almost impossible for the attacker to complete it satisfactorily without starting all over again with a new attack. *Anything* you say that has this effect, and is not just more verbal abuse, will be an improvement over going right into Step 2 of the chain.

Problems with the Technique

The major problem with this technique is not that it's difficult, or hard to remember, or anything of that kind. The major problem is that people sometimes have trouble putting it into practice. They say, to me, "I understand what I should have done — BUT I COULDN'T BRING MYSELF TO DO IT." And they offer me, always, one of two reasons.

First. They couldn't do it because they just couldn't let the attacker "get away with it."

Second. They couldn't do it because they felt so guilty. Both of these explanations rest on a serious misunderstanding of what verbal abuse is, and why verbal abusers practice it. Let's examine them more closely.

"I JUST COULDN'T LET THEM GET AWAY WITH IT."

What the verbal abuser wants is THE CONFRONTATION. The scene. The fight. The row. Like a child who misbehaves because it would rather be punished than be ignored, the verbal abuser wants your full and undivided attention and is willing to go through any amount of ruckus to get it. The bait itself is trivial to verbal abusers, valued only for its potential to provoke you.

They do not really care about your lateness to work or your smoking or your weight or your extravagance or the effect your actions may have on your parents, or whatever else they dangle in front of you as a lure. Unlike the rude Leveler, they have no interest in your answers to their questions, or your replies to their challenges. They care about holding your attention; they care about tying you up for fifteen minutes or more in the scenario they have planned for you. They care about demonstrating that they have *power* over you and can control your behavior.

Therefore: ANY TIME YOU TAKE THE BAIT IN A VERBAL ATTACK AND PARTICIPATE IN THE VERBAL VIOLENCE LOOP, YOU *ARE* LETTING THEM GET AWAY WITH IT. That fact — not the irrelevant statement that you found so insulting or hurtful — should be your concern. Their tactic must not work — you must not join them in the game and play the role of verbal victim or counterattacker. Any participation on your part *is* letting them get away with it.

"I FELT SO GUILTY, I JUST COULDN'T DO IT."

This ordinarily happens when your attacker doesn't fit your *image* of an attacker. Perhaps the person who has come at you verbally is a small child, or a very frail and elderly person, or someone you outrank in so many ways that you perceive him or her as essentially helpless against you. In your internal grammar the word "attacker" is marked with the features [+ LARGE], [+ PHYSICALLY STRONG], [+ IMPOSING], etc. You feel obligated to respond to the verbal abuser who does not fit this definition as you would to an infant who was trying to hurt you. You feel an obligation to be kind.

Again, there is a misunderstanding here. VERBAL ABUSE IS AN ADDICTION, JUST LIKE DRUG ADDICTION. The verbal abuser uses the verbal attack to satisfy a need. As with any other dependency, if you feed that need, it will grow, and the abuser will need more and more of the same in order to satisfy the need. It is not kind, it is not caring, it is not nurturing, to serve as a verbal abuser's victim. Just as it is not kind to hand a drink to an alcoholic. The two situations are equivalent, and the linguistic addiction is as dangerous as the chemical one.

Remember the first and second metaprinciples of *Gentle Art* syntonics: anything you feed will grow; anything you starve will fester or die. No matter which of the *Gentle Art* syntonics techniques you decide to use, these metaprinciples apply. When you play verbal victim to the verbal abuser, you feed the habit of verbal abuse and strengthen it. If you do this on a long-term basis, you are participating in the abuse as part of a co-dependency. The only way you can break a verbal abuser of the habit is by making sure that the attacks never work and therefore fail to provide what the abuser wants. There is absolutely no reason for you to feel guilty about doing that.

SPECIAL CIRCUMSTANCES

Non-native Speakers.   Always remember that the verbal attack patterns described in this chapter, and the others like them that come your way, are part of the GRAMMAR OF AMERICAN ENGLISH. If the person you are interacting with is not a native speaker of American English, be careful — make generous allowances. It is entirely possible that the person is unaware that the utterance is an attack. It may have been learned in a language class, or picked up from a television show or in a conversation, without any awareness of the special meanings carried by the unusual intonation pattern. As a rule of thumb, if the speaker does not have native fluency in American English, assume that the utterance is NOT an attack until you have some independent evidence to the contrary.

Similarly, never take it for granted that a non-native speaker understands the attack patterns when you (or others) use them. This is a serious problem in multinational business and professional interactions, where there is a tendency to assume that because the foreigner knows the English *words,* the message has been understood. English uses intonation to express verbal abuse, to convey anger and annoyance, and to demonstrate severe displeasure with others. It's never safe to assume that another language does this — it may use quite different methods.

What we need in order to improve crosscultural communication are the *equivalents* in other languages of the verbal attack patterns in this chapter. We don't have them, and they aren't going to be easy to get.

— Because when you ask a non-native speaker for a translation of those patterns, what you always get is the translation of the *neutral* utterance with the same words. That is, when you ask for a translation of "WHY did you leave so EARly?", you are given the translation of "Why did you leave so early?" instead.

Written Language. The English system of punctuation is nearly useless for indicating intonation. Editors are making special exceptions when they permit writers to use capital letters as I have used them in this book — to differentiate abnormal stress from the normal stress that is indicated by underlining or italics. Linguists use musical notes and arrows and exotic graphic arrangements in an attempt to show the melodic pattern that intonation imposes on sequences of language, and that doesn't begin to do the job. Ordinary written language will not have even these minimal clues. It is therefore *never* safe to assume that you have been verbally attacked on the basis of written language alone. Remember that a single word or phrase — "Idiot!" will do for an example — can mean "You are so stupid that I am shocked into saying an ugly epithet about that stupidity!" or "What you've just done for me is so wonderful that I don't know how to tell you what it means to me!" or a host of other things corresponding to many different emotions both negative and positive. This is one situation for which the cliché "You had to *be* there!" holds true.

When the written language comes from someone you have routine access to, you can usually manufacture a way to find out what was intended. Suppose the suspect sequence is in a memo addressed to you: Spill coffee on it. Then take it to the person who wrote it, announce that you have spilled coffee on it — which is true — and that you can no longer read it. Ask them to to tell you what it says, and listen to the intonation. If the message is handwritten you may be able to just say you can't read it. Any excuse that will serve as a legitimate reason to let you hear the sequence from the speaker's own lips will serve.

Secondhand language. Everything I've said about written language applies equally strongly to *reports* from Person *X* that Person *Y* said something or other. You can never know what intonation the utterance had in Person *Y*'s mouth from the intonation Person *X* gives to it. Unless you can find a way to hear the sequence from the alleged attacker's lips, as with written language, or find additional evidence that the language was an attack, assume that it was a neutral utterance.

DEFINING VERBAL VIOLENCE

I want to turn briefly to the question of how the word "violence" should be defined. If your definition of violence stops at such things as bombs and bullets and beatings, you may be finding my term — "verbal violence" — hard to deal with. This is a reality gap, and a major one, responsible for vast amounts of confusion and chaos. It appears to be one of the "only semantics" issues that breaks down along gender lines.

Let's set aside for now the *moral* questions about violence. They are touchy questions, and there is no shortage of materials in all the media dealing with them. Let's consider simply the *economic* questions, which are not controversial.

I am certain that even the most ramboesque and militant among us will agree that violence in society costs us money: money that could be spent to expand the economy; money that could be used for investment and rebuilding; money that could be used to reduce the tax burden; money that could be used to improve the environment; money that could go to research and development in the sciences and the arts. A VAST AMOUNT OF MONEY. And it must all be devoted instead to the servicing of violence.

Consider what you personally spend for security, for insurance against vandalism and burglary, and for taxes to support your local law enforcement and criminal justice systems. Not to mention the whopping bills for healthcare, for the rehabilitation of substance abusers, and for lost productivity, all due to the effects of violence on the members of the work force. VIOLENCE IS AS MUCH A PART OF YOUR COST OF DOING BUSINESS OR PRACTICING YOUR PROFESSION AS YOUR LIGHTS AND WATER AND PHONE BILLS ARE. You cannot *afford* to be indifferent to the subject.

When M. D. Blumenthal and her colleagues investigated this matter in a research study in 1972, they found that 57 percent of the 1400 American males in their study said that when police shoot looters that is *not* violence: 58 percent of the same group stated that when people burn their draft cards it *is* violence. In a similar study in 1975, Blumenthal asked American males where on a seven-point violence scale they would rank a protest meeting held without a permit. Sixty percent put the meeting on the VIOLENT end of the scale; 32 percent gave it the most violent rating shown. Blumenthal's research (from these and later studies) can be translated into semantic features that seems to be applicable to the majority of the male population in this country.

By and large, for American males, "violence" is marked [+ FIERCE], [+ STRONG], [+ UNNECESSARY], [+ AVOIDABLE], and [+ BAD]. When one of these features is missing, the word "violence" is not perceived as the proper label. Burning draft cards is seen as avoidable, while the shooting of looters by police is not: therefore, the otherwise innocuous action is labeled as violence and the one in which people suffered genuine physical harm is not.

It is common to hear individuals who have attacked family members physically state that what they did was necessary and unavoidable, and therefore not *bad*. War, in which violence is the name of the game, is always considered necessary and unavoidable. When we look at the set of semantic features established by Blumenthal's studies, such statements cease to be surprising. They allow us to predict that when the actions taken by members of teenage gangs terrorizing our streets are dictated by the code of the gang, the perpetrators will not consider them violence. They make it easier for us to understand why drug addicts insist — and insist, the news stories tell us, "without any sign of remorse" — that they are not violent criminals. Notice that the defining features make no reference whatsoever to the *results* of the actions. Those results clearly are not considered relevant.

If you are someone who believes that injury resulting from an action taken against another person's will makes that action violent, you are going to have great difficulty communicating with people who define violence as the Blumenthal subjects did. For each of you, the other person's language will seem to make no sense, because you will not be speaking the same language.

The implications for criminal law, the justice system, law enforcement, human service agencies, education, healthcare, and the economy at large, are obvious — there's no need for me to point them out to you. But there is something important that is not so obvious: THE ROOTS OF PHYSICAL VIOLENCE ARE IN VERBAL VIOLENCE.

Defining "violence" with no reference to the harm it does to people requires just one thing: callousness. Human infants are not callous. By the age of six months, if they are set down near another infant who is crying and in obvious distress, they will make unmistakable efforts to comfort the other child. If those efforts fail, they will begin to cry in sympathetic chorus. Callousness has to be taught to children — and we do teach them. We listen when they tell us that little Mary and little Johnny were upset by their words, and this is the sort of advice we give them:

"Oh, don't worry about it — they'll get over it."
"They're just making mountains out of molehills."
"They just don't know how to take a joke."
"They're just acting like babies — they'll grow out of it."

That is: we tell them that when their language causes pain in others they should not concern themselves about that pain — it is the fault of those who *feel* the pain. We carefully ignore the very physical consequences in the real world of what we call "hurt *feelings*." We should therefore not be surprised when the children grow up to be callous adults with little concern for the wellbeing or property rights of others.

If we are going to stamp out the epidemic of physical violence that hits us so hard in the pocketbook and has so many other disastrous social consequences, we will have to begin by putting an end to the *verbal* violence that is its breeding ground. The techniques presented in this book make that possible.

The Verbal Violence Two-Step

Chronic verbal abusers and chronic verbal victims, faced with the facts of their situation, respond with dismal predictability. Verbal abusers begin by insisting that their victims are simply "touchy" and "neurotic"; that's Step One. Step Two comes in two versions: "I didn't mean any harm" and "I was only kidding." Verbal victims let the abusers lead, beginning with "I guess I'm just neurotic" and "I guess I just make mountains out of molehills." And then they move to the *defense* of their abusers, staunchly insisting that "they don't really mean any harm" and "after all, they're only kidding."! I don't think I've ever given a presentation on this subject without at least one person in the audience saying, "But since they don't really mean any harm by it, it doesn't *count*, does it?"

This might be of some minimal interest if — as is often assumed — meaning were something you could hand from person to person like a parcel. It's *not* like that.

> THE ONLY PRACTICAL MEANING AN UTTERANCE HAS IN THE REAL WORLD IS THE MEANING THE LISTENER UNDERSTANDS IT TO HAVE.

If what you say to someone is understood to be an insult or an attack — or a compliment, for that matter — what you intended it to mean makes little difference. The other person's response and subsequent behavior will be based not on your intended meaning but on his or her *understanding* of that meaning.

Furthermore, the intentions are irrelevant. Consider what you would do if a business down the road from you were discharging toxic chemicals into your water supply. Certainly you know that this isn't being done for the specific purpose and with the specific intention of harming you. It's being done because it's convenient and because it saves money and perhaps because "that's the way we've always done it." But you do not for one moment say, "Oh, well — since you don't mean any harm by it, it doesn't count!" and let the practice continue unchallenged. You insist that it be stopped, regardless of intentions, because it puts you at risk.

The only reason people don't behave the same way toward language pollution is that most of the information demonstrating its dangers is relatively new. When I first began working with verbal violence and verbal self-defense twenty years ago, sympathy for verbal victims was *literally* nonexistent, and that is only just beginning to change. But once you are aware of the facts, it makes *no* sense to say that verbal abuse will be accepted as long as there's no deliberate intent to do harm.

In business and the professions, things are looking up. It has now been formally established that Malpractice Of The Mouth is grounds for legal action. The concept of "emotional abuse" has now been recognized as grounds for official intervention and redress. But when the relationship is a personal one, and one that you are unwilling or unable to terminate, you still have to do the cleanup work yourself. We are very slow to recognize the fact that it is *also* malpractice when personal responsibilities — such as the responsibilities of spouses or parents — are carried out carelessly or maliciously or incompetently. Let me offer a few encouraging words, to be referred to when progress seems slow. Let's talk cattle for a minute.

The only reason cattle can be confined by an ordinary barbed wire fence is that they have no idea they can jump over it. If they ever do, by bizarre chance, jump a fence even once, they are liberated cattle thereafter. No ordinary fence will ever hold them again.

People are precisely the same way about the language barriers that verbal abusers set up to hold them back. The only reason such barriers work is that people have no idea they can get past them. A person who does get past, even once, is no longer a prisoner of verbal abuse in the same way. And such barriers will never hold that person back in the same way or to the same degree again.

The Man/Woman Problem

The September/October 1988 issue of *Executive Female* had an article by Linda Heller titled "The Last Angry Men? What Men *Really* Feel About Working With Women." According to the men (almost every one of them, at their own request, anonymous):

> Women "haven't developed the grace of leadership that comes naturally to men . . ."
>
> Women's "poor political skills," "emotional tendencies," and "lack of leadership abilities" hold them back.
>
> Women "haven't been socialized to become team players . . ."
>
> Women are "very sensitive to perceived slights . . ."
>
> Women "get cowed too easily and back down, even when they have a good point . . ."

Women "lack proper social presence when they're not making business conversation . . ."

Women "don't know how to play the corporate game . . ."

Women tend to "be more emotional and to personalize professional matters . . ."

And much more of the same, all from men who insisted that the women in question were intelligent, capable, good at their jobs, and in every other way admirable colleagues. Clearly this problem has not been solved by the women's liberation movement. What's going on here?

We've already discussed the problems many women have functioning as team players in the strategic games of their firms and organizations. But there's another game that's equally unfamiliar to women, that has not yet been discussed, and that is largely responsible for male opinions like those quoted above.

Many men use the verbal attack patterns of English, together with overt Blaming behavior, NOT TO GET ATTENTION, OR TO DO HARM, BUT AS A SPORT. This is especially true when they are with other men in business or social settings. They toss out verbal attacks exactly as they would serve a ball in tennis or throw a pass in football, and they keep track of "points scored" as a result. This can get very ugly — as football can get very ugly — BUT IT IS IMPORTANT TO REMEMBER THAT THE INDIVIDUALS INVOLVED ARE HAVING FUN. There are plenty of men who dislike this game — but they recognize it *as* a game, and they understand the two most important facts about such verbal contests:

☐ The attacks are not meant personally.

☐ A good time is being had by all.

I cannot emphasize too strongly that many women are not aware of these facts, that many who *are* aware find it hard to tell when verbal sparring is sport and when it is for real — and that for most women, even those who are themselves highly skilled at this game, it is most assuredly not FUN.

If you are a woman, I have one simple suggestion: WATCH THE MEN. If the seeming verbal carnage is all a game — no matter how fierce and perhaps outraged the words being used may be — the men's body language will show only alertness and pleasure. That mismatch, with none of the signals of pain and anger that would ordinarily result from verbal violence, is your best guide. And then, *learn* from your observation. Don't hesitate to ask for help when a session is over; say, "Okay — how much of that was for real and how much was just kicking the ball around?" There's no shame associated with not knowing how to play, as long as (a) you're willing to learn, and (b) you're willing to accept the instruction given you, gracefully.

What if you prefer not to play? Fine — that's your choice. But it must *be* a choice, not an accident born of ignorance. And it must be a choice you make after you know what it is you're turning down and what the penalties are for your decision.

If you are a man, there are things you can do that will help. First and foremost: REMEMBER that the women present in these verbal contests are novices; be alert to their signals. Second: When women ask you for clarification and help in this area, either give it without being patronizing and sarcastic or turn them over to someone who can. Third: when a woman becomes obviously rattled and distressed by verbal sparring, don't take *that* personally.

NOTES

1. *Contemporary Ob/Gyn's* "Malpractice Update" column for September 1986 (page 207) carried the following instructive item: "A Georgia appellate court ruled that a physician had to stand trial on charges of using abusive language. The higher tribunal found a trial court had erred in granting summary judgment for the doctor. The patient had brought suit, charging intentional infliction of emotional distress through use of abusive statements."

2. Remember that multiple strong stresses on words or parts of words are characteristic of Blaming and Placating language.

Workout — Chapter 6

1. Where are the toxic waste dumps in your own language environment? What are the places — and the times — that you know in advance will be filled with verbal abuse? If you were preparing a spacetime map for yourself, where would you write "Here There Be Language Dragons"? Make a list, date it, and file it. Check it again a year later to find out (a) which dump sites have been cleaned up and (b) whether new ones have been added.

2. What does the word "violence" mean to you? Use semantic features and reality statements and prepare a definition. As always, it would be useful to get some other definitions from within your circle for comparison with your own.

3. For at least two weeks, keep a record of every Verbal Attack Pattern example you encounter. Make a note on each one to indicate whether you were present as abuser, as victim, or as innocent bystander. The totals will give you a rough idea of your own Verbal Attack Pattern profile. Do this again six months later and compare the two profiles to determine what changes have taken place over that period.

4. For another two-week period, keep a record of verbal attacks you encounter that are in the form of obscenities, curses, racial and sexist epithets, open insults such as "You're an IDIOT!" and similar garbage. Compare it with the record you prepared for #3 — which type of abuse is more common in your life? What kinds of people and situations are involved in this cruder kind of abuse? Are they Leveling or Blaming?

5. In "Litigation sickness," published in the April/June 1987 issue of the *Newsetter of Americans For Legal Reform*, Harold J. Moskowitz claims that clients hear so much from lawyers about more pain and suffering equaling a bigger settlement that they continue to suffer pain long after their injuries are gone. Lawyers, he says, are "the leading cause of 'jurisgenic' disease." He's trying to draw a parallel with "iatrogenic" disease (disease due to the actions of physicians) and perhaps "nosocomial" disease (disease due to the actions of hospitals.) Do you agree? Is there any other profession that could be added to the set?

6. The May 1986 issue of *Science 86* had an article by William F. Allman, titled "Mindworks." Allman offered the following lines as an example of the mind's amazing ability to supply missing information:

> There was a young maiden from Kew,
> Whose limerick stopped at line two.
>
> There was an old pirate from Dunn.

Simple, right? But why? How did you know? And now that you know why and how you know, demonstrate your skill with the patterns involved by writing a few more verses. "There was an old lawyer from Bree. . . ."

SIGHT BITES

1. "If we are to control the increasing expressions of violence which threaten our society, it is imperative that we seek every technology at our disposal to understand the nature and the character of those who would use violence as their weapon. What better source could we hope for in our understanding of such individuals than their own words?"

   (Murray S. Miron, expert on coercive language, quoted in "Between the Lines of Threatening Messages," by Berkeley Rice, in *Psychology Today* for September 1981; page 64.)

2. Asked why he left in the film called *Hitcher* a scene in which a young woman is tied between a pole and a truck and torn in half, director Robert Harmon said he was trying not to "emasculate the script."

   (Reported in the *Los Angeles Times Calendar* for February 23, 1986; page 37.)

3. "What is conversationally implicated by an utterance depends not only on the utterance but on what other utterances the speaker could have produced but did not."

(From "Conversational Implicature and the Lexicon," by James D. McCawley, in *Syntax and Semantics*, Vol. 9, Academic Press 1978; page 245.)

4. "Why do women have such a hard time breaking through to the top? E. Pendleton James, former head of personnel for the Reagan White House, points to a process he calls 'BOGSAT — A Bunch of Guys Sitting Around a Table . . . .'"

   (From "Corporate Brides, Is It Worth It?" by Nehama Jacobs and Sarah Hardesty, in *Management Digest* for November 1988; page 5-12.)

5. "The adolescent population is the only age group in America with an increasing mortality rate during the past 25 years. Violence remains the leading cause of adolescent deaths, with accidents, suicides, and homicides accounting for more than 75 percent of teenage mortality."

   (From "Risk-Taking Behaviors in Adolescence," by Donald E. Greydanus, in *Journal of the American Medical Association* for October 16, 1987; page 2110.)

6. "What we find in talking to high school kids is that they don't characterize a lot of what they're experiencing — grabbing and slapping — as violence."

   (David Adams, quoted in "Swinging — and Ducking — Singles," in *Time Magazine* for September 5, 1988, page 54.)

7. ". . . people in corporations are going to have to find new ways to express anger, and this without scaring each other to death, offending anybody's professional dignity, or plunging the company into anarchy."

   (From "Facing Up to Executive Anger," by Walter Kierchel III, in *Fortune* for November 16, 1981; page 208.)

7

Language and the Time Domain

SCENARIO TEN   John Martin glared at his wife, his eyebrows knotted and his jaw grimly set. He'd been down this road before, and he was very tired of it. "What do you mean, you don't have enough time?" he demanded. "You have just as much time as anybody *else* does!"

"I do *not!* How can you SAY that? You know perfectly well that I work at least a seventy-hour week! There's no WAY I can go to Jamie's play, and you KNOW it!"

"Well, what do you think *I* do, lie around the pool all day? I spend just as many hours working as *you* do, and there are plenty of weeks when I spend MORE!"

"That sounds logical, John," Elaine Martin said doggedly, "but it's not the same. It's not the same at all. You have a *choice* — I *don't.*"

"Wrong!" John declared. "It's *exactly* the same. You have work to do — I have work to do. And *one* of us has to postpone some of that work long enough to go with Jamie next Friday night. I went last year; it's YOUR turn — and if you REALLY cared about either Jamie OR me I wouldn't have to point that OUT to you! My work is just as important as yours, Elaine, and just as hard to put off — WHY can't you see that? WHY can't you ever consider the *facts* instead of your ridiculous FANtasies?"

Elaine stared at him, outraged. "*Listen!*" she said. "If *you* decide to take the day off, or go home early, nobody gives you any static! But if *I* want to do that, I'm *help*less, because people will DIE if I'm not there! You can't tell ME that's not different!"

John stood there silent for a minute, staring at her. And then he stepped back and made an elaborate deep bow, his arm sweeping before him, like a medieval courtier with a plumed hat in hand. As he straightened up, he spoke to her, the smile on his face as false as the absurd gesture had been.

"Oh, yes — I'd forgotten how you see the world, Elaine! *You* are the *MDeity*, without whose radiant presence the ordinary person could not surVIVE. That picture had SLIPPED MY mind, in SPITE of the way you *harp* on it day and night! Pardon ME, *Doctor* Martin!"

She turned her back on him, shaking, determined that he would not see her cry. And she answered him in icy tones. "You don't understand," she said. "It's not possible for someone who is not a doctor to understand. A doctor's time is not his own. Doctors have responsibilities they cannot set aside. Patients cannot *wait*; advertising campaigns *can*."

Elaine didn't jump when the door slammed; she had been expecting it. *Now* she could cry.

In the past twenty years much has been written about the way that perceptions of time vary from one culture to another. In *The Dance of Life*, Edward T. Hall writes of France, where acquiring a customer means acquiring several generations of a family and is expected to take years of effort. He tells us about Brazil, where how long you have been in a line or on a list is irrelevant, because only people who have no connections and don't know how to get along with others ever have to wait on lines or lists. He describes the Pueblo Indian culture, in which no project can begin until all the right *thoughts* are present — which would be an impossible impediment to scheduling, since no method exists for determining how long that will take.

But such differences are not confined to different nations and ethnic groups. As Scenario Ten shows, two people who share the same cultural background can still be situated perceptually on opposite sides of a reality gap that has to do with time. This often leads to vicious arguments, and language that is hard to forget even if it is forgiven. Our scenario shows a time fiasco taking place between spouses, but the same altercation could have taken place in any professional or business context. The only difference between the two is that wounds are likely to be *deeper* when the person you're fighting with knows you well — because people who know you well know far more about where you are vulnerable.

Few people, if you asked them to complete a reality statement beginning with "Time is . . . " would do so with ease; even fewer would provide you with anything like Einstein's clear and emotionally neutral "Time is what the clock says." But you do need this information — because a significant portion of your ability to predict others' behavior must be based on how they would complete that statement, and how their statement might differ from your own.

One way to investigate perceptions of time is by finding out what ROLE time fills in someone's image of reality. Consider the following simple sentence:

"John hit the golf ball with the club."

In this sentence John fills the role of DOER; he *does* the action described. The golf ball's role is the role of OBJECT — what the action is done *to*. And the club fills the role of INSTRUMENT — what John does the action *with*.

The language you speak determines the assignment of these roles. And if your language allows you to assign something this OBJECT role (not to be confused with the schoolroom term "direct object"), it encourages you to perceive that thing as something over which you have power. In English we say "Harry rode a horse," and because the horse is the OBJECT, we perceive Harry as *doing* something *to* the horse. In Navajo the horse's role is not OBJECT but ASSOCIATE, so that the equivalent sentence means "Harry and the horse went about together." In Hopi, the horse's role is INSTRUMENT — Harry *uses* the horse to go about *with*, just as he would use a fork to eat with. And in French the horse has roughly the role of PLACE; it's just where Harry happens to be located as he rides. Such linguistic phenomena have powerful effects on the way we think and the way we behave.

English has a revealing metaphor (originally Benjamin Franklin's): "Time is money." For much of the American population, this metaphor dominates their image of reality, and they assign time the OBJECT role accordingly. They *do things to* time. They spend it, save it, waste it, give others a few hours of it, and resent the squandering of precious moments of it. For them, everyone has a personal inventory of units of time, just as they have a personal inventory of units of money, and this inventory is something under their control, to be *managed* in the same way a stock portfolio is managed.

John Martin's language in Scenario Ten fits this metaphor. He says things like . . .

" . . . have enough time"

" . . . have just as much time as anybody else"

" . . . spend just as many hours working"

But Elaine Martin's language makes it clear that she does not perceive time as something she controls. On the contrary. She uses the very strange sentence, "A doctor's time is not his own," which contradicts itself.[1] She complains of her helplessness in terms of time. And she becomes so upset, and so afraid of showing her emotions, that she turns her back on her husband and switches to Computer Mode.

Changing this situation is the proper business of a novel; it won't be attempted here. But there are useful things to be learned from examining — and rewriting — Scenario Ten. Obviously, if your dominant reality statement is TIME IS MONEY and you are forever fighting with someone *about* time, you should investigate the possibility that your opponent doesn't subscribe to that metaphor. If time, as he or she perceives it, fills the role of DOER rather than OBJECT — if time passes, and drags, and flies, and runs out, and goes by, and it is that image set that is dominant — the two of you are involved in one of those "It's only semantics" situations. You're not speaking the same language; you're not syntonic; and meaningful communication between you will demand careful attention to that problem. Knowing this — like knowing that someone perceives failure as [+ FINAL] — will help you understand behavior that would otherwise be mysterious and perhaps infuriating.

Another possibility is that the individual does share your metaphor, but believes himself or herself to be a *failure* at the task of managing time. Again, careful attention will be needed if the two of you are to communicate successfully.

Time Out for a Brief Review and a New Technique

Other things are going on in Scenario Ten, and you will have begun to be aware of them in a systematic fashion instead of at the level of "gut feelings." It's worth stopping for a moment to review the characteristics of language behavior that you will have noticed as you were reading the scenario. For example:

SATIR MODES ANALYSIS:

John Martin stays in Blamer Mode throughout the entire scenario. Elaine Martin *begins* by Blaming back (which results in a predictable escalation of the fight) but becomes alarmed and switches to Computer Mode before it's over.

SENSORY MODES ANALYSIS:

John Martin shows a strong preference for Sight Mode, while Elaine Martin repeatedly uses Hearing Mode vocabulary.

VERBAL ATTACKS ANALYSIS:

John and Elaine not only use the verbal attack patterns of English — in addition, the multiple heavy stresses in their sentences signal almost incessant verbal attacks even when the patterns don't appear.

Matters would improve if one of these two people would match the other's preferred Sensory Mode or refrain altogether from sensory vocabulary. Matters would improve if they would stop feeding one another's Blaming loops. Matters would improve if they would moderate their intonation to get rid of the sarcasm and hostility it conveys.

Those improvements might well keep John Martin from losing his temper — as we have already seen him do at the office — and throwing both undignified body language and deliberately vicious words into a pot already boiling over. And they might make it possible for Elaine Martin to explain her feelings more competently.

Rewriting the scenario to reflect these changes would be a good exercise. But before you start rewriting, I want to tell you about another technique that would be helpful to John and Elaine Martin. They need a better way to express their COMPLAINTS. Let's begin by considering their perceptions of what they have to complain *about*, and then go on to the technique.

JOHN'S PERCEPTION:

John's complaint is that Elaine considers the time she spends working as a physician far more important than the time he spends working as an executive; he wants her to change that attitude. From his point of view, she has as large a supply of time in her inventory as he has in his. There are twenty-four hours in her day, just as there are twenty-four hours in his. And she is as free as he is to decide how she spends that inventory. Nobody is making her work at gunpoint. As he sees it, her only possible reason for insisting that *he* give up time at work to go to their child's play is because she views his work as so trivial that interruptions don't matter.

ELAINE'S PERCEPTION:

Elaine's complaint is that John believes she has power over her schedule when in fact she has none. He doesn't appear to understand the urgency and critical importance of work that involves human beings rather than products. She knows he is too intelligent and too decent to consider a dying patient and a dying product one and the same; she doesn't want to believe that he would be cruel for no reason. And so she falls back on a comforting platitude: that ordinary people cannot possibly understand the problems of doctors.

People *need* to complain, and not only in their personal lives. If you are in a dominant position in your work, you will often find yourself obliged to tell other people that you want something about them, or about their behavior, changed. If you're not in a dominant position you will find yourself obliged to pass on similar messages on behalf of your superiors — telling other people that the superior is not satisfied with them as they are and wants something changed.

There is an automatic negative reaction to complaints, based on the fact that they *are* complaints, independent of whether they are accurate or logical or justified. The result of this automatic resistance is that most complaints are not listened to. They are *heard* — but they are not listened to. What we need is a way to structure complaints that will provoke less of this kneejerk negativism. There is an effective one, based on the work of Thomas Gordon, called "The Three-part Message Technique." Let's take a look at it, with a view to incorporating it into the revision of Scenario Ten.

Using the Three-Part Message

Suppose you feel that your chief administrator — who likes to yell at staff members in public — is too domineering and unwilling to consider the feelings of others. Suppose you feel that someone has to tell him about this before he alienates valuable people and drives them away for good. Typical formulations of such a complaint include:

1. "Jim, you've got to stop being so domineering. You've got to start considering other people's feelings." (LEVELING.)

2. "Jim, I am SICK and TIRED of you acting like some kind of imperial potentate, with NO consideration at ALL for the feelings of OTHER people!" (BLAMING)

3. "People who insist on being domineering and who ignore the feelings of others are certain to regret it sooner or later." (COMPUTING)

4. "Jim, we all KNOW that you don't really MEAN to act like some kind of imperial potentate — shoot, WE know you consider other people's feelings! We realize that the way you act is just your MANner! But we can't help wondering . . . is there ANY way we could get you to just moderate your behavior a LITTLE BIT?" (PLACATING)

All of these complaints will provoke hostility in the person they are directed to; some are worse than others. All of them suffer from the same three critical flaws:

☐ They don't tell the administrator what element of his behavior should be changed.

☐ They don't tell him what effect that behavior has on the complainer.

☐ They don't tell him why the objection is being made.

In addition, they are vague, judgmental, and confrontational. And every one of them is an invitation to a fight.

Gordon's three-part messages are very different. They are constructed to fit this pattern:

WHEN YOU *X*,   I FEEL *Y*,   BECAUSE *Z*.
      1   2   3

Each of the variables, *X, Y, Z,* must be filled with something that is directly observable and verifiable in the real world. For example:

"When you yell at the secretaries, I feel angry, because they start crying, and they can't type while they cry."

Part One, "When you yell at the secretaries," is something the person has actually done, and will remember, and its reality is presupposed by the word "when." Never begin your complaint with the word "if" unless there is no possible way to avoid it, because "if" presupposes that something does not exist or has not happened. Use "when" instead; it's the most neutral of the words that could fill this slot.

Part Two, "I feel angry . . . " is directly observable and verifiable in the real world because of the speaker's body language.

Part Three, "because they start crying, and they can't type while they cry" is also concrete, directly observable, and verifiable in the real world. The secretaries can be seen crying, and their performance can be seen to be impaired by their crying.

This complaint message tells the administrator *exactly* what he does that is being objected to, exactly what reaction it produces in the complainer, and exactly what real world phenomenon the complainer considers to be justification for making the complaint. There is no moralizing, and there are no vague undefined terms to quarrel over. Certainly, yelling at the secretaries to such a degree that it reduces them to tears *is* "acting like some kind of imperial potentate" and should be stopped, but this is a much more efficient way to transmit that message.

It's important not to tinker with the pattern of the three-part message, because the possibilities for ruining it are so varied and so unlikely to occur to you in situations of stress and tension.

Be sure that the first part — "When you *X*. . ." — refers to something REAL. It must not be "When you act like . . . " or "When you treat people like . . . " or "When you do the awful things you do . . . " or "When I have to put up with your . . . " None of those are verifiable.

Be sure that the second part — "I feel *Y* . . . " — is filled in with an *emotion.* Don't use "I feel like a second-class citizen" or "I feel like quitting." Be sure it begins with "I feel" and not with "you make me feel like . . . " something or other. Even "You make me angry" is a mistake; for two reasons: (a) it is a *separate* complaint and should not be cluttering up the major one; and (b) it says, "You have the power to decide what emotion I will feel." This may be true, but it's bad strategy to admit it. The only time that sequence should appear in a three-part message is when it's the *first* part of a message that is genuinely necessary. For example:

"When you make me angry, I feel panicky, because I hit people I am angry with."

Be sure the third part — "because Z..." — like the first, refers to something concrete in the real world. It must not be "because nobody should have to put up with that" or "because it's unfair and unreasonable" or "because that's a terrible way to act" or "because if this goes on I won't be able to stand it."

These messages will be tricky to put together at first. When you have to make a complaint without any lead time you may have difficulty constructing one. You should therefore write them down — or say them into a tape recorder and listen to the result — whenever you *do* have time to plan ahead. You're more likely to get them right if you do that; it gives you an opportunity to practice the pattern at leisure, so that when you must use it off the cuff it will come to you more easily; and you will find out if the complaint is one you really want to make. Here's an important rule to remember:

IF YOU CAN'T FILL IN ALL THREE PARTS OF A THREE-PART COM-PLAINT MESSAGE, YOU'RE NOT READY TO COMPLAIN YET.

When you don't know what you want the other person to do, or how it makes you feel when they do it, or what effect their behavior has that justifies the request, it's not reasonable to expect *them* to know. When you know what it is you want them to stop doing or do differently, and you know what emotion you feel when they do it as they do it now, but you haven't the faintest idea what comes after the word "because" (the most typical problem), you aren't yet ready to make your complaint. For example:

"When you forget my birthday, I feel sad, because ...."

Because what? Not "because that means you don't care anything about me." Not "because it shows you have no manners." Those statements are not verifiable in the real world.

If what comes after "because" turns out to be something you'd be ashamed to say, far better to find that out *before* you say it. It's very common to discover, while working out the three parts of the message, that it isn't worth complaining about after all — and you may find yourself amazed that you could have been so upset about whatever it is. It's easy to feel resentful about something trivial, and to let that resentment fester, and then to lose track of what it was you were really angry about. Constructing a three-part message before you complain will refresh your memory and save you needless embarrassment.

WARNING. For any three-part message, no matter how carefully you word it, remember to say it in Leveler Mode, with neutral intonation. Try reading this sentence aloud, as marked:

> "When you YELL at the SECretaries, I feel ANGry, because they start CRYing and they can't TYPE while they're crying!"

Hear that abusive melody? It makes no difference *what* words you set to that tune; if you stress them that way, they become a verbal attack.

Three-part messages are also extremely useful when someone is angry or distressed and you don't know why. If the individual will cooperate with you, explain the three-part message pattern to him or her and ask that one be provided as clarification. If you can't get that sort of cooperation, try constructing the message yourself, and then saying to the person: "I've been trying to decide why you're so angry, and I think I've figured it out. Would you listen to this, please, and tell me if I have it right?" Followed by your candidate for their complaint. It's a rare person who can resist correcting your version if it's *not* right! If time allows (Time the Doer) or if you have enough time (Time the Object), it's best to ask the person to write down the message for you in privacy and mail it or hand it to you later. Be prepared to be amazed at what you read. The usual reaction is, "Is THAT ALL HE'S ANGRY ABOUT???"

The Three-Part Message as Negotiation Technique

There is an extended use of the three-part message pattern that I have been recommending for a number of years now — one that works magnificently well in situations where two groups are "at each other's throats" and ordinary negotiation hasn't helped. We'll refer to the groups as Group A and Group B; they could be doctors and nurses, employers and workers, teachers and students — they could even be "groups" of only one person, like a husband and wife, or a parent and a teenage child. Here are the steps you follow:

1. Each group meets alone to draw up a list of its complaints about the other group. The list is typed up, to keep it as anonymous as possible. And NOTHING is allowed on the list that can't be formulated as a three-part message.

2. The groups exchange their lists, and meet again separately. Group A looks at Group B's list of complaints, and vice versa. Each group works out what it is willing and/or able to do to meet the complaints of the other group.

3. Then — and only then — the two groups have a *joint* meeting, for negotiation. At this point everyone knows what the source of controversy is, how everyone else feels about it, what the consequences are, and what people propose to do to resolve it.

Highly recommended; this will save vast amounts of time and energy and emotion!

If you are involved in a situation where customer/client feedback is important to you, consider providing a stack of blank forms with skeletons of three-part messages on them, and one completed example, for people to turn in as "Suggestions" or "Satisfaction Surveys." If you receive a dozen sheets that say, "When you keep me waiting for two hours, I feel angry, because then I miss my bus," you won't try to increase satisfaction by redecorating the waiting room. If you are like many of us and have an old computer sitting on a shelf somewhere that no longer meets your needs, put *it* in your waiting room with a simple program that will prompt people to type in three-part messages, and use them as you would written responses.

Finally, you may also find it helpful to use this pattern to convey — or solicit — messages of *praise*. ("When you see me on time, I feel pleased, because I get away in time to catch my bus." "When you speak to the secretaries politely, I feel pleased, because they get their work done without being interrupted by crying.") Many people are suspicious of praise, anticipating that there will be a catch somewhere; three-part praise messages help to reduce this suspicion.

The three-part message is a fine application of Elgin's Corollary (to Miller's Law): "In order for other people to understand what you are saying, you must make it *possible* for them to apply Miller's Law to your language." That is, you must make it possible for them to assume that what you say is true, and to imagine what it could be true of. Using a typical complaint — "When you do the things you do, you drive me crazy, because nobody should have to put with that!" — sets up communication barriers that only a psychic could get past.

Perceptions of Time (and of Spacetime . . .)

We ordinarily think of time as separate from space. It's more convenient to do so. But it's important not to lose track of the fact that the two cannot actually be separated, just as verbal communication and nonverbal communication cannot actually be separated. Space and time interact to form a single element (spacetime) within which we LOCATE things and creatures and events. We reference locations in time with the word "when" and locations in space with the word "where" — and Sunday morning at ten o'clock is as surely a location as the corner of 72nd and Vine is. We divide space into units — inches and yards and miles — just as we divide time into hours and days and years. We grant status to people who control large amounts of *either* space or time. Our words "take up space" in time; our body language "takes up time" in space. Notice the way the two vocabularies of time and space have been merged into the single vocabulary of spacetime in this quotation:

> We have, as part of our European heritage, a deeply ingrained belief that space is something outside us that can be cut up into little cubes and that time is a one-way street, which we can mark with convenient intersections. . . . We divide the time of our life into intersections we call hours, and we have established neighborhoods of early morning, noon and afternoon within the city limits of our days, and we recognize (although it has not for many years been necessary) a distinction between night and day — sort of county lines we have set up in time.

Don Fabun, *The Dynamics Of Change*, 1967.

For all their interrelatedness, however, our perceptions of time and space, and our processing and expression of those perceptions, differ in significant ways.

1. WE PERCEIVE SPACE AS RELATIVELY STABLE, AND AS IMPERVIOUS TO THE EFFECT OF WORDS; WHAT LITTLE WE ARE ABLE TO DO TO CHANGE OUR PERCEPTION OF OUR "SUPPLY" OF SPACE THROUGH LANGUAGE IS DONE WITH *NONVERBAL* COMMUNICATION ALONE.

2. WE PERCEIVE TIME AS RELATIVELY ELASTIC, AND WE ARE ABLE TO DEAL WITH OUR PERCEPTIONS OF TIME DIRECTLY THROUGH WORDS *PLUS* NONVERBAL COMMUNICATION.

3. WHENEVER WE FEEL THAT WE DO NOT HAVE ENOUGH OF EITHER TIME *OR* SPACE — AND WHENEVER WE ARE UNCOMFORTABLE FOR THAT REASON OR FOR ANY REASON WHATSOEVER — WE PERCEIVE TIME AS EXPANDING.

To make space seem larger (or smaller), then, we have to turn to architects and interior designers; we have to spend money, often very large amounts of money, on the surfaces of the space around us and the objects we use to fill that space. When we deal with *time*, however, we need no outside experts and no cash — all we need is our competence as native speakers of our language.

Using Language to Control Time

One of the most constant complaints people make about professionals and executives is that they charge a great deal of money for very small amounts of their time. But the perception that you are hurrying through your interactions with them can be significantly altered by the way you make use of language while you are together.

First, your body language. The two most important things you can do to make time spent with you seem longer to people are: (a) to sit down while you are interacting with them and (b) to avoid any movement that makes you seem to be checking on how much time has passed. (You could of course make the time stretch drastically by making people absolutely miserable in some way; I don't recommend that as an alternative.) Sit down, in as relaxed a fashion as is natural for you. Don't look at your watch or at a clock on the wall. If it's critical for you to be aware of the passage of time, put a clock somewhere unobtrusive where you can see what it says without having to glance away from the person you're talking with or ask a staff person to call you.

Nothing will shorten the perceived time for your client (or patient, or student, or subordinate) more drastically than watching you stand at a door with your hand on it, poised to flee. If you have only two minutes to spare, that posture will make those two minutes seem like only one to the person you're speaking with, and you will have canceled out 50 percent of those precious minutes. Sitting on the edge of your chair, standing behind your desk — *any* "poised to flee" arrangement — will have the same effect.

Warning. Be aware that sitting down and assuming a relaxed posture will also make the time seem longer to *you*; don't be misled. Many professionals are convinced that if people are not constantly reminded about time constraints they will abuse the privilege and talk endlessly — this is a myth. I strongly suggest that for a few days you make a note of the exact time when an interaction begins and ends, so that you can determine whether your perceptions are accurate. The most common pattern is for professionals to estimate that everyone involved has used at least twice as much time as the clock will verify.

Next, the words you use with your body language. There are things you can say — and refrain from saying — that will convince people you have given them more time than has really transpired.

Eliminate the word "only," with all its negative presuppositions, from your time vocabulary. Don't say, "I only have ten minutes," or "I can only talk for a few seconds," or "We only have half an hour." State how much time you have, but drop the "only." Announce that you have ten minutes as if you were delighted about it — your tone of voice should carry the metamessage "I've got ten whole minutes to spend with you! One-sixth of an hour! What terrific luck!"

There is a device much used by dentists that can usefully be adapted for other professions. Dentists will tell patients, "Now this will hurt, and it will take a few minutes. BUT IF YOU TELL ME TO STOP, I WILL." The patients, who now believe that *they* are in control of the time spent on the procedure, will put off asking the dentist to stop, thinking "I can handle this just a little longer." And much of the time, when they do say "Stop!", the procedure is already over. What is important is the illusion of power and control over the time involved.

Adapt this by saying that you have ten minutes (not "only" ten minutes), "but if you need more time than that, just say so, and I will stay." Do the same thing when you are talking on the telephone. Once a month someone will take you up on it — and you must honor your commitment or you will not be believed thereafter. But over the long term, not only will it be easier for you to stick to the schedule you've chosen for yourself, but the people who interact with you will come away with the *perception* that you always offer them an ample amount of your time. All of it that they want, as a matter of fact! THAT PERCEPTION IS MONEY IN THE BANK.

The alternative is a perpetual undercurrent of resentment, which will make *both* sides of the interaction tense and cross, with an everspreading ripple effect on everyone around you. The alternative is an ongoing perception that you — like Elaine Martin — feel that your time is more valuable than the time of others. Whether that's true or not is irrelevant — the resentment it creates is real, and so easily avoided that allowing it to arise is absurd.

Using Personal Space to Control Time

Another factor that can change perceptions of time, and that involves both verbal and nonverbal communication, is your use of what is called *personal distance*. That is, the amount of space you put between yourself and other people when you are talking with them. Medical and dental professionals often must be extraordinarily close to patients during actual procedures and cannot alter that distance, no matter how uncomfortable it makes them *or* the patients. This is an exception that adults are aware of and will accept. In all other cases you would be wise to use the principle of the feedback loop as a way to match your personal space requirements to those of the person you're talking with.

Suppose you are an American native speaker of English and you meet your Hispanic client briefly in an airport corridor. As you talk, your client will seem to you to be too close, and you will back up a bit. To your client, it will now seem that you are too far away, and he will move toward you to correct the mismatch. Which will cause you to back up . . . which will cause him to move toward you again. And shortly you will be standing with your back to a wall at the corridor's end, with your client, who now feels that you are at "talking distance," contented at last — and you very ill at ease because he is "too close for comfort." TIME YOU SPEND FEELING THAT YOUR CLIENT IS TOO CLOSE — AND TIME THE CLIENT SPENDS FEELING THAT YOU ARE NOT CLOSE ENOUGH — WILL EXPAND SUBSTANTIALLY.

It's not hard to learn to communicate at distances that are smaller or larger than those you prefer, once you are aware that it matters. The cliché situation just described usually happens because the people taking part in it are *not* aware that space is the problem. They only know that something is wrong, and they are trying to fix it. Once you understand the concept of personal space preference, you are not likely to make this mistake, and a little practice talking at various distances from a willing partner will put you in control of a variety of personal distance "dialects."

The information about Anglo/Hispanic preferences for personal space is well known. But you may need to interact with people of many different cultures and subcultures, for whom you don't have the facts in advance. That's all right — just pay attention to the body language of the other speaker, and proceed as follows:

1. Choose a location from which to talk, and begin.
2. If your partner moves toward you — or backs away from you — stand your ground until he stops.
3. Once the other person has chosen a location and is talking comfortably, you know that's his preferred personal distance; respect it.

Don't waste your time memorizing preferred personal distances for Japanese speakers, Laotian speakers, Italian speakers, and so on. Make your adjustments to the individual on the spot. This has the advantage of helping you avoid mistakes with persons whose space requirements differ from those expected for their culture. Make a note of what you learn, so that you can look it up when you are considering such things as seating arrangements for a conference or social event, and then don't clutter your memory with it.

If your goal is to make another person *un*comfortable, violating their personal distance by talking to them from either too close or too far away will accomplish that. Such violations will cause people to perceive the time spent in your company as drastically extended — the more uncomfortable they are, the longer the time with you will seem to be. There are times when that is *exactly* what you want. But be sure you are doing it deliberately, as part of a consistent strategy. Never let it happen by accident because you are unaware of what is taking place.

Talking Time and Writing Time Down

When you are choosing from the set of prepositions of location in space — "under, over, between, through, beside," and the like — your task is straightforward. Except for a few stylistic choices, like the choice between "under" and "beneath," there's little you can vary for strategic reasons. But the prepositions that translate perceptions of *time* into words are a very different matter. Because they carry with them presuppositions that can be extremely useful to you. Compare the following sentences:

1. "Until you get that contract, you won't be eligible for a promotion."
2. "After you get that contract, you will be eligible for a promotion."
3. "When you get that contract, you will be eligible for a promotion."

Notice the presuppositional differences. The sentences beginning with "when" and "after" presuppose that you *will* get the promotion. The sentence beginning with "until" does not — it reinforces the message "You won't be eligible for a promotion." Not until you get that contract, you won't. A very negative message! If you want to encourage someone and express your confidence, you will rule out the word "until." And your choice between "when" and "after" will be based on your knowledge that "after" expresses that confidence more strongly than the neutral "when." All *three* choices are better than using no time word at all and saying "If you get that contract, you will be eligible for a promotion" or the multiple-negative "If you don't get that contract, you won't be eligible for a promotion."

Adults in our society resent complaints and react to them with automatic resistance. They respond even *more* negatively to direct commands. A careful choice of time words will let you transmit the command message "You will do *X*" without structuring it *as* a command. Suppose that you want Charlie to take the Andersons out to the Country Club this weekend. You could just tell him to take them, but that will put Charlie's back up, and when Charlie is annoyed he doesn't do his best work. Don't do it that way. Instead, say things like these:

☐ "While you're at the Country Club with the Andersons next Saturday, I'll be here in the office waiting for your call."

☐ "When you're at the Country Club with the Andersons next Saturday, you'll notice that the club has redecorated the whole dining area."

◻ "During your lunch at the Country Club with the Andersons next Saturday, they're sure to tell you what they think of the new golf course. I'd be interested in knowing."

The time words "while, when, during" allow you to *presuppose* "You will go to the Country Club next Saturday with the Andersons," but they do it with much less loss of face for Charlie than the naked command does.

You can combine this strategy with what Gregory Bateson called "the illusion of choice," and make Charlie even more likely to cooperate willingly. Like this:

"After your lunch at the Country Club with the Andersons next Saturday, would you rather bring them back here to the office or just take them on home?"

This works for the same reason that the "I'll stop when you tell me to" statement works for dentists. Many studies have proved that people react with far less stress to unpleasant stimuli — like loud noises and electric shocks — if they feel that they can turn those stimuli off whenever they want to. Even if they never push the CANCEL button, they show milder reactions than people facing exactly the same phenomena without a cancel option. What matters to them is the PERCEPTION that they have some control over what happens — a perception of power. You may have little or no control over "what the clock says," but a careful use of language will give you substantial control over *perceptions* of time.

When you hand Charlie a choice between two elements that don't matter to you, as in the "would you rather *X* or *Y*" patterns, you also hand him a perception that he retains some of the power and can control the situation at least in part. It may or may not keep him from noticing that you're taking it for granted that he will go to the Country Club with the Andersons. But either way, it will reduce his automatic kneejerk resistance to your having told him to do so.

There is almost *never* any reason to give a direct command to an adult unless the situation is one of life or death and you must shout "Duck!" or "Run for your life!" Direct commands, like lies, are almost always the evidence of linguistic incompetence.

For variety, you can leave out the time words and begin with space words that have the same effect, like this:

◻ "In Dallas, you'll notice that they sell sourdough bread at the airport."

◻ "At the Country Club, you might very well see some of the new people from Clak-Tak."

Every sentence, without exception, presupposes some element that fills the roles of TIME and SPACE — everything, without exception, happens "at some time" and "at some place." If you make only one of the two specific, the other is still presupposed in its less definite form. For every native speaker of English, that "In Dallas" sentence means "AT THE TIME WHEN you are in Dallas, you'll notice that they sell sourdough bread at the airport."

You already know all these things — of course you do. They are part of your internal grammar of your language. But unless you are accustomed to using them strategically, your communication will not accomplish as much as it could accomplish. There's a strong tendency to rely on slapdash "Oh, it doesn't make any difference — they all mean the same thing!" judgments. That's a failure to take advantage of the power of language at your disposal. Very rarely do they mean the same thing, and much of the time it makes a *lot* of difference. When a writer tells you that cancer kills "one American per minute" today, instead of "525,600 people a year," the number of people killed is the same, but the effect is not. We don't easily grasp the concept of half a million people, but we are stunned by the clarity of "one person per minute." That, we understand. And when we do not bother to choose our words for expressing time so that they give us that kind of maximum impact, we are wasting one of our most valuable sources of power.

"I Don't Have Enough Time" — The Time Monster Myth

Once in a great while you meet someone for whom this is *literally* true. Someone who loves what he does so much that he wishes he had ten more hours in each day to spend doing it. Someone who would skip sleep altogether if she could figure out a way to do that, because there are *really* not enough hours to spend in the activity she values above all others. People like this tend to sleep on a battered couch at the office or studio or store, to have no car, to own only one suit (which fits badly), and to die with a drawer full of uncashed checks. These people are rare, and unless they are also perceived as geniuses (Einstein was like this, for example) they are looked upon with alarm and distaste. For most people, "I don't have enough time" actually means "I don't have enough THINGS."

American adults have astonishingly little forced upon them. No law requires them to own or rent a place to live, or a car, or furniture, or appliances, or what is called "decent" clothing or food or medical care. If you try to wear *no* clothing, or to eat *nothing*, or to lie at a busy intersection and quietly bleed to death unattended, someone will interfere and force things upon you — but you have to go to that extreme. Check with the homeless, if you doubt me.

Yes, there are a multitude of pressures on you to be a conforming American. But let's Level here: Except at the most extreme minimum of possible possessions, you freely CHOOSE whether to have things or not. The way you get the things you do choose to have is by exchanging money for them; the way you get that money, for the vast majority of the population, is by working for it. (For purposes of this discussion, we will consider crime to be work — not *honest* work, but not leisure.)

I'm not setting all this down in such detail because it's an opportunity for me to philosophize. I'm doing my best to make a point that is directly related to your physical and mental health and to your ability to succeed and achieve your goals. Here it is: because all of what I said in the previous paragraph is true, it is also true that YOU CONTROL YOUR TIME.

It's critical for you to realize that. Because the wear and tear on your mind and body caused by the false perception that you "never have enough time" does you serious damage. This idea takes the form of language that you say to *yourself* over and over again, as well as language that you say to other people around you, creating your own personal language toxin that you take with you everywhere you go. That's dangerous. Because people who feel that they are always far behind, always desperately trying to catch up, are in deep trouble — that perception taints everything they say and do, and it leaks into the lives of everyone they interact with. It constitutes a permanent perception of themselves as VICTIMS, trapped and powerless.

Obviously, this is a bad situation. Let's use the technique of reformulating it in other language terms, with other labels and other reality statements, so that we can see it more clearly.

When I was a young woman I was poor, and I had a household to provide for. Like any young person, I saw things I was tempted to buy. But in those days baked beans cost ten cents a can — and many of the meals I put on our table consisted *only* of baked beans. I therefore converted prices to Baked Bean Units. I might have given in and bought something that cost only five dollars; I *never* succumbed to that temptation when the price was fifty cans of baked beans. In the same way, you can step outside the standard system of assigning value by reformulating prices as units of *time*.

Suppose you earn twenty-five dollars an hour, and you're considering the purchase of a two hundred dollar suit. To decide whether you want it badly enough to buy it, stop saying, "That suit costs two hundred dollars." Instead, say, "That suit costs eight hours." Eight hours of your time. Now, do you choose to exchange those eight hours for the suit or not? IT IS YOUR CHOICE.

You are *not* a helpless victim at the mercy of a machine grinding away somewhere, doling out time to you from some mysterious and cruel National Ministry Of Time that you cannot escape. It's not like that at *all*. If you — like Elaine Martin in Scenario Ten — work a seventy-hour week, you do it for one of two reasons:

1. You love your work more than anything else you could use your time for.
2. You have decided, of your own free will, that you would rather have seventy hours a week worth of *things* than a week of time to use as you wish.

Remember the research indicating that people suffer far less from unpleasant stimuli if they believe they have control over it and can stop it whenever they like? The same principle holds for your dealings with time. Knowing that you are in charge — that you have power over your time — dramatically reduces your level of stress and strain and anxiety. No law forbids Elaine Martin, in Scenario Ten, to practice medicine forty hours a week instead of seventy; she makes that choice, and her time *is* her own. Her life, and John Martin's life, would be vastly improved if they were both consciously aware of that fact.

You may find it hard to remember that no merciless Time Monster exists for American adults. You may find it *inconvenient* to remember, if you're accustomed to using "I don't have enough time" as an excuse. You may find it socially awkward to translate that to "I don't choose to spend my time doing what you asked me to do." If so, for the sake of your mental and physical health, make a set of small signs and put them up in places where you'll see them at least once daily. They should say something like this: "I don't have to do this. I am free to walk away from this whenever I like and go do something else. I am doing this because I CHOOSE to." With the "do this" phrases filled by whatever applies to you. "I don't have to go to the hospital/office/restaurant/bank." You need those words staring you in the face, until your perceptions have shifted sufficiently so that you'll never forget them again.

The point is not to reduce the hours you spend in work. Most of us *do* want the house and the car and the clothes and all the rest, for ourselves and for our families. The point is to return to you the power, the confidence, and the serenity that comes from knowing *you* are the one in charge.

Helping Time's Victims: "What Would Happen If ... ?"

When you find yourself involved with persons whose view of time is that they are its helpless victims — like Elaine Martin — problems are inevitable. That perception will be accompanied by great tension and stress, and people under severe stress cannot function at their maximum level of efficiency or effectiveness. Such people betray their dilemma by their frequent use of statements like those listed below, accompanied by body language that indicates distress:

☐ "I never have enough time!"

☐ "It's *impossible* for me to do everything I have to do!"

☐ "I don't know where the time *goes*."

☐ "If only I had more time!"

☐ "I'll never get through, I know I won't — there just isn't enough *time*!"

☐ "Somehow I've got to find more *time*!"

☐ "*Nobody* could do all the things I have to do today!"

If you are in a long-term relationship, either professional or personal, with one of these people, you may want to explore the situation to determine whether it can be changed.

Begin by finding out how tightly the individual is locked into this perception. The simplest way to do that is by the traditional "What Would Happen If . . . " technique, as in the following dialogue between a lawyer and a doctor.

LAWYER: "You say you cannot possibly work fewer hours than you do now. What would happen if you cut those hours back?"

DOCTOR: "My patients would die."

LAWYER: "Only if you were on a desert island. Your patients might not be pleased about it, friend, but if you weren't there to see to them some other doctor would be. Or a nurse would be. Or failing that, a bystander would *get* a doctor or a nurse for them."

DOCTOR: "Maybe. But my practice would be ruined."

LAWYER: "What would happen if your practice was ruined?"

DOCTOR: "My income would be ruined, too! What a stupid question!"

LAWYER: "And if you had less money, what would happen?"

DOCTOR: "I wouldn't be able to pay for my mortgage, or my car, or my kid's tuition."

LAWYER: "WHICH MEANS THAT YOU ARE IN FULL CONTROL OF YOUR TIME."

DOCTOR: "Explain that."

LAWYER: "It means that you have decided, of your own free will, that you prefer your house and your car and your kid's tuition to having more non-work hours. That's *your* decision, under *your* control, and you could change it tomorrow if you chose to do so."

When this works, the result is a grateful, "I never thought about it that way, but you're *right!*" When it doesn't work, it leads to infinite regress. In the dialogue above, the doctor would insist that he *had* to have the house and the car, and that his child *had* to go to college. And the lawyer would have to explore each of these, with "What would happen if you lived in a smaller house?" "What would happen if you drove a secondhand car?" "What would happen if your kid didn't go to college?"

It's worth exploring a few more of these levels of alleged helplessness. But once it becomes clear that every "what would happen if" has another one behind it, *ad infinitum*, you are wasting *your* time and tormenting your associate to no purpose. Let it go.

At this point, the most useful thing you can do for the other person is to provide one of the many books (or tapes, or videos) on organizing and managing time, and encourage him or her to try some of the ideas suggested. If even one idea is helpful — proving that it *is possible* to be less at the mercy of time — there are two potential benefits. One is that it may alter your associate's perception enough to serve as an opening wedge toward greater change. The other is that the feeling of having *some* control over time, however limited, may decrease the level of tension and stress, making it less destructive and less dangerous.

If *you* are the person victimized by time, you can do this exploration by yourself. Just write down the questions, as someone else would pose them to you, and then write down your answers. — Until you have either come to the end of the "what if's" and realized that in fact you do control your time, or until you can see that it's useless to go farther. In which case you buy yourself the time management book or tape or video, and put it to use.

The Man/Woman Problem

In *The Dance of Life*, Edward Hall divides perceptions of time into what he calls "monochronic time" and "polychronic time." In monochronic systems — like the American one — only one thing is done at a time, and it's finished before some other thing is started. He explains that in polychronic systems, on the other hand — as in much of the Arab world — people do many things at once. And then Hall stops to clarify matters, saying that yes, it's true that American time is monochronic. But not *all* American time! For American men, he says, it's true. But American women function on *polychronic* time.

Hall is correct. A very large percentage of American women must cook the dinner while they watch the children while they help with the homework while they fold the laundry while they answer the phone while they listen for the baby to cry while they study for an exam. The luxury of doing each task separately, of finishing one before beginning another, is not part of their lives.

This goes a considerable distance toward explaining why women who step into formerly male roles are so often perceived as "disorganized" or "having no sense of time." It explains why women have trouble with the traditional corporate long-range planning process. And perhaps most important of all, it explains why so many women don't seem to have any firm concept of *how long* it will take them to do things, or how long it will take others. THEY ARE NOT ACCUSTOMED TO EVER KNOWING HOW LONG ANYTHING WILL TAKE, BECAUSE IT ALWAYS DEPENDS ON HOW MANY TIMES THEY ARE INTERRUPTED.

Conversely, it may also explain why so many *male* professionals are made irritable and tense by scheduling systems that require them to run back and forth between various consulting or examining rooms instead of completing each transaction before beginning another one; for males, accustomed to monochronic time, this is bound to be maddening. Women should be far better at it.

ABOUT CRYING, WHILE WE'RE HERE

Vast quantities of material have been written about the fact that it's all right for women to cry, but not all right for men to, and offering reasons both genetic and environmental for that concept. Most of this stuff is claptrap. But the problem of crying is a serious one for women, nevertheless.

Consider the reaction to Congresswoman Patricia Schroeder's tears when she announced that she would not be running for President in 1988. Here's a representative sampling.

"I got back to New York just in time for Pat Schroeder's three-Kleenex declaration she wouldn't be going to run."

— James Brady, in *Advertising Age* for October 12, 1987 . . . .

"Schroeder's tears got her more media attention than anything else she said or did during her campaign. While many women were sympathetic, others were embarrassed by her crying, feeling that it gave credence to men's worst fears about women . . . "

— Mindy Schanback, in *Executive Female* for May/June 1988 . . .

"Yet even Mrs. Schroeder's friends said they wished that she hadn't cried — at least as much as she did. Perhaps a tear or two — but not the weeping."

— Bernard Weinraub, in the *New York Times* for September 30, 1987 . . .

NOBODY said of this incident, "Oh, it was all right for her to cry, because she's a *wo*man!"

In the piece quoted (which was entitled "Presidential Politics: Are Female Tears Saltier Than Male Tears?") Weinraub noted that "former Senator Gary Hart grew tearful on a campaign stop when he visited his birthplace in Kansas to talk about his roots, Gov. Michael S. Dukakis of Massachusetts brushed tears from his eyes at the dedication of a park in honor of President Kennedy . . . and President Reagan has choked up on numerous occasions, including the funeral service for the crew of the space shuttle Challenger. It seems perfectly appropriate, at least nowadays, for men to be tearful." And then he asks, "But what about Patricia Schroeder?" The clue is in his own phrase "perhaps a tear or two."

Let's get this straight once and for all: whether it's okay to cry has nothing to do with whether you are male or female. The problem with crying is that you can't talk while you cry, nor can you carry out the other aspects of language interaction that are included in "talking," such as listening and observing body language. WHEN YOU CRY — MORE THAN A TEAR OR TWO — YOU CAN'T TALK; WHEN YOU CAN'T TALK, YOU CAN'T NEGOTIATE; WHEN YOU CAN'T NEGOTIATE, YOU'RE VULNERABLE. Crying in public strips you of all power in American society today in almost precisely the same way that being naked in public would — the only difference is that public crying is not forbidden by *law.*

The reason little boys have been trained to cry only when it was appropriate and expeditious, while little girls have been allowed to grow up without learning to bring their crying behavior under their conscious control, is that until very recently only American males did any negotiating in public.

Knowing that Congresswoman Schroeder couldn't keep from crying on such a public and important occasion struck fear into the hearts of the voters, who translated their uneasiness into the murky sentence, "She didn't seem very Presidential." *Not* because she was a woman, and not because crying per se is considered unacceptable, but because she would have been vulnerable at the negotiating table.

NOTES

1. The sentence is also strange because this woman MD uses the masculine possessive term, "his." Try saying "A doctor's time is not her own," and see how odd it feels in your mouth — you'll understand why she said it as she did. This will tell you something about the validity of the common claim that masculine pronouns are "generic" and "don't really mean" [+ MALE].

Workout — Chapter 7

1. The three-part messages in this chapter were all done in Leveler Mode. There are times, however, when a power gap or some other circumstance might make it difficult to come right out and say "When you X, I feel Y, because Z." In such situations, you have the alternative of translating the message into Computer Mode. Like this:

   ORIGINAL MESSAGE: "When you throw your lunch on the floor, I feel angry, because I have to stop and clean it up."

   TRANSLATION INTO COMPUTER MODE: "When a lunch is thrown on the floor, there will be anger, because someone has to stop and clean it up."

   Write some similar translations, for complaints in this chapter and complaints of your own.

2. Choose a few tasks you (or others) routinely carry out, and reformulate them in various time units to see what effect that has. Is there any difference, for example, between these two complaints?

   a. "When it takes you an hour and a half to sort those files, I feel angry, because I can't start my work until that's done."

   b. "When it takes you ninety minutes to sort those files, I feel angry, because I can't start my work until that's done."

   Which *takes* longer — an hour and a half, or ninety minutes? Is it worse to have to wait three hours or one hundred and eighty minutes?

   Which makes you feel more rushed — a lifetime expressed as "seventy years" or a lifetime expressed as "twenty-five thousand five hundred and fifty days"? My own perception is that a lifetime expressed in days needs "only" in front of the number; do you agree?

3. From your own experience, select five complaints that you make over and over again. "Your payment is late." "You got a D-minus in math." "Your renewal didn't come in until after the issue was already mailed." "I've been sitting here waiting for more than two hours." Write them down (or tape-record them) and then reword them as three-part messages. The next time you need to make those complaints, use the three-part message format. Pay close attention to the reaction you get, and to the results of making the complaint.

4. Suppose your employee, Jack Jones, considers himself a competent worker who does things quickly and efficiently; suppose he ordinarily assembles seven widgets an hour. What happens to his self-image — and his definition of "quickly" — if you announce in a meeting that "the ten-widget-per-hour

man is invaluable to this company"? According to Thomas J. Bruneau, many people "measure their own self-worth and self-esteem in terms of their abilities to beat clocks, . . . go faster than a pacing device, or regiment themselves with clock time." How can you make use of this information?

5. We're accustomed to sentences like "She assembles seven widgets an hour" or "He types eighty words a minute." We evaluate people by asking them "How fast can you [DO SOMETHING]?" We don't ask them "How fast can you [KNOW SOMETHING]?" However, studies show that many people who fail timed tests would pass if they were allowed to work for a longer period of time. Aren't we defining "failure" as "not being able to know this set of facts fast enough"?

Suppose I have the power to pass legislation dividing all doctors and lawyers into two groups: those who can pass their certifying exams in three hours and those who need six. Does knowing which group an individual falls into tell me anything about his or her competence and skill as a doctor or lawyer? Would you vote for a ballot initiative like that? Or for one that doubled the usual examination time but told you nothing about how long an individual needed to complete the exam? Or for one that gave diplomas showing *exactly* how many minutes that professional needed to complete the exam?

SIGHT BITES

1. "To require everyone to hurry and scurry through their waking day not only produces fatigue, but also such demand reduces the possibility of inquiry, reduces the possibility of personal interaction necessary for the development of trustful relationships, and reduces the possibility of the formation of groups whose purposes may be contrary to organizational purposes. . . . Wittingly or unwittingly, the control of objective tempo can be a powerful persuasion tool. A proposition may be in order: Those who control or potentially control objective tempo also control space and motion through space. People who control clocks control people.

   "Chronemics can be . . . defined as the study of human tempo as it related to human communication."

   (Thomas J. Bruneau, "Chronemics and the Verbal Nonverbal Interface," in Mary Ritchie Key, editor, *The Relationship of Verbal and Nonverbal Communication*, Mouton 1980; pages 113 and 114. Objective tempo is time regulated by a device, as opposed to subjective tempo, which is *perceived* time.)

2. "It is often said that the difference between American and Japanese business attitudes is that Americans plan for the next quarter while the Japanese plan for eternity."

   (From "The Money Culture: Japanese Takeout," by Michael M. Lewis, in *The New Republic* for October 3, 1988; page 19.)

3. "In one study, patients were found to have three problems on their mind, on average, when they entered the room to consult a physician, but their accounts were cut off by the physician within the first 18 seconds of the interview. Most of the patients never got beyond the first problem."

   (From "Physicians May Bungle Key Part of Treatment: The Medical Interview," by Daniel Goleman, in the *New York Times* for January 21, 1988.)

   "As many as one third of all patients who switch physicians do so because their doctors cannot communicate effectively with them."

   (From "Communication is Key to Keeping Patients Pleased," by Michael J. McGowan, in *Private Practice* for April 1987; page 15.

4. "In one study, tickets to a lottery were sold for a dollar. . . . Participants in one group were simply handed their tickets; in another group, the participants were allowed to choose their own. Just before the drawing, ticket holders were asked if they were willing to resell their tickets. The average resale price asked by those who had been handed tickets was $1.96. Those who had chosen their own tickets asked an average of $8.67. Being in control of the selection process apparently made people think they had a better chance of winning."

   (From "Staying Alive in the 20th Century," by William F. Allman, in *Science 85* for October 1985; page 33.)

5. "The manager's pinstripes convey a message: 'As a well-heeled member of the establishment, I am in control of myself — and of you.' The scientist's jeans, sneakers, and open collar say in effect: 'Knowledge is power, appearance nothing; you need me more than I need you.' "

   (From "Science of Business: Different Breeds," by John Pfeiffer, in *Science 86* for January /February 1986; page 22.)

6. "To learn how Union Carbiders are doing in their status-free building. . . . Cynthia Froggatt, now associated with a New York architectural and design firm, studied employees' reactions.

   . . . Her most significant finding: the big-man-big-space tradition, dating back to the pharaohs and beyond, could be scrapped without arousing massive resistance. In fact, the response is solidly positive.

   "Japan represents an entirely different attitude toward work and work space. . . . Privileged executives regard the offices they occupy as the company's, not their own, and certainly not as symbols of personal prestige."

   (From "Science of Business: Democracy by Design," by John Pfeiffer, in *Science 86* for March 1986; page 19.)

7. "Most medical educators do not consider teaching students how to talk with patients an essential aspect of training for professional responsibility."

   (From a review of Eric J. Cassell, *Talking with Patients*, titled "Reviews:

The Doctor-Patient Conversation," by Jay Katz; in *Hastings Center Report* for June 1986; page 41.)

8. Asked to explain how anyone could possibly get as much done as he does, Martin E. Marty answered that you must "make a distinction between being 'busy,' 'occupied' and 'scheduled.'" He says that "busy" is a horrible word and that "occupied" is even worse. "I try to substitute the concept of 'scheduled' for 'busy' or 'occupied.' If something takes up a space in the calendar book, something else cannot be in the same place."

(From "Advice From a Scheduled Man," by Martin E. Marty, in *The Christian Century* for December 7, 1988; page 1135.)

8

Language and the Public Relations Domain

Introduction

As an executive or professional you are sure to spend some of your time on public display, functioning as a celebrity. Celebrity status varies in *scale*, from serving as a role model for two or three people in your immediate circle to becoming a household word — but in strategic terms, it's all the same thing. How well you carry out this role will be reflected directly and dramatically in your financial statements. It is a skill critical to your success. For executives and professionals — whose public image does not depend on how fast they can run, how high they can jump, or how talented they are in the arts — it is by and large language-dependent. Remembering that the public in question may be composed of only a few people, *this* is PUBLIC RELATIONS.

The Universal Fifteen Minutes Of Fame predicted by Andy Warhol comes along on the basis of trivial and temporary factors — what you happen to be wearing or driving, who you happen to be talking to, and the like. Such fame involves not public relations but blind luck, and its benefits are as fleeting as the fame itself. It's not worth trying to achieve or avoid, and it's not worth worrying about.

Celebrity status that *lasts,* and that has genuine value for you and for your group, has little to do with luck. It requires *effort,* both to establish and to maintain. It is a matter of causing other people to perceive you as someone they would like to be like, or — if that can't be managed — as someone they admire more than they do the average person. (I will not be discussing either the [+ NEGATIVE] celebrity role called "notoriety," in which people remember who you are because you are so much *worse* than the average person, or the role of *full-time* celebrity, which cannot be maintained while functioning successfully in any other activity.)

Being a celebrity means being a person whose spoken or written words are considered so important that people are willing to exchange items of value such as money or time for them. And because public reaction *to* you is based on public perception *of* you, scrupulous attention to public relations is required if you are to achieve that status.

This chapter is about the positive side of celebrity, on any scale, and about the construction and maintenance of your *image*. Images — which are composed of perceptions — are based on feedback loops established and maintained by your language behavior, with three predictable steps involved.

- ☐ STEP ONE: Because you are *perceived* as an unpleasant person, people will treat you as one.

- ☐ STEP TWO: Your sense that you're being treated as an unpleasant person will cause you to *act* like one.

- ☐ STEP THREE: Your behavior will then confirm the perception people had of you in the first place, which brings us around once more to STEP ONE.

This cycle, which is both self-fulfilling and self-perpetuating, is shown in Figure Ten. Your goal is to produce not a negative cycle like the one shown, but its positive equivalent.

There are five celebrity slots that you can reasonably expect to be called upon to fill at one time or another, that you can fill without becoming a full-time celebrity, and that you can deliberately seek out if you desire. They are:

- ☐ YOU AS PROMINENT LOCAL CITIZEN: When you are asked to give brief talks for your local schools or civic organizations; when you are expected to write brief items for your local newspaper or regional publication.

- ☐ YOU AS AVAILABLE EXPERT ON SUBJECT X: When it is a matter of public knowledge that anyone who wants a brief presentation — spoken or written — about Subject *X* can call on you with confidence.

- ☐ YOU AS REPRESENTATIVE OF A FIRM OR GROUP: When you are asked to speak or write not as a private person or member of your community but as a representative of a particular firm or other group.

- ☐ YOU AS MEDIA FOCUS: When you are asked to appear on radio or television; when a publication requests an interview from you.

- ☐ YOU AS DRAGONSLAYER: When you are chosen as spokesperson in the middle of a real mess — an industrial accident, a tampering scare, a scandal of some kind — that must be explained to the public or some select portion of the public; when you become the spokesperson, perhaps reluctantly, in an emergency.

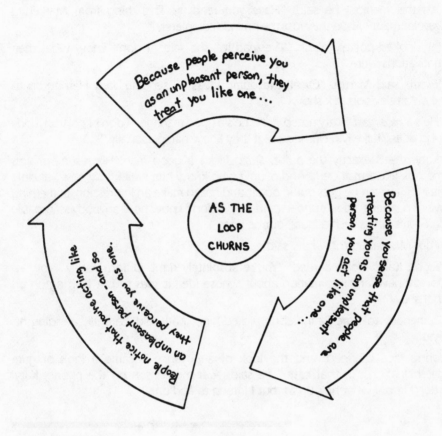

FIGURE 10.

These five categories will overlap. You may have to do your Dragonslaying on television. You may give your talk to the local Kiwanis club on behalf of your corporation. The skills and information required will overlap extensively as well, since no matter who you are talking to or writing for your performance goals will be much the same. It's therefore most efficient to first discuss those things that all five have in common and then close the chapter with the leftover bits. We'll begin with a scenario.

SCENARIO ELEVEN   John Martin smacked the top of the desk with his fist and said a rude word, making Katy jump.

"What's wrong, Mr. Martin?" she asked. "Can I help you with something?"

"It's this memo," he said. "Have you read it? This thing from Marketing Development? Have they lost their minds completely?"

Katy looked politely blank. "I've read it," she said. "I don't know what their motivations were."

"*Blast!*" said Martin. "Of all the dumb ideas — sending Jack Harrington to be on a television talk show!"

"He's a *nice man*," Katy noted. "and he's a good manager. I don't know anybody who doesn't like Mr. Harrington, if they know him personally."

"Katy, that's exactly the point. *Sure*, Jack's a good man! His résumé makes *me* look like a mail clerk. And people who know him well know how valuable he is. But when he gets out in public and has to make an impression, something weird happens. I don't understand it . . . I don't know how anybody so capable can come off as such a klutz, but he does."

"Poor Mr. Harrington," Katy said.

"Right, Katy!" John agreed. "You're absolutely right. Unfortunately. Now — do you have any information about whose idea it *was* to put Harrington on that show?"

"Somebody told me Paul Nelson picked him," Katy said, carefully avoiding his eyes.

John's face changed, and the look of annoyance became a look of grim determination. "In that case," he said, "get me Nelson on the phone, Katy! I don't know what he's up to, but I intend to find out."[1]

A conversation like this going on behind your back, with your name in there instead of Jack Harrington's, is everybody's nightmare. If you suspect that when people hear you're going to make a public appearance they are appalled at the prospect, you can't help feeling devastated. The only thing worse is the knowledge that you *did* make the appearance, and that you were just as bad as they expected. A survey done a few years ago reported that Americans who were asked to list and rank their worst fears put public speaking at the top of the list, ahead of either death or disease.

Public writing — that is, writing for public consumption — doesn't evoke a terror quite so deep. But that's only because you can't see the people who read what you write and they can't see you. You would still be wounded by complaints that it was an ordeal to have to read what you had written. And written flops, like recorded spoken ones, live *on*, coming back to haunt you at the most unexpected and inconvenient times. These two activities — public speaking and public writing — are referred to in the *Gentle Art* system as *public language*.

There are many possible reasons why John Martin would not want Jack Harrington appearing on a talk show where his performance could affect the company image. Harrington might not be well-informed. He might have a tendency to panic or to lose his temper. He might be boring. He might be careless about his dress and grooming. He might be rude. But notice what John says:

> "*Sure*, Jack's a good man! His résumé makes *me* look like a mail clerk. And people who know him well know how valuable he is. But when he gets out in public and has to make an impression, something weird happens. I don't understand it. . . I don't know how someone so capable can come off as such a klutz, but he does."

In my experience, this description corresponds to only one problem — a problem that has consistently plagued George Bush, but that nobody seems willing to bring out into the open — the problem of VOICE QUALITY. President Bush's voice quality (and the rest of his body language) are going to interfere every step of the way with the perception that Americans and others around the world have of him.

Americans have demonstrated that they are entirely capable of separating the person from the issues and coating the person with perceptual Teflon, if seeing the issues attached to him or her would be uncomfortable. The positive or negative things Bush has already done are not sufficient to determine whether he is perceived as "presidential" — the quality of his voice *is*, however illogical that may seem. Just as Reagan's wonderful from-the-burning-bush deep baritone has always been sufficient to make people like him and vote for him even when they disagree with the words the voice is saying. It was the quality of Michael Dukakis's voice — a deep and rich and unmistakably patriarchal voice — that made it possible for him to break out of the homogenized pack of would-be Democratic candidates in 1988 and compete believably against the otherwise overwhelming advantages the Vice Presidency afforded to his Republican opponent. When we hear the voice of Michael Dukakis, we hear the voice of everybody's mythical father — the one you can always rely on. It's boring, and it wasn't enough to whip the Reagan/Bush candidacy, but it's definitely the voice of a reliable adult male.

George Bush, on the other hand, has the voice of a whiny little boy who is overtired. For that reason alone, he has to do everything *twice* as well as other men do just to achieve the same goals (a situation that ought to give him tremendous sympathy for American women).

The reason women react so negatively to George Bush is that women are 100 percent of all mothers and at least 80 percent of all elementary school teachers. THEY SPEND A LOT OF THEIR TIME DEALING WITH WHINY LITTLE BOYS, AND THEY KNOW EXACTLY WHAT THAT

INVOLVES. Women who feel positively about George Bush either know him personally — which allows them to learn his value as a person on the basis of experience — or they enjoy whiny little boys.

Nothing that Bush's expensive image makers can do for him — no objects they trim him with or surround him with, no insertion of his person into power boats or farm machinery cabs or kindergartens — is going to correct this situation. He needs a good voice coach on a crash priority basis. This is so overpoweringly obvious that it has surely been pointed out to him many times. He must refuse, for reasons of his own, to follow through on the counsel he is given.

Immediately following his election to the presidency in 1988, many Bush-watchers (and Bush-listeners) noted that his voice seemed to have dropped markedly in pitch and become richer and fuller. Not like Reagan's, to be sure; but still a tremendous improvement on the pre-election version. However, careful attention to this seeming transformation quickly showed that his voice pitch was providing us with an unambiguous index to his state of mind. When Bush is at ease with what he's saying, and otherwise comfortable, the pitch drops; when he is under stress and ill at ease, it rises again. Far from being unique to Bush, this transparency is a common phenomenon in the speech of almost everyone. But it is so exaggerated in the President's speech that it constitutes an impediment to diplomacy, and is something he would be well advised to bring under his voluntary control.

George Bush personally may be everything those who know him well say he is — certainly his record of achievement points that way. But his record is irrelevant to how *other* people are going to interact with him in the real world, and most of us can never know him well. As Lyn Nofziger puts it (in *Business Week* for August 22, 1988, page 28): "If there's one thing that George Bush cannot be, it's a 'regular guy'." FALSE PERCEPTIONS HAVE REAL CONSEQUENCES. Look again at Figure Ten — it applies here. If people perceive Bush as weak, or as ineffectual, they will TREAT him as if he were weak. Or ineffectual. And that will hold him back, and diminish his effectiveness in serious ways. His voice quality is the primary reason for the problem.

The first step you take, then — to make sure that what *you* say is not heard through a negative perceptual filter that handicaps you in advance — is to assess the quality of your voice and do everything you can to bring it to its full potential.

Perfecting The American Voice

Every individual interested in achieving goals in this world needs a valid assessment of his or her voice quality, as it is perceived within the culture.

In America today, preferred voices are low and resonant and full, and of moderate volume, and the contours they follow as they speak are smooth curves rather than flat lines or sharp angles. If the voice has all the characteristics just listed, it's all right for it to be *slightly* nasal — but only slightly. This profile is demanded of both males and females. The worst voice of all, in current American fashion, is the voice that is both high and nasal, no matter what its other characteristics. The high nasal voice is the WHINY CHILD voice, and it is a severe handicap and a barrier to success.

It is not true, by the way, that women's voices must "naturally" be higher than the voices of men. The gender-dependent physical differences involved are minor and trivial. Many men have voices higher than many women. (Compare George Bush with Barbara Jordan, Jeane Kirkpatrick, Elizabeth Dole, or Phyllis Oakley.) There are many countries in which men's voices are usually higher than the voice of the average American woman and where that is considered the "natural" male voice.

These facts do not keep the high nasal voice from being an especially serious problem for American women. It is the voice we associate with the image of the whiny child, and women are *already* struggling with a stereotypical image of childishness. When this image is reinforced by a childlike voice — a voice which typically becomes even higher and more nasal, even more childlike, when the woman is under stress — the results are overwhelmingly negative.

For George Bush, I suggested a voice coach. That is because he needs spectacular results FAST. If your ambition is to be a Shakespearean actor (or President of the United States) I suggest a voice coach for you, too. But if you are only interested in being certain that the words you say do not have to fight their way through a perceptual filter that says "YOU ARE LISTENING TO A SMALL CHILD," a voice coach is not necessary. You can reach this particular goal yourself, at your own convenience, on your own time, and in privacy. Here are the steps you follow:

1. Make a baseline tape of your own voice, twenty to thirty minutes long, speaking naturally. Talk about something that interests you — taxes, or the economy, or tort reform, or golf, or what you dislike most about liberals/ conservatives. Talk about the teacher you liked or disliked most in school, if that would be easier. The subject is not important, as long as it triggers natural speech.

2. Listen to the tape. Ask yourself: is that a voice I would enjoy listening to, if it weren't my voice? Is it too high? Too nasal? Too loud or soft? Too monotonous or too dramatic? Do I talk too fast or too slowly? THIS IS IMPORTANT. If you can't rely on your own judgment because of a natural bias in your favor, get a few second opinions from people you trust. Do not fall for the soothing idea that you sound terrible to yourself because you aren't used to hearing your voice on tape. It's true that it can be a

shock, but with today's recording technology it's also reliable. THE WAY YOU SOUND TO YOU IS PROBABLY THE WAY YOU SOUND TO EVERYONE. To get an idea of how much nasalness is too much, listen to Senator John Danforth or Congresswoman Patricia Schroeder, whichever gender is appropriate for you. Both are good speakers; both have excessively nasal voices that make them less effective than they could be.

3. If the result of Step 2 is general agreement that you have a clear and compelling voice with no negative qualities, congratulations — you're through with this process. Otherwise, the next step is to get a tape of someone whose voice *does* fit that description, who is the same gender you are, and who makes an impression that you would like to make. This tape will serve you as a model. It should be roughly half an hour long, and should be taped speech, not taped theater. If you know someone personally whose voice fits the bill, tape that person. Otherwise, choose a public figure readily available on tape (or on radio or television, from which tapes can easily be made.) For women, Diane Sawyer or Jeane Kirkpatrick are good choices; for men, Peter Jennings or almost any of the anchormen on National Public Radio are equally good. Do not choose someone whose voice — like Barbara Jordan's or William Buckley's — is highly distinctive. You don't want your listeners to be thinking "What an unusual voice!" or "What a wonderful voice!" You want your voice to be so effective that they listen to what you say without any *awareness* of your voice, either positive or negative.

4. Now you work with the tape — at your own convenience, at your own pace, and in privacy. What you're going to do is speak *with* the tape. Not after it, as you may have done in foreign language classes, but with it. Work on one sentence at a time. Don't write the sequence down or memorize it; just listen to it until you're familiar with it and then do your best to say it simultaneously with the speaker. If you get bored with the tape, get a new one. If you come to know it so well that you can *recite* it, get a new one. Unless you have to listen to the speaker model as you talk, your brain won't be able to make the constant adjustments that correct the mismatch between your voice and the model.

5. After you've spent roughly twenty hours at this task, make a new baseline tape of your own voice and check again. When you find the improvement adequate, it's time to stop.

6. Repeat Step 5 again after every six hours of practice until you are satisfied with the results.

This technique, which is based on the work of Leonard Newmark, works very well. You don't have enough conscious knowledge of how the human voice works physiologically and neurologically to make the neccessary changes in your voice on your own. It's not particularly useful to know those details, unless you are an acoustic phonetician. But your mismatch detector — your magnificent brain — is fully capable of monitoring the two streams of speech and making adjustments until they match, if you simply give it the opportunity. In fact, this works so well that it's possible to overdo it. Your goal isn't to be able to do a flawless imitation of your speaker model; stop your practice before you reach that stage.

You can use this same technique as a way of acquiring an accent other than your natural one, if you like. Some accents are fashionable and are assets to you professionally; others hold you back. If you know that your accent is a barrier to your success, get a suitable tape by a speaker who has the accent you want to use instead, and work with that tape. Similarly, if you would like to be able to switch competently among several different dialects, use tapes as models and work with them as described above.

It is becoming ever more apparent that knowing the language of the people you're doing business with gives you a great advantage. (The Japanese provide an enlightening example.) If you are trying to learn a foreign language, speak *with* your language tapes or records instead of repeating after the foreign speaker in the pause provided. Repeating afterward, which adds the task of remembering what you've just heard, only trains you in your errors — especially errors in intonation, the most important area to get *right*.

There's only one significant difference between working with a tape in your native language and a foreign one. With a foreign tape, for which you may only be able to say half a dozen words instead of full sentences at first, always say a partial sentence from the end of the sentence, not from the beginning. Suppose you were a Japanese speaker trying to learn English, and the recorded sentence was "The value of the stocks issued by Metamega Corporation steadily increased during the month of October." You would work with that sentence using the following chunks:

1. " . . . during the month of October."
2. " . . . steadily increased during the month of October."
3. " . . . the stocks issued by Metamega Corporation steadily increased during the month of October."
4. "The value of the stocks issued by Metamega Corporation steadily increased during the month of October."

This makes it possible for you to preserve the intonation of the sentence; working from the beginning, a few words at a time, has the contrary effect.

You can also use this technique as a way of improving your body language. Just switch to videotape. Have yourself taped when you are talking with a small group about some subject of interest and while you are giving a brief speech — you need at least fifteen minutes of each. If watching this baseline video convinces you that improvement is needed, select as a model someone whose nonverbal communication you admire and for whom videotapes are available. Then work with the model tape, matching the body language as well as the words, just as you did with the audio tape. Again, stop before you appear to be doing an impersonation of your model!

The reason I have given so much space in this chapter to voice quality and other body language is that — although it is entirely illogical and unfair — NOTHING ELSE IS AS IMPORTANT TO YOUR PUBLIC SPEAKING AS YOUR NONVERBAL COMMUNICATION, AND VOICE QUALITY IS THE MOST POWERFUL *PART* OF NONVERBAL COMMUNICATION. No matter how superb the words you say, poor voice quality and body language will cancel the impact of those words and drain them of power. You can hire the finest speechwriter, you can wear the most expensive clothes, you can surround yourself with the most impressive trappings — that won't do it. Unless your nonverbal communication is effective, your speech will not be effective either, and you will have wasted your money. Conversely, a speaker whose body language is as effective as Ronald Reagan's can deliver the most abominable claptrap and it will go over like a new Gettysburg Address.

Nonverbal Communication and Written Language

With written language, the critical importance of nonverbal communication factors works both to help and to hinder. No one who is reading your words is exposed to your voice and your body language while reading. If they're not very good, that's a help to you. If they are excellent, not being able to use them is a drawback. You will have noticed that very little is *written* by Ronald Reagan, who is well aware of where his strengths are.

The actual words you write are much more important than the actual words you speak. However, the three elements corresponding to nonverbal communication that are available for written language — PUNCTUA-TION, GRAPHIC DESIGN, and PACKAGING — can wreak havoc with your written words in exactly the same way that facial expression, postures and gestures, and voice quality can wreak havoc with your spoken ones. And this is often something over which you have little control.

When your personal "packaging" is shabby, but your words and body language are well chosen and well delivered, you can override the packaging problem. But when you have written something fine, and a publisher packages it abominably, or gives it a stupid title, you can't be present to correct the bad impressions. At that point, it's too late. Here's the rule to remember:

THE BEST INSURANCE YOU CAN HAVE AGAINST EDITORS OR
PUBLISHERS TREATING YOUR WRITTEN LANGUAGE BADLY IS

SKILL IN DEALING WITH THEM *VERBALLY, BEFORE* YOUR MATE-
RIAL APPEARS.

The *Gentle Art* techniques provide you with that skill.

There is one other thing you can do to protect yourself. Most people,
when given the opportunity to review the written work of others, feel
an irresistible temptation to change *some*thing. This is a way for them
to demonstrate that they did read the material, that they gave it careful
consideration, and that they have power over it and its writer. Making
a change, be it ever so trivial, allows them to make a *dominance display*.
This is as true when you submit two paragraphs to your company
newsletter as it is for an article you submit to the most prestigious
professional journal.

THIS IS EXTREMELY IMPORTANT. Whenever you submit
anything written — whether for publication or for presentation — salt
it with items you don't mind losing, set out prominently enough to attract
attention. Your strategy is to maximize the chances that *those* will be
axed instead of things that do matter to you. Always expect dominance
displays; always provide for them. The more people there are who will
examine your material, and the more they are likely to be struggling
for power over one another, the more extensive the dominance displays
will be. Plan for that. And give in graciously — but reluctantly — when
your plan succeeds.

Producing Public Language

It's traditional to claim that there's little connection between the language
of public speaking and the language of public writing. At the extreme
ends of the linguistic spectrum, this has a certain amount of validity.
But for the type of public language we are concerned with in this chapter,
it is false. Speaking and writing for public consumption have four major
characteristics in common:

☐ Unlike ordinary language, both are planned in advance.

☐ Both are more highly valued in our society than ordinary language is; you
are therefore expected to take sufficient care and trouble to provide good
value.

☐ Both are variations on the language you use every day, and are based on
the same internal grammar.

☐ Both use a set of basic techniques of *rhetoric*, the purpose of which is
not to make your language fancier, but to make it easier to read or listen
to, easier to understand, and easier to remember.

You will want to keep these characteristics firmly in mind when
you are involved in producing public language. Always work in both

directions. Whether you will be speaking the words from notes or reading them aloud in full, write them down and read the text. Once it's written, read it aloud and tape it so that you can listen to your performance (or listen and watch, if you have convenient access to videotaping facilities). If you are preparing written language, always read that aloud also, and tape it, and listen to it. Written language that can't be read aloud comfortably is *badly* written language. You cannot know the full effect of your language unless you use all four language skills — reading, writing, speaking, and listening — when you evaluate it.

Now we can move on to the subject of choosing your words and arranging them. Remember, as we turn to this subject, that you should incorporate into your public language all of the *Gentle Art* syntonics techniques presented in this book. Verbal attack patterns, improperly chosen Sensory Modes and Satir Modes, direct commands and badly constructed complaints, random twirks[2] or twirks with negative impact on your audience, are just as counterproductive in your public language as they are in any other area of your language behavior.

CHOOSING AND ARRANGING YOUR WORDS FOR PUBLIC LANGUAGE

Whenever you speak or write for public consumption, you have four essential tasks. You need to:

□ Make it easy for the audience to apply Miller's Law to your language — to assume that it is true and to imagine what it could be true *of*.

□ Make it easy for the audience to read or listen to your language and to understand it.

□ Make it easy for the audience to organize and remember your language.

□ Make it easy for the audience to be persuaded by your language.

We'll be discussing these four topics one at a time, but there is much overlap among them. An improvement in any one of the four will automatically improve the other three as well. The easier your words are to believe, the more persuasive they will be, and vice versa. The easier your words are to read or listen to, the less burden there will be on language processing mechanisms, which makes understanding and remembering more likely. And so on. In tennis, people are forever talking about "the wrist" or "the forearm" as if they were not attached to the rest of the body; the separation of the four items on the list above is a similar convenient fiction.

MAKE IT EASY FOR THE AUDIENCE TO APPLY MILLER'S LAW

You can do two things to minimize the chances that people will react to your language with dubiousness or outright disbelief.

First. Don't *lie* when you are speaking publicly. Later in this book you will find an entire chapter on lies and lying. For now, let me take this opportunity to quote Ronald Reagan (in "Yankee Doodle Magic," by Laurence I. Barrett and Barrett Seaman, *Time Magazine*, July 7, 1986) on the subject. He said: "If you don't believe the line you're speaking, the audience will know it, and they won't believe it either." And that is true. Your voice and the rest of your body language will give you away. This does not mean that you must get up and bare your soul. Rather, it means:

YOU MUST FIND A WAY TO CONVEY THE MESSAGE YOU WANT TO CONVEY WITHOUT SAYING THINGS THAT ARE *CONTRA-DICTED* BY YOUR BODY LANGUAGE.

That's almost always possible; it just requires careful thought.

Dishonesty in written language is not as immediately obvious, because there's no accompanying body language to betray you. But unless the lie is trivial (in which case it would have been easy to avoid) you are likely to find yourself trying to defend it aloud at a later date, with all the problems that poses. You have time, with written language, to choose a careful wording that contains no false statements. Failing to do so is taking unnecessary risks, with no probable gain sufficient to justify them.

Second. People act on what they believe. Facts and logic have little to do with whether they believe something or not. Facts and logic demonstrate that smoking will kill you, and that people should be terrified of cigarettes the way they are terrified of AIDS. This not only doesn't stop smoking, it hardly even slows it down. Facts and logic prove that the single most effective step people could take to extend their lifespan would be to buckle their seat belts — but this doesn't make them do it, even when they're taking megadoses of vitamins and eating a diet of fiber and fish oil and spending huge sums on exercise machines and health clubs. You need something more than facts and logic.

If your audience already agrees with everything you're saying, this is not a problem. If they have no previous opinion about what you're saying — and if they perceive you as informed and reliable and innocent of malicious intent — it's not a problem. But when something you want them to believe is in conflict with something they *already* believe, you run into what Leon Festinger called *cognitive dissonance*. DISHARMONY IN THE HEAD. Reality mismatch, perceived by the brain and provoking immediate resistance. People suffering from cognitive dissonance will always try to fix it, and the most common fix is to protect the belief they already have, just as it is — not to change it or accept the idea that contradicts it.

The recent history of pain control offers us a fine example of cognitive dissonance and its effects. American mainstream culture had a reality statement that went like this: "Chemicals control pain." Then along came hypnosis and acupuncture — neither one of them a chemical — and it became impossible to hide the fact that *they* controlled pain. Americans disliked this intensely, and they were absolutely unwilling to give up their reality statement. Whereupon, our scientists got busy and "discovered" that the human body produces, all on its own, pain-controlling chemicals called *endorphins*. Now it was possible to remove the cognitive dissonance and restore harmony. Because now you could say that hypnosis and acupuncture stimulate the body to produce endorphins, which is not in conflict with "Chemicals control pain." This has been very helpful. Now, if your neighbor's headache disappears as a result of the application of a quartz crystal to his brow, you can dismiss it without cognitive dissonance by saying that it's "only endorphins."

In any culture, including the culture of a firm or organization, reality statements with no scientific implications can cause an astonishing amount of cognitive dissonance when challenged. Anything of which it can be said that "We've always done it that way" is a potential source of trouble when a decision is made to introduce change.

Obviously, you avoid language that will provoke cognitive dissonance if you can. When you can't avoid it, two strategies will make it less traumatic and disruptive:

□ INTRODUCE ANY NEW ELEMENT AS GENTLY AS POSSIBLE.
□ ALWAYS TIE THE UNFAMILIAR TO THE FAMILIAR.

To get people to accept spaceships, tell them — gently — how many ways spaceships are *like* sailing ships. To get them to accept a sudden temporary increase in their working hours, tell them — gently — how much that is like a baseball team playing an extra inning.

Go over the language you plan to use. Ask yourself: Are there reality statements important to my audience that I am going to be in conflict with? In order to believe what I say, will my audience have to discard something they already believe, or revise it drastically? If the answer to either question is yes, that material must be presented with great care. And you must find something familiar to your audience, preferably something they admire and value, that you can compare the new element to as you talk or write.

MAKE IT EASY FOR THE AUDIENCE TO READ OR LISTEN, AND TO UNDERSTAND

Five strategies are available for your use in accomplishing this task:

1. Pamper the short term memory.

2. Use metaphors to provide additional context.

3. Use parallelism.

4. Include a structure that will serve as index.

5. For spoken language, provide written backup.

Pamper the short-term memory.

More than twenty years ago, George Miller proved that the human short-term memory (also called "working memory") has a limited capacity which can be stated with reasonable precision: it is *seven*, plus or minus two. Your sensory systems take in units of information and combine them into chunks for processing; your short term memory can handle five to nine of those chunks at a time. Less than five chunks are *very* easy to remember. More than nine chunks means that some of the information is going to be lost. Not because it isn't transferred to long term memory — so far as we know, *everything* gets transferred — but because it is transferred without an index. It's there, all right, but you can't get at it except by accident.

Advertisers — marketers and packagers and product promoters — are the only American professionals who make consistent use of valid psycholinguistic information. And they are very careful indeed to use Miller's "magical number seven plus or minus two." It's not an accident that phone numbers are seven digits long, divided into a chunk of three numbers and a chunk of four numbers. Or that when the area code is added, it is added as a separate chunk. Your short-term memory can manage pretty well with (501) 112-3479; it would have a terrible time hanging onto 5011123479. When the post office decided to introduce zip codes, it made them five digits long; when it decided to add four more digits to the codes, pushing the limits of short-term memory, it was careful to package that as five digits *plus* four digits, with a dash to mark off the chunks, rather than as a nine-digit sequence.

If you construct your sentences in such a way that you overburden the capacity of the short-term memory, people cannot understand you. In speech, another sentence will come along while they are still trying to figure out the preceding one, and they will soon fall hopelessly behind. In written language, which must be read at 200 words per minute to coordinate the speed of the visual system with the speed of language processing in the brain, the badly constructed sentences will slow readers down below that minimum speed — and they will soon be hopelessly lost.

Now this does *not* mean that your sentences must all be less than ten words long. It means that ANY SEQUENCE THE SHORT-TERM

MEMORY HAS TO HANG ON TO WHILE MORE LANGUAGE IS STILL COMING *IN* MUST BE LESS THAN TEN WORDS LONG. Consider this sentence:

> "That the stock market crash of October 1987 was not the first step in a major depression surprised many economists."

That sentence is hard to process — thus hard to understand and to remember. The reason it's hard is that its *subject* is seventeen words long. When we read a sentence, the first thing we do is find the *verb*, and then we assign roles to the other pieces of the sentence in terms of their relationship *with* the verb. Reading "John sold the stocks on Wednesday," we first locate "sold" and then assign John the role of DOER, the stocks the role of OBJECT, and Wednesday the role of TIME. When you read the example sentence about the stock market crash, you have to hold that entire subject — "That the stock market crash of October 1987 was not the first step in a major depression" — until you get to the verb "surprised." That overburdens the short term memory. There is a better way to do it, like this:

> "It surprised many economists that the stock market crash of October 1987 was not the first step in a major depression."

Now the verb is right up front in the sentence. The revised sentence is actually one word longer than the original — but it is vastly easier to understand and remember.

The same problem occurs in all of the examples below, in which access to the all-important verb is delayed by a sentence element more than nine words long.

1. The product that was designed by the Marketing Division prior to the arrival of the new CEO in early April sold better in the Northeast than had been anticipated.

2. The results of the survey — although everyone knows that they must be viewed with a certain skepticism and that no poll is ever completely reliable — indicated that smart investors should put their money into maglevs immediately.

3. I am here today to introduce a man who, after overcoming almost inconceivable obstacles, none of which had ever been encountered in the Asian market previously, and any one of which would have meant failure for the average executive, saved the company from bankruptcy.

Long and cumbersome sentences can be handled more easily in written than in spoken language, because readers can go back over the sequence as many times as may be necessary to determine what you mean. BUT THEY HAVE TO WANT TO DO THAT. Great writers know many clever ways to put their sentences together so that lots of words are packed into a single chunk; they know how to write material so compelling that readers are willing to work to understand it. But unless you are a great writer, you would be well-advised to do everything you can to accommodate yourself to the short-term memory's capacity.

Use metaphors to provide additional context.

The speaking and writing that you do should be BRIEF. People will forgive you for not being inspiring or brilliant; they will *not* forgive you for taking too much of their time. No speech you give should ever last more than twenty minutes. To find out how long your written pieces should be, take a successful speech that you can deliver comfortably in twenty minutes, get it typed up in manuscript format and from then on write something approximately that size. (For me, this will be seven double-spaced pages.)

If you are involved in presentations that must go beyond those time limits — for example, if you are leading a seminar or workshop — divide the extensive material into sections, none of which should be longer than twenty minutes. Then allow ten more minutes in each section for taking questions and comments from participants.

It's hard to get much detail into twenty minutes or seven pages. But if you have a unifying metaphor, one that is shared by your audience, they will automatically fill in the details you had to leave out. Metaphors say "*X* is *Y*" or "*X* is like *Y*." (Metaphors with "like" are traditionally called "similes.")

To impress people with your brilliance, try for a metaphor that is fresh and new and surprising. But for pampering the short term memory, choose one so familiar that you can count on everyone to know all about it. The Old Western Frontier is an excellent example. Suppose you have to give a pep talk for a new sales campaign. You start like this:

"The first thing I want to say to you this morning is just two words: WAGONS — *HO!*"

All right? That sentence says, "This sales campaign is like the campaign to develop America's Western Frontier." You do not then have to go on and tell people which parts of the operation are like the drivers and which are like the covered wagons . . . and the deserts and the wagon trails and the whips and the oxen . . . they know all that. The entire schema for the trek west in covered wagons is nicely stored and indexed in their long-term memory and is readily available to you at all times as a set of pigeonholes for sorting and indexing *new* material. (This — not an ability to win trivia games — is why it's important for students to learn trivia. So that they will instantly recognize and be familiar with the shared metaphors of their culture.)

Find a metaphor that will fit your message and that can be established with only a few words — like "Wagons—*ho!*" When people hear you say, "Gentlemen, the starting whistle has blown, the first quarter has begun, and we are on the field!" they automatically set up three more index slots in their memories, one for each of the three additional "quarters" they know are included in the game. They set up a slot for the various members of the team and are prepared to toss people's names into those slots when you announce them. Metaphors do much of your detail work for you and expand the content of your words. So that you can gain a reputation — a reputation everyone would like to have — as someone who can be counted on for the *brief* effective talk or article.

Two warnings are necessary before we move on. First: No matter how clever a metaphor may seem, always stop and think about its presuppositions before you use it. Telling the group that a sales campaign is like a famous battle is fine, but don't choose Waterloo.

Second: Watch out for the Stowaway Metaphor — the metaphor you never intended to present, that you did not put into the "*X* is (like) *Y*" pattern, but that is in effect presupposed by your words. In the October 1-14 1985 issue of *Obgyn News*, the International Medical News Service quoted a professor of obstetrics and gynecology as follows:

> "A formula for setting an obstetrics fee that can be easily explained and justified to the public could start with the local fee for embalming, which falls into the $500-$800 range in many localities. Two or three times this amount is an appropriate base fee for the care of a pregnant woman and the delivery of a baby."

We can safely assume that the professor did not intend to set up the metaphor "Taking care of a pregnant woman and delivering her baby is like taking care of a corpse and embalming it." But the corpse, and the coffin, and the hearse and the embalming fluid and the mortician are all stowaways here. And they match up most elegantly point for point with the pregnant woman, and the delivery table, and the ambulance, and the intravenous fluids, and the physician.

The professor has made a considerable fool of himself in print, and his words have indeed come back to haunt him; his editors have in this case either made no effort to save him or failed to notice the danger. We can only hope that physicians around the country are not following this advice and saying to their patients, "Certainly, Mrs. Jones, I'd be happy to explain why I charge $2000 for prenatal care and delivery. Two thousand dollars is exactly four times as much as it costs to embalm a corpse here in Happytown!"

A Stowaway Metaphor is one of the quick roads to notoriety instead of celebrity. You cannot always count on the people who pick up your blunder to be as merciful as I have been and leave your name out of the story. In fact, the more important and successful you are, the more certain you can be that your name *will* be mentioned, along with details about where you work and what your product or service is. Have someone whose judgment you trust go over your speech or article and make certain nothing like an embalmed corpse is lurking in it anywhere.

We will return to the subject of metaphors in more detail in Chapter Ten.

Use parallelism.

Parallelism is a device for making sequences of language syntonic — for making them *match* one another. In the same way that mentioning one element of a metaphor prepares your audience to read or hear about the rest of its parts, parallelism helps people anticipate what is coming next and reduces the memory burden. When John F. Kennedy said, "Ask not what your country can do for you; ask what you can do for your country," that was parallelism. He could have said "Don't ask what your country can do for you; find out how you can be of service to your nation." He, and his speechwriters, knew better. And after he had used that structure once, he could be sure that each time he said, "Ask not *X*" the audience would be prepared to hear "ask *Y*." Oliver North used the famous "the good, the bad, and the ugly"; he was too skilled to say "good things, and some things that are bad, and also ugly things."

People worry far too much about the need for *variety* in their public language. YOU ONLY NEED VARIETY IF YOU TALK OR WRITE TOO LONG. Otherwise, it's difficult to overdo parallelism. If you need examples of the various patterns that make parallelism possible, you'll find an ample supply in any textbook on rhetoric.

Include a structure that will serve as index.

At the beginning of your speech or article, say, "I am going to discuss four points. First: . . . " This prepares people to anticipate three more points. Then, as you say "Second: . . . " and "Third: . . . " and "Fourth: . . . " they know where you are in your argument and what pieces should be stored together in their memory.

As you go along, use transitional words and phrases that help establish the indexes for the material you want remembered, such as "therefore" and "as a result" (or the less formal "so") and "in addition" ("also") and "which brings me to my next point."

At the end, unless the item is so short that it would be ridiculous to do so, sum up. Especially for spoken language. With written language, the audience can always go back and look over the material again. That isn't true for speeches, and a fast review of your major points is usually an excellent idea. (If you find that you can't construct such a review, it usually means you don't *have* any major points — it's better to find that out early, so you can fix it.)

Don't be a fanatic about this. There's a military version that says to tell them what you're going to tell them, then tell them, then tell them what you told them. That's overdoing it. Don't tell them what you're going to tell them. Just tell them how many indexes they should set up in memory, so that it's easier for them to sort the information and store it as they listen or read. That's not "talking down" or "writing down"; it's courtesy and linguistic competence.

For speeches, provide a written handout.

You don't need a handout for the six-minute talk; you don't need one for a talk that is an introduction to someone else's speech. But beyond that, a single page that gives your audience an outline of what you intend to say is helpful, in the same way that a table of contents for written language is helpful. You will have had to prepare an outline for your own use in any case; it's neither difficult nor expensive to run off copies for the people listening. Like summarizing your main points, preparing the outline is an excellent way to give your talk a quick physical — if you can't outline it, it's in bad shape and must be restored to health before you make it public.

If you'll be using names and terms your audience has not heard before, or introducing formal concepts that will be unfamiliar to them, putting those items on a written handout will keep people from getting lost while they wonder what you said or try to write it down. On page 169 is a one-page handout that I might distribute at an introductory verbal self-defense workshop for the general public, to show you the sort of thing I mean.

You don't need the copyright line for something genuinely informal, but it's much better to have it and not need it than the other way around. If you would object to having someone else use the material in your speech without your permission, do put your copyright line at the bottom of the page. If this is a matter of major concern to you, add another line that says the material is not for quotation or duplication or distribution. I don't think this is paranoid at all. It won't keep people *from* quoting you and talking about what you said, but it will keep them

THE GENTLE ART OF VERBAL SELF-DEFENSE

I. INTRODUCTION

- A. The problem of verbal violence
- B. Verbal abusers and verbal victims
- C. The Four Basic Principles

☐ Question-and-answer session

II. THREE TECHNIQUES FOR VERBAL SELF-DEFENSE

- A. Recognizing and responding to Sensory Modes
- B. Recognizing and responding to Satir Modes
- C. Recognizing and responding to the verbal attack patterns of English

☐ Question-and-answer session

III. CONCLUSION

- A. Why it matters
- B. What's in it for *you*
- C. How to explore the subject further

☐ Question-and-answer session

REFERENCE ITEMS

1. Miller's Law: In order to understand what another person is saying, you must assume that it is true and try to imagine what it could be true *of.* (George Miller)

2. *Presupposition.* A presupposition is anything that a native speaker of a language knows is part of the meaning of a sequence of that language, even if it isn't present on the surface of the sequence.

— Suzette Haden Elgin, Ph.D.

from appropriating the material wholesale. And it will serve notice that you would prefer to be contacted before they proceed. You do not have to register a copyright of this kind (or any other copyright) with the government.

There is one additional advantage to having a brief written handout when you're doing a talk. It gives people who are not good listeners, or not willing listeners, a way to keep track of how far along you are. This tends to soothe them, and they may listen after all.

Make it easy for the audience to organize and remember.

All of the communication strategies listed here so far will help you reach this goal — use them. In addition, I strongly recommend making use of a venerable rhetorical device known as the "Rule of Three". Here is an example from the opening paragraph of an article titled "The Torch Is Passed," (*Time Magazine*, August 22, 1988, by Laurence I. Barrett):

> "First in graceful defeat, then in glorious triumph, and finally as a reassuring symbol of the presidency itself, Reagan became the conservative constant through two decades of Republican resurgence."

We are *extremely* comfortable in this culture when things come along in threes. We learn about the goodness of threes as children, when we encounter the Three Bears, and the Three Little Pigs, and the Three Billy Goats Gruff. We learn that in fairy tales you get three wishes, and we carry this three-preference into adulthood. We like for things to have a beginning, a middle, and an end; we know you get three strikes before you are out; and we know the third time is a charm. When one item is introduced in a set and no other information is provided, audiences expect two more; if you live up to their expectations a time or two, they will assume that is a rule for the duration of the speech or article. This helps them organize the material and puts them at ease.

Barrett's sentence above is a flawless example. He lists three contexts in which Reagan had the leading role: defeat, triumph, and as symbol of the presidency. Then he uses parallelism as a way of making the list memorable: "in graceful defeat" . . . "in glorious triumph" . . . "as a reassuring symbol." He goes on to repeat the same structure of one modifier plus one noun in "conservative constant" and "Republican resurgence." It's not too much. On the contrary, it works extremely well. Here is the same message, written slapdash (by me) for comparison:

> Reagan took his initial defeat gracefully, and followed it up with a big win, becoming a reassuring symbol of the presidency. This made him the conservative constantthrough two decades of Republican resurgence.

When you set up your outline, use the Rule of Three. The outline below is considered old-fashioned, but I use it without exception and recommend it without reservation. It has never failed me yet.

TITLE

I. INTRODUCTION

II. MAIN BODY OF PIECE

    A. FIRST POINT OR EXAMPLE

    B. SECOND POINT OR EXAMPLE

    C. THIRD POINT OR EXAMPLE

III. CONCLUSION

For instance . . .

MEMORANDUM

I know you've all been wondering why we haven't put in the new computer system that was planned for early February. There are three good reasons for the delay.

First, the manufacturer did not complete production of the computers by the December 10th date that had been announced. Second, the unexpected increase in our sales in January convinced us that we needed a more elaborate software package than we had ordered originally, and clearing that up took time. Finally, the recent series of blizzards in the Midwest has caused one serious delay in shipping after another.

Fortunately all these problems now seem to be solved, and I am able to announce with confidence that you will have your new computers within the next ten days.

— J.T.

If you find yourself with some other number of points or arguments or examples instead of three, try reworking them. Usually there is one that you can divide into two, or there are two that you can combine. A large number should be divided into three sets. For example: the four arguments about cost; the two arguments about location; and the three arguments about delivery dates.

What about all the admonitions to keep your writing *lean* — pared of every nonessential word? After all, I've been stressing the urgent necessity to be brief. Isn't this Rule of Three business, along with the parallelism, going to lead to padded writing?

No. Even Herschel Gordon Lewis, whose specialty is the writing of ad copy — where you *really* must make every word count — cautions us not to confuse leanness with anorexia. And I would add an additional warning: Don't confuse *osteoporosis* with leanness, either.

You don't want fat in your public language. But you must have bone and muscle or it will collapse. The rhetorical techniques described here provide the underlying structure necessary to make your language strong enough to carry your message. *Padding* is something that happens when people recognize that their language is weak and they have no solid structure to use in strengthening it.

Make it easy for the audience to be persuaded.

There are things everyone does as a means of persuading readers and listeners. Some of them — like providing facts and logic — are not very helpful, although by philosophical standards they surely ought to be. Others — like the use of culturally loaded vocabulary items that can be counted on to trigger particular emotions in the group — are highly reliable, although by philosophical standards they should not be so effective with rational adults. Beyond those traditional tools there are two useful linguistic patterns: *nominalizations* and *factives.* They represent a single familiar communication strategy that you've seen before in the *Gentle Art* syntonics system:

USE PRESUPPOSITIONS TO CONVEY CHUNKS OF MEANING THAT YOU DO NOT WANT TO MAKE OPEN CLAIMS FOR.

This is exactly the same strategy people *mis*use in verbal attack patterns, but for quite different reasons. People who confront you with verbal attack patterns want to persuade you to give them your full attention for as long as they can keep the confrontation going. They do their best to cause you pain. Not because they are sadistic but because they are no good at getting attention by causing pleasure. They could care less whether you are convinced of the *content* of the attacks. When this strategy is used as part of public language, however, its primary purpose is to persuade people to accept the content of the speech or written piece.

NOMINALIZATIONS

Every English verb and adjective can be turned into a noun or noun phrase — a nominal. You can do it by adding "-ing" to a verb or putting "being" in front of an adjective. For many verbs and adjectives, you can do it by adding a special nominalizing ending to the word. For example:

1. "Swim" becomes "swimming" —
    "Swimming is good for you."

2. "Sick" becomes "being sick" —

"Being sick is a nuisance."

3. "Resign" becomes "resigning" or "resignation" —

"Her resigning surprised the firm." — or — "Her resignation surprised the firm."

4. "Careless" becomes "being careless" or "carelessness" — "Being careless is dangerous." — or — "Carelessness is dangerous."

(This process is in fact the quickest test for finding out whether a particular word *is* a verb, adjective, or nominal.)

In English, if an item has "the, this, that, these, those" before it, or one of the possessive forms like "his" or "her" or "Ted's," it is presupposed to *exist*. Thus, you can openly make the claim, "I have a yacht" or you can presuppose the existence of a yacht owned by you by saying "my yacht." Similarly, you, can openly make the claim, "You destroyed the software" or you can presuppose it by saying "Your destruction of the software . . . " Notice the difference in strategic terms.

1. "You destroyed the software." CLAIMED; MUST BE SUPPORTED

2. "Your destruction of the software surprised everyone."

PRESUPPOSED: You destroyed the software.
CLAIMED: This surprised everyone.

In your public language, then, write down the claims you want to make and see how many of them you can tuck into presuppositions by nominalization. Instead of saying, "We have succeeded, and it makes us very proud," say, "Our success makes us very proud," which presupposes the success and only claims the pride. Instead of saying "We discovered the cure for Syndrome Q," say, "Our discovery of the cure for Syndrome Q . . . " and finish the sentence with something innocuous. Suppose you need to persuade people of five separate propositions — if you can presuppose four of them, that leaves you free to concentrate on the fifth and make it your focus.

People may still challenge your presupposed claims. But it's more complicated for them than challenging an open claim, and thus is less likely. That is why politicians on the campaign trail say "My opponent's inability to understand X endangers this brave nation" instead of "My opponent doesn't understand X, which endangers this brave nation." Especially in speech, when the language goes by so fast, the audience is likely to accept such presupposed chunks without question. Nine times out of ten, your audience will accept that sentence about your opponent as a sentence about whether the "inability to understand X" is a danger to America or not. They will not stop to question the claim hidden in the presupposition.

You can strengthen these presuppositions considerably by adding a descriptive word or phrase to the pattern. "You are late" is an open claim. "Your lateness surprises me" presupposes "You are late" and claims only that it surprises me. "Your chronic lateness surprises me" presupposes not only "You are late" but also "You are late all the time." "Your chronic unexplained lateness" adds "You never have any explanation for why you are late." With each increasing layer of presupposition it becomes harder to get at the original claim, "You are late." Similarly, "my expensive foreign car" makes the presupposition of ownership much stronger than just "my car" does; "my expensive foreign car with the mag wheels" makes it even more likely that there really is such a car. "Car" is already a noun and freely available for this strategy; the process of nominalization makes it possible for you to achieve the same effect with verbs and adjectives.

FACTIVES

English verbs and adjectives are either factive or non-factive. When you use a factive and follow it with an embedded sentence (a sentence inside a larger sentence), the embedded sentence is *presupposed* to be true. This is not as complicated as it sounds. Look at the following examples:

> "I knew the stock was a good buy."
> "I didn't know the stock was a good buy."

Because "know" is factive, it makes no difference whether you say you did know or you didn't know — the embedded sentence, "the stock was a good buy," is presupposed to be true. Contrast this with:

> "I thought the stock was a good buy."
> "I didn't think the stock was a good buy."

Notice what happened? When you made the verb "think" negative, the sentence "the stock was a good buy" was no longer presupposed to be true. This tells you that "think" is not a factive verb.

Using a factive verb before a sentence lets you *shelter* it so that it's less vulnerable to attack. That's what makes "regret" so useful; any statement you claim to "regret" is presupposed to be true, as in "We regret that all the tickets have already been sold." To test a verb for factive status, just put it into the pattern shown in the examples above. If the embedded sentence continues to "feel" true even when you make the verb negative, that's a factive verb.

A group of physicians once asked me for help with a common problem. Suppose you are a rheumatologist. Another doctor in town, who is in a different medical specialty, calls you up and tells you, "I've got a patient with rheumatoid arthritis in my office," and asks you which of two drugs you recommend. Now you have a problem, and it's not that you can't make the requested recommendation. The problem is that you don't trust your colleague to diagnose RA correctly — but you can't say so without giving offense. The solution is to use the factive, "be aware." You say, "As you are aware, Doctor Jones, many conditions can be mistaken for rheumatoid arthritis." And then go on to add the needed information.

Use the same strategy in addressing an audience. When you want them to be persuaded to accept some claim, tell them you know they are already aware of it. Say, "As you are all aware . . . " Say "As every thinking person knows . . . " and then insert your claim. You may have a completely confident Leveler in the audience who comes right back at you with "Wait a minute! *This* thinking person does *not* know . . . " whatever it was. But completely confident Levelers are rare. Most of the time, that won't happen.

Filling the Five Celebrity Roles

YOU AS PROMINENT LOCAL CITIZEN

The material we've just gone through will make it easy for you to prepare effective brief talks for any situation, including the situation of minor crisis. And we have thoroughly covered the necessity for good voice quality and for body language that supports your words, as well as techniques for achieving both. Just one matter remains, and it has to do with the method you use to deliver a speech.

It is my personal opinion, based on fifty years of experience as both speaker and listener, that you should feel absolutely free to *read* speeches aloud. I know this is not the usual position, but I am not giving you this advice without good reason. If the fees people pay to hear me speak are any indication, I am a good speaker. I think they must be, because I'm not a public figure who would be booked to speak for my status alone. AND I *ALWAYS* READ MY TALKS AND SPEECHES. No one has ever complained yet, or failed to book me again. No one evaluating my presentations has ever written, "She would have been a pleasure to listen to if she hadn't been *reading* her talk."

If you are totally at ease speaking extemporaneously or from brief notes, by all means do that. I congratulate you. Otherwise, *read your speech*. I see speakers struggle through their talks in obvious distress, bungling and getting lost and backtracking and apologizing and wiping their fevered brows. I see speakers go droning on interminably while the audience grows more and more restless and resentful, because they do not have their material organized and cannot find a way to bring the ordeal to a graceful end. I see speakers who have *memorized* their talks, but who — because they are not professional actors — deliver them like wooden dummies. (Such memorized speeches are usually accompanied by a bizarre facial expression, because the speaker is "reading" the text off an internal screen invisible to the rest of us.) These people would be much better off reading from a page. And reading, done properly, doesn't have to be second best.

Type or print your talk in bold black letters on white or yellow paper, so that you will be able to read it easily without *peering* at it. Carry your pages openly, so that it's clear that you intend to read and feel no reluctance about doing so. Look at the pages as often as you need to, without making any attempt to hide what you're doing; look your audience in the eye the rest of the time. As you finish each page, put it at the bottom of the stack — or, if you think your audience is restless, put it to one side so that they can see what a small stack remains to be read.

CONSIDER WHAT THIS WILL MEAN TO YOU. You won't have to worry about remembering what comes next. You won't have to worry about forgetting something important. You will be going through an experience that you've been able to rehearse thoroughly, so that you can be certain you're doing it well. You won't have to worry about the speech being either too short or too long, because you will have read it in advance and timed it to be sure it fits your allotted time slot. You will have listened to your reading on your tape recorder and become satisfied with the way it sounds, so that you can relax and enjoy yourself — which makes you sound like a highly skilled speaker.

When the speaker is suffering, the audience is in agony; by reading your speech you can put an end to this problem. Your speech teacher might not approve — but your audiences will.

YOU AS AVAILABLE EXPERT ON SUBJECT X

One way to enhance your public image is to build a reputation as an expert on some interesting subject. You will then be called on for public language about that subject whenever the occasion is suitable. And you will have an excuse ready at hand when you are called on for something outside your specialty. The only problem is the selection of your topic.

It should always be a small topic, suitable for general audiences, and not controversial. Choose "Antique Violins," not "Antique Musical Instruments." Choose "Click Languages Around the World," not "The Bilabial Glottalized Fricative Consonant." And choose "Farmers in Colonial America," not "Satanists in Colonial America."

If there is some subject of general interest that you feel passionately about — something that genuinely interests you, and that you would keep up with whether you were asked to talk or write about it or not — the thing to do is to specialize in that subject. If that convenient solution doesn't present itself, I have a fail-safe suggestion. I suggest the venerable, and always satisfying topic, " . . . IN SHAKESPEARE." "Medicine in Shakespeare." "Lawyers in Shakespeare." "Reptiles in Shakespeare." "Public Policy and Political Science in Shakespeare." "War in Shakespeare." Shakespeare wrote about everything, and in the intervening years someone has catalogued and commentaried every word. The material is so broadly applicable that it can be adapted for any audience whatsoever, including your child's grade school class. And the resources that you can find for your subject are not only vastly abundant but easy to find and usually inexpensive.

Once you've chosen your topic, buy the necessary basic books and subscribe to the essential publications, so that you stay current. If there is an organization associated with the topic, join it. You may not want to spend time participating, but paying your dues will keep you aware of conferences, new publications, and the like.

This will allow you to build up a database from which to prepare your talks and articles. It will mean that when someone calls on you to produce public language at a moment's notice, you won't have to go through the "What on earth will I talk about?" hassle. It will guarantee fulfillment of Dale Carnegie's sage recommendation that you should always know a great deal more about your subject than you're likely to need. And you will have solved, without extra effort, a problem that plagues your family and friends. Now, at gift-giving time, they can always choose something to add to your collection of materials on your chosen subject. This is a fringe benefit that should not be underestimated. As the years go by, and you do not have to face every birthday knowing that there will be yet one more box of handkerchiefs, one more boring tie, one more bottle of nondescript cologne, you'll appreciate it.

YOU AS REPRESENTATIVE OF YOUR FIRM OR GROUP

The only thing different about this role is the limitation it places on your freedom. As a private individual, or a private expert on some subject of interest, you can say almost anything that isn't legally actionable. As the representative of a firm or other group, however, you must constantly keep in mind that everything you say reflects on others. Your own common sense and courtesy, and your knowledge of the image the group prefers to maintain, will guide you safely through this role.

One thing you can do to make your public language safer is to use Computer Mode very extensively. Use generalizations and abstractions rather than examples that are specific. Throw in an occasional personal anecdote if it is appropriate and if its cast of characters cannot be identified;

except for that, avoid "I" or "You" language. Talk of "people" instead. Use passive constructions in order to get rid of any identifiable DOERS in your sentences — saying "Chemical waste has been dumped in our harbors" does not require you to mention who did the dumping. Maintain neutral tone of voice and neutral body language in general. This may not keep your audience on the edge of their seats, but it does not have to be boring, and it will not harm the group image you must be wary about. Just write your talk or your article in the usual way, and then go back and translate as much of it into Computer Mode as you reasonably can without robbing it of all vitality.

YOU AS MEDIA FOCUS

The important difference between speaking for the media and other public speaking — including the talking that you do as part of an interview for later publication — has nothing to do with what you wear or how you look. You can always ask someone about that part of it. Just call up the studio (or the publication's photographers) and Level. Tell them you want to look your best; tell them you have no idea how to accomplish that; ask for their advice; do what they tell you to do.

The important difference is that when you talk for the media you give up your *control* over what you will say. No longer are you in a position to decide exactly which words you will use and exactly how long you will spend saying them. Now you have to deal with producers and directors and reporters and talk show hosts and camera crews — all with their own ideas about what's going to happen — and with the clout to put those ideas into practice. NEVER accept a media person's word that certain things will or will not happen. If it looks like a good story or a good picture, that promise will be forgotten. You may get an apology later, and it may be sincerely meant — but the damage will be done.

Find out everything you can about the appearance or interview. Ask whether there will be people calling in by phone. Ask whether there will be commercial breaks, and how many. Ask who will be on before and after you. Find out who will be introducing and interviewing you — and make a point of listening to this person while someone *else* is appearing, so that you can get a feeling for the style you will be facing. If you discover that the goal of the occasion is to make the guest look like an idiot, withdraw your agreement to appear — unless you enjoy sparring with an adversary in public, in which case this event is tailor made for you.

When all of this has been done, you're ready to prepare for the occasion. Prepare exactly as you would prepare if you were going to go to court and testify. Write down every question you can imagine that you might be asked, and write thorough answers for each one; tape them and listen to yourself, so you can be sure that you sound the way you want to sound. DO NOT MEMORIZE YOUR ANSWERS, JUST BECOME VERY FAMILIAR WITH THEM. Take along your notes and your references, and don't hesitate to look at them if you really need to do so.

And then you have four simple rules to follow.

1. When asked a question that you don't know the answer to, say, "I'm sorry — I don't know the answer to that question."

The worst thing that can happen after you admit you don't know something is that you can be criticized for not knowing or for forgetting. This is trivial by comparison with the awful things that can happen when you try to *answer* a question you don't know the answer to.

2. When asked a question that — for whatever reason — you don't *want* to answer, go to Computer Mode and stay there.

Asked, "Why did your CEO accept a bribe last Tuesday night?" you say, "Few things are more mysterious than the motives of other people."

3. Try — try hard — never to say "That's a good QUEStion!" or "I'm GLAD YOU ASKED me that!" And try hard never to say "No comment."
4. Be aware that *something* will go wrong. It always does. One thing going wrong is acceptable and not to be worried about. When it happens, don't torment yourself about it. Most of the time, you'll be the only person who notices.

YOU AS DRAGONSLAYER

Once in a while, unless you are extraordinarily lucky, you are going to find yourself elected as spokesperson to explain, excuse, or in some other way deal with a MESS. Messes are of two kinds: internal, like the Watergate burglary; and external, like the Tylenol tampering scare.

The markedly different examples provided by Richard Nixon and Lee Iacocca have made it clear that the only way to handle the *internal* mess successfully is to transmit the following message: YOU'RE RIGHT — IT WAS A STUPID THING TO DO. WE'RE SORRY WE DID IT, AND WE PROMISE YOU IT WILL NEVER HAPPEN AGAIN. If you are so unfortunate as to be personally responsible for the entire problem, you will have to say "I" instead of "we"; if taking full responsibility is a good strategic move, say "I" instead of "we"; otherwise, don't change a thing. If Nixon had done this, he would have saved both himself and the nation a great deal of trouble and grief, and he would not have had to resign.

The appropriate message for handling an *external* mess — one that happens *to* you or your group, and in which you are essentially blameless — differs by only a few words. It goes like this: YOU'RE RIGHT — IT WAS A TERRIBLE THING TO HAVE HAPPEN. WE'RE SORRY THAT IT HAPPENED, AND WE PROMISE YOU WE WILL DO EVERYTHING HUMANLY POSSIBLE TO MAKE SURE THAT IT NEVER HAPPENS AGAIN.

In both cases, internal or external, your goal is to transmit the *same* metamessage: TRUST ME — EVERYTHING'S GOING TO BE ALL RIGHT. Never lose track of the fact that the most important tool in your Dragonslayer Kit for this purpose is body language — your nonverbal communication and its skimpy equivalent resources in written language. There is no better model than Ronald Reagan, described here in the January 9, 1986, *New York Times*, by R. W. Apple, Jr.:

> To most television viewers who saw him emerge from behind a closed door, stride purposefully down a long, imperially furnished, red-carpeted corridor, then fairly bound onto a platform framed in the doorway to the East Room, much of the message — vigor, authority, relaxation — had been communicated before he spoke.

NOTES

1. Because this is not a novel, and because I am not an unkind person, I am going to *tell* you what Paul Nelson was up to in Scenario Eleven. Metamega wanted John Martin to be on that television talk show, but people knew he would refuse if asked directly. They asked Nelson to help, and he agreed: the way to get Martin to do the show, he told them, would be to pretend that Jack Harrington was going to do it, and that the choice was Nelson's idea. He assured them that it would work — and it did. As for Jack Harrington, who was in on the plan from the beginning, he was grateful not to have the duty and happy to be of service.

2. A twirk is a characteristic of language behavior that draws excessive attention to itself. See pp. 242-246 for a discussion.

Workout — Chapter 8

1. According to communications consultant Arch Lustberg , there are three basic facial expressions: the closed face — when you frown, making a vertical line between your eyebrows; the open face — when your brows go up, together, quickly, making one or more horizontal lines across your forehead (like Ollie North); and the neutral face — on which only the *mouth* moves

(like George Schultz.) Practice using these three basics while you're talking, with the help of a mirror for feedback. Your goal is to become aware of what your facial muscles are doing and to get them under conscious control. (Lustberg's remarks appeared in "Tips On Speaking — Lincoln Didn't End at Gettysburg by Saying 'Thank you!'" in an interview in *Physician's Financial News* for April 30, 1988; page PB8.)

2. Listen to the *MacNeil/Lehrer News Hour's* otherwise very capable Judy Woodruff when she asks *questions*. Notice her voice quality, especially at and near the *end* of questions. Count the number of strong stresses she uses in questions. Notice your intonation. What's your evaluation?

3. Here are two examples of poor word choices. For each one, decide what the problem is and reword the example to fix it.

   a. "We are grateful to God for His unspeakable gifts." (A rural church bulletin.)

   b. "Our study is an attempt to answer part of this question. Unfortunately, its most critical component — whether people are sicker or remain in ill health longer when they do not receive medical care — cannot now be answered." (From "Uncompensated Care by Hospitals or Public Insurance for the Poor: Does It Make a Difference?", by Robert J. Blendon et al., in *The New England Journal of Medicine* for May 1, 1986; page 1161.)

4. A language style tied to a particular role is called a *register*. To see what happens when the content of an essay and its register are deliberately mismatched, read "Aristotle's Garage: A Mechanic's Metaphysics," by Don Sharp, in *Harper's* for March 1981, pages 91-93. Sharp uses the *academic* register to discuss automobile brake repair, and the result is elegant. What do you think would happen if a piece went the other way, using a blue collar register to discuss an *academic* subject? Would that be as effective?

5. Here is a finely crafted sentence, with a double use of the Rule Of Three; rewrite it so that it's ruined.

   "To defend the infringement of liberty, to refuse to uphold the Constitution in a crisis, to support the alien methods of despotism — surely that in a republic is shameful, disgraceful, and unpatriotic."

   (Walter Karp, in "Republican Virtues," in *Harper's* for July 1979; page 27.)

6. On page 235 of this book, I wrote the following sentence: "The usefulness of the ability to detect signals of lying when they are present is obvious." The subject of that sentence is fourteen words long, which overburdens the short-term memory; the sentence is awkward. Why would I write it that way, instead of "It's obvious that the ability to detect signals of lying when they are present is useful"? (Hint: Analyze the *nominalizations* used in the awkward version.)

7. Rhetorical devices can accomplish astonishing things. Consider the one known as "apophasis," shown in the examples below:

   a. "I am much too polite to tell you that your socks don't match."

   b. "I would certainly never mention to you the fact that you aren't Ph.D. material."

   c. "I wouldn't think of allowing you to find out how little respect your junior executives have for you."

   Can you write a rule for this structure? What's the pattern?

8. When·you are asked an outrageous question, respond forcefully and confidently — with something that is not a lie, is not a response to the question, and cannot be challenged. For example, when Jane Pauley asked a young Japanese teacher on an August 1985 *Today Show* whether she thought there was any justification for the dropping of the bombs on Hiroshima, the young woman smiled serenely and said, "As a teacher, it is my responsibility to provide the information about the facts." Make a list of the five questions you would most dread being asked in public, and write responses of this kind for each one.

9. Here are two questions you can use to practice your skills at public language — both are guaranteed to produce spirited language. The first is my own; the second is based on a quotation from an editorial by George D. Lundberg and Laurence Bodine, on page 3157 of the December 4, 1987 issue of the *Journal of the American Medical Association*.) Either one will serve well as a subject to talk about when you prepare a tape to judge your own voice quality by.

   a. Would you be willing to go into combat beside a female soldier? Why or why not?

   b. "Doctors and lawyers in our society have benefited greatly from the abundant opportunities made available to them from the fruits of our plenty. We believe that all doctors and all lawyers, as a matter of ethics and good faith, should contribute a significant percentage of their total professional efforts without expectation of final remuneration. ... We believe that 50 hours a year — or roughly one week of time — is an appropriate minimum amount." Do you agree? Why or why not?

10. Does "Don't worry" mean the same thing as "Let not your heart be troubled"? If not, what's the meaning difference?

11. For a detailed discussion of current knowledge about judging emotions from listening to voices, read "Vocal Indicators of Psychological Stress," by Harry Hollien, in *Annals of the New York Academy of Science* for 1980, pages 47-72. Hollien takes up the use of judgments based on voice in law enforcement, health care, forensic medicine, aviation, etc., and provides an excellent bibliography.

SIGHT BITES

1. "To describe perceptual phenomena ... we in American use the term 'extrasensory perception', or 'ESP'. Russians, however, speak of biological information or bioinformation. Much can be said for the wisdom of this choice, for, as several American scientists have noted, any inference that events might be extrasensory or beyond the range of the senses creates immediate hostility."

   (From "Parapsychology in the U.S.S.R.," by Stanley Krippner and Richard Davidson," in *Saturday Review* for March 18, 1972: page 57.)

2. "I'm six feet two, and when I go out on the campaign trail, people say, 'We thought you were a short guy.'"

   (George Bush, quoted in an interview titled "I've Been Underestimated," in *Time Magazine* for August 22, 1988; page 20.)

3. "All politicians say as little as they can. Only the very greatest can get away with saying nothing. Abraham Lincoln in his 1860 campaign did not make a single speech ... "

   (From "Hurrah for Politicians," by Garry Wills, in *Harper's* for September 1975; page 46.)

4. "Often the best way to disarm a hostile press is to embrace them; 'love bombing', some call it."

   (From "Nancy steals the show," by Hedrick Smith, in *Advertising Age* for June 13, 1988; page 38.)

5. "As a hypothetical illustration, consider Lincoln's 'Gettysburg Address' as it might have been written by Dwight Eisenhower, probably beginning something like 'Eighty-seven years ago, I think it was.' "

   (From "The Problem of Style in Presidential Discourse," by Ronald H. Carpenter, in *Concepts in Communication*, edited by Jimmie D. Trent, Judith S. Trent, and Daniel J. O'Neill; Allyn and Bacon, Inc. 1973; page 110.)

6. "When I was a boy, I was told anybody could become President; I'm beginning to believe it."

   (Attributed to Clarence Darrow. Try this sentence with a variety of different intonations and notice (a) how the meaning changes as you go along, and (b) how hard it is to indicate those differences in written language.)

9 Semantic Modulation

SCENARIO TWELVE   "**W**hat do you mean, I can't have these books?" John Martin had been leaning on the high library counter with both elbows, listening to Mary Forthright; now he stood up straight, shoved both hands into his pockets and stared at her. "Why not? I *need* them."

"It's too many books," she said stiffly. "Too many at one time."

"It's six books," he said.

"Yes. And that's too many."

"Well, what's the rule?"

"The rule?"

"Yes, Mrs. Forthright — the *rule*. What's the upper limit on the number of books I can take out?"

She had been meeting his stare; now she dropped her eyes and her lips tightened. "It's not an actual formal regulation," she said stiffly. "It's simply common sense."

"You mean there isn't any *rule*? And you're still holding me up like this? Time is *money*, Mrs. Forthright, and I don't have any more of it to waste!"

"Any thinking person knows;" said Mary Forthright, "that six books is *too many books* to take out of a library at one *time*."

"Not *this* thinking person!" He was angry now; every minute he had to spend standing here arguing with this ridiculous woman was one more minute delaying the research he had to get done before Monday's meeting. "*This* thinking person happens to know that the function of a library — which is paid for by this thinking person's taxes — is to provide books for this thinking person to check out! And unless you can show me a written regulation that forbids it, Mrs. Forthright, I am going to take these books. *All* of these books."

Mary Forthright had a brilliant flush high on her cheeks, and her fists were clenched at her sides. "I can't stop you," she said bitterly.

"No. You can't," said John, "Now please — do whatever it is you have to do, so I can get out of here and get on with my work."

From John Martin's point of view, the librarian's behavior is not only infuriating, it is also incomprehensible. Why on earth should she care how many books he checks out? He's a responsible adult, he always returns the books on time, and that's what the books are *for*. If he had proposed to remove an entire car full of books — so many books that it might conceivably have diminished the supply of books for other people — her attitude would have made some minor degree of sense. As it is, it makes *no* sense, and Martin fully intends to make a formal complaint to whoever runs the library system in his area; when he gets home, he makes a note to have his secretary find out who that is, first thing Monday morning.

We have all run into people like Mary Forthright; if we *are* people like Mary Forthright, we have all run into people like John Martin. And although the fate of nations does not revolve around a situation like the one in Scenario Twelve, it will serve us very well as an example with which to learn a new technique. Because no matter what profession or business or field we belong to, we have all shared the experience of using a library.

The problem here is that Martin and Forthright face each other across a reality gap, and neither of them can understand the other's behavior. This creates resistance and hostility on both sides and is entirely counterproductive.

Incidents like Scenario Twelve will cause Mary Forthright to demand that a change be made in the library regulations, to provide her with a written rule stating the upper limit of books that can be checked out at one time. Incidents like Scenario Twelve will cause John Martin to demand that a change be made in the library regulations to prevent librarians from interfering with the rights of patrons in such matters, and to insist that they *serve* the public as they are hired to do. Both demands for change will create even more resistance and hostility, and this loop, fed energetically from both sides, will grow. Soon, unless something is done to prevent it, there will be public meetings at which someone from the library will have to present its case while citizens of the town present theirs, and arguments will rage. On both sides, there will be people saying, "I don't think you understand our point of view," and they will be right.

In order for change to work — that is, for it to be met with cooperation rather than opposition, whether that opposition is open or hidden —

two conditions must be met. It must be introduced *slowly*, and the new elements must be tied to the old. Semantic modulation is a technique for achieving those conditions, using the linguistic device of the *metaphor* as a working tool.[1]

Metaphors — A Brief Review

For any common situation in daily life, people develop a set of specifications; often these are encoded as a metaphor. If the metaphor is named, or if enough of its elements are mentioned to bring it to mind, everyone involved will have a great deal of shared information that can serve as the context — the background — for communication *about* that situation thereafter.

For example, when someone says during a business negotiation that "the bases are loaded" or "we're at the top of the ninth," the metaphor of The Baseball Game is evoked; everyone present knows that and can supply missing details. When someone says, "It's time to circle up the wagons," the metaphor of The Old Western Frontier is brought in to serve as the context. The Reagan administration's frequent references to things happening on someone's "watch" brought up the metaphor of The Ship Of State.

It's not necessary for anyone to actually say, in so many words, "This is a baseball game" or "This is the ship of state." Just as "You don't really love me" is presupposed by "If you REALLY loved me . . .", the metaphor is presupposed by those of its parts appearing on the surface. Popular metaphors are in many ways like holograms — any recognized part will serve to carry the information of the whole.

In any negotiating situation, ask yourself the following two questions:

1. WHAT METAPHOR IS IN OPERATION HERE?
2. IS EVERYBODY OPERATING FROM WITHIN THE *SAME* METAPHOR?

These questions are related to the questions about what game is being played and who is playing it, but they are not the *same* questions. Metaphors are much less formal and their rules are far less specific than is true for games. This is why reformulating experience in terms of a good metaphor is so helpful — metaphors have a lot of *give*. They allow great flexibility, without the risk of major breakdown.

Librarian Mary Forthright's metaphor is: A LIBRARY IS A REPOSITORY. It is a repository — a storehouse — for knowledge, in the form of books placed in order on shelves and carefully indexed. Marketing executive John Martin's metaphor is: A LIBRARY IS A DISPENSARY. It is a dispensary — a fountain — of knowledge, in the form of books placed in order on shelves and carefully indexed. They have much shared meaning here, but it's not enough to prevent a confrontation. This tells us that there must be other semantic areas that are not shared, and that do not match.

John might have been able to gain a better understanding of the situation by applying Miller's Law — by asking himself the following question: "Suppose that what she says is true? Suppose it's true that people ought to take as few books as possible out of a library? What would that be true *of*?" If that was sufficient to allow for productive negotiation, it would be an excellent outcome. When you find yourself involved in a confrontation of this kind, always *begin* with the application of Miller's Law. But then, if the only answer you are able to come up with is "Darned if *I* know what it could be true of!", you can use semantic features composed of ordinary English words, backed up by reality statements when you need them, to work the problem out. I've done this for John and Mary in Figure Eleven.

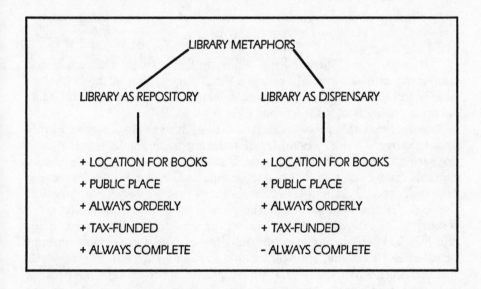

FIGURE 11. LIBRARY METAPHORS

Up to the feature [ALWAYS COMPLETE], the two metaphors match, but they break down at that point. Mary Forthright's image of a library is one in which every book is *there* at all times — the collection of books is always complete. She is of course aware that people are going to take some of the books away, but she feels threatened by this and tries to discourage the practice. In many ways this metaphor makes her a *good* librarian. She can be counted on to shelve books promptly, to put them in their proper place on the shelves, to mend them when they are damaged, to take action when they are not returned, and so on — all essential duties of the competent professional librarian. She will even encourage people to *use* the books, as long as they remain in the library — which will make her very helpful to researchers working there, to children who will sit at the library tables while they read, and to browsers. It is only when someone wants to take the books *away* that she begins to subvert the purpose of a public library.

It's extremely important to realize that PEOPLE ARE NOT USUALLY AWARE OF SUCH METAPHORS. This is not ordinarily *conscious* knowledge. But it's accessible if an effort is made to get at it. One good way to begin is with the three-part message pattern. Suppose that Mary Forthright and John Martin were asked to complete the following messages:

> When people check a lot of books out of the library at one time, I feel upset, because . . .

> When the librarian tries to keep me from checking as many books out of the library as I need, I feel upset, because . . .

It might take Mary a little while, but eventually she would add something on the order of "because the library is where the books are SUPPOSED TO BE." And John would eventually provide something like "because taking books *out* is what a library is FOR."

Sometimes this process of clarification, in itself, is enough to bring about change. That is, when Mary Forthright understands what is going on here she may well say, "I had no *idea* I was looking at the library as a collection of objects that had to be guarded every minute! I'm amazed at myself, and I'll do my best not to fall into that way of thinking again!" Especially if the negotiators of the change have been careful to point out to her the extensive areas of perfect agreement between her metaphor and John's. With encouragement and support, and a reasonable amount of patience all around, she will be able to follow through. She may still feel a twinge when she sees a library patron approaching the checkout desk with a half dozen books, but she will understand where the twinge is coming from and will disregard it.

Suppose, on the other hand, that the facility is not an ordinary public library but a location for a special collection of great rarity and value, for which the librarian rightly serves as a vigilant guard. Investigation of the metaphors involved might well bring John Martin to say, "I really wasn't aware that I was treating this place like a public library! I'm surprised at myself, and I'll do my best not to fall into that way of thinking again!" Thereafter, a polite but firm "Mr. Martin, this isn't a public library" should be sufficient to keep matters on an even keel.

When the change you want to bring about is not something as simple as the number of books that can be taken from a library — when it's a major reorganization of a large corporation, or a shift from one product line to another, or the hiring of women for positions traditionally reserved for men, or the introduction of a radically new curriculum at a college — the scale is different, but the process is the same. If you are the spokesperson for this change, if you must persuade others to accept and support the change, if you encounter resistance (or know that resistance is inevitable), you follow the same steps. You want information about the reality perceived by the resisters. It may be that the simple application of Miller's Law will give you the information you need; if it doesn't, use three-part messages to hunt for the metaphor mismatch causing the difficulty. Here are some examples.

> When you tell me we have to drop our course in Ancient Greek Literature to make room for a course on women writers, I feel angry, because . . .

> When you tell me that we are going to combine the Dawnthunder Line with the Nightlightning Line, I feel alarmed, because . . .

> When you tell me that none of the managers are going to have secretaries any longer, I feel distressed, because . . .

The "because" statements produced this way may fit the three-part message pattern very badly. They may not refer to concrete items that are directly observable and verifiable in the real world. That's all right. THE FUNCTION OF THESE MESSAGES IN SEMANTIC MODULATION IS NOT TO SERVE AS A PERFECT COMPLAINT, BUT TO PROVIDE INFORMATION AND CLUES TO MORE INFORMATION. However flawed the because-statement may be, listen to it carefully. If you're dealing with a number of resistant people, collect as many such statements as you can and consider *all* of them carefully. They are the foundation from which you will work.

You may be thinking that when you want to effect a change you don't have to go through all of this. You have the authority to *order* the change, and if people don't like it that's too bad — they have to do it anyway. That may be true in your particular case; you may have that sort of power. But people who go along with change unwillingly — as a result of coercion either mild or severe — are never going to give you good performance. They will do what they absolutely must, as badly and as slowly as they dare, and they will seize on any safe opportunity to sabotage your goals. If the necessary change is an emergency matter, you may have to settle for this initially. But you would be wise to begin a systematic attempt to persuade people to support the change voluntarily, the instant the acute crisis has been dealt with. CHANGES BROUGHT ABOUT BY FORCE WILL NEVER WORK

PROPERLY. They generally cause far more trouble than they are worth and often they have to be scrapped or reversed.

Suppose you come upon an animal that is trapped against a barbed wire fence. It doesn't know how to go back the way it came, and it doesn't know how to go forward over the fence. You have two choices, if you want to help. You can muster whatever force is necessary to lift or shove the animal over the fence. Or — more gently, and more usefully — you can cut the barbed wire so that the animal can move forward on its own, *learning* as it goes.

The *Gentle Art* system uses the second of these choices. It is not intended — as many therapies and self-help systems are — to *force* people over fences. It is intended to remove the obstacles in their paths that keep them from moving forward on their own. And semantic modulation is one of the most powerful and effective tools available for that purpose. It's not like surgery, it's like *hygiene* — without which surgery is closer to murder than to medicine.

Even when you and the other individual share the *same* metaphor, a semantic feature difference may turn out to be critical for solving problems. Perhaps you and a payroll clerk have a shared metaphor for the accounting structure in question, but the clerk keeps making it difficult for people to obtain their paychecks. Or you may share an inventory metaphor with a supply officer whose primary goal appears to be *preventing* the distribution of supplies.

It's unlikely that the clerk views the payroll as a collection of money that should not be disturbed, or that the supply officer views the supply inventory that way. Much of the time this phenomenon occurs because individuals have — almost always without realizing it — attached the feature [+ PERSONAL] to the money or supplies and have come to feel that it is their *own* property that others are trying to take away. Or, in a variation on this theme, someone has attached [+ PERSONAL], but not on his own behalf — rather, he views the materials as the personal property of his immediate superior and guards it fanatically on the superior's behalf. The procedure for dealing with the variation is the same.

You would begin the task of finding out if something of this kind is happening by simply *asking*. Do this in private, if that's possible; if not, be sure to do it discreetly, to avoid causing needless embarassment. In the case of the payroll clerk, you would say something like this:

> "Maybe I could help clarify what's going on here. Listen, please, and tell me if I'm stating your feelings accurately. 'WHEN PEOPLE COME TO PICK UP THEIR PAYCHECKS, I FEEL DISTRESSED, BECAUSE THEY'RE TAKING AWAY MONEY THAT BELONGS TO ME." (Or "THAT BELONGS TO THE COLONEL.")

Be careful to do this with neutral intonation, so that it does not sound mocking or sarcastic or negative in any other way. You are just asking for information — you are not making a judgment.

This may not work. Sometimes people are not sufficiently in touch with their feelings to be able to answer you truthfully. Or they may be afraid, or ashamed, to do so. Nevertheless, it is worth a try. It may cause them to think about what you have said, starting a process that will lead to an improvement eventually. If it does work, the information is very valuable. Because there is a big *difference* between a clerk who doesn't give out paychecks because he is incompetent or lazy or uncooperative, and a clerk who doesn't give out paychecks because she has lost track of the difference between her own money and the organization's money.

If the response is a puzzled, "Why in the world would I feel that way about the government's money?", that may or may not be reliable. WATCH THE INDIVIDUAL'S BODY LANGUAGE; LISTEN TO THE INTONATION OF THE VOICE. When people are aware that they are not telling the truth, their nonverbal communication will give them away. (See pages 229-249 on *lying*, for further details about what to watch for.)

Changing the Metaphor: A Case Study

Let's assume that you have gotten to the root of your problem. You have been able to determine from within what metaphor those who are resisting your change are functioning. Now what? Now you want to bring about a semantic modulation — a change in the semantic features that are responsible for the resistance. It will be easier if the resister's metaphor is the same as yours and all that needs to be changed is the plus or minus (or the ranking in pluses or minuses) for a single feature, as in the library example. If you are correct about the need for change, and if it does not involve something monumental such as a religious belief, you can proceed with confidence. In such cases, a thorough discussion of the matter will probably clear up the difficulty — unless that payroll clerk, discussion or no, is determined to convince everyone that the payroll really IS his or her personal money, in which case no amount of discussion is going to help.

When resistance to change is like that — when it is in fact unquestionably irrational — you approach the situation differently. The payroll clerk who looks you in the eye and says, "But it IS my money, and people keep trying to take it AWAY from me!" needs expert help; unless you are an appropriate expert, it's time to call one in. However — and not to be sneezed at — when your discussion evokes a statement like that, genuine progress has been made. Now at least the source of the problem is out in the open.

In music, when the goal is a harmonious change from one key to another, you can do it abruptly — *if* the two keys are close enough to one another in musical space to make the leap painless to the listening ear. If the distance between the two keys is large, however, you move from the first key to one nearby, and then judge the distance again; if it's still too great, you move to yet another one. Until, step by step, you are close enough to move to the key that is your final goal.

To change from one *metaphor* to another, use the same procedure. Consider the metaphor your resister is starting with — how far away is it from the metaphor you *want*? If the distance is large, don't try to make the change in a single leap. Instead, make several smaller moves in the proper direction. The metaphors in between the original one and the target are called *bridge* metaphors.

We can refer to the situation in which pointing out the source of the reality gap and discussing it are sufficient to motivate the change as "The Eureka Leap". When this happens, it's swift and efficient and a marvel to behold; it's the ideal outcome. For a reality gap of the size and scope experienced by John Martin and the librarian, it's a *probable* outcome. But the more complicated the change is, and the more people there are involved, the more unlikely The Eureka Leap becomes. Let's move on to discuss a situation where the Eurekas will be few and far between.

Suppose you're dealing with a group of six executives, each provided with a personal secretary (each in turn provided with a personal typewriter.) Let's assume that this arrangement, once satisfactory, has become downright quaint in the context of your business. Your goal is to change the arrangement so that in the end there will be six secretaryless executives, each provided with a personal computer. And there will be six secretaries, each with his or her own personal computer, functioning together as a combined clerical unit when needed, but also carrying out additional tasks that had to be sent elsewhere in the past.

This is not a small change — this is a revolution. You don't have six eager go-getting executives and six forward-looking secretaries, all chafing at the bit to be updated. You have people who are very comfortable as they are, thank you, who will have to be dragged kicking and screaming into the future if you don't do this very carefully. A gentle semantic modulation is recommended. We are going to take a look at the steps involved, with the various stages summarized for reasons of space.

1. You identify a suitable metaphor for the situation as it is now — the status quo. In our example case, that metaphor turns out to be THE ONE BIG HAPPY FAMILY.

2. You select a suitable metaphor for the situation that is your target — your eventual goal. For this example, it would be THE PROUD SPACESHIP CREW.

3. You compare the status quo metaphor with the target metaphor, to see how much semantic distance lies between the two. In this case, a happy family in its cozy home is one heck of a long way from a proud crew in a spaceship of *any* kind — and it's probable that for the business described, the employees will perceive it as a spaceship going where no one has gone before. Resistance is almost inevitable and will be severe; you need a bridge metaphor.

4. Now, if you have not already done so, you do a feature analysis of the two metaphors, using reality statements as a check on the process. You will find that the following feature inventories are the critical ones:

THE ONE BIG HAPPY FAMILY *THE PROUD SPACESHIP CREW*

[+ SMALL]   [+ SMALL]

[+ + CLOSE-KNIT]   [+ + CLOSE-KNIT]

[+ + TRADITIONAL]   [- - TRADITIONAL]

[+ + FOCUSED INWARD]   [- FOCUSED INWARD]

[- IN MOTION]   [+ + IN MOTION]

5. Now you need to select your bridge metaphor(s). You will compare the feature inventories for their similarities and differences, and then you will ask yourself: what else is there that shares these features and would be appropriate? What else needs a small close-knit group of human beings and could be described as [IN MOTION], but is not quite so untraditional as a spaceship? The answer is a *ship*. And that allows you to modulate through two stages of metaphorical change — THE WOODEN SAILING SHIP'S CREW, and THE ENGINE-POWERED SHIP'S CREW.

6. Prepare semantic feature inventories for your bridge metaphors and compare them with the other two. Like this:

THE WOODEN SAILING SHIP'S CREW: [+ SMALL], [+ CLOSE-KNIT], [+ TRADITIONAL], [+ FOCUSED INWARD], [+ IN MOTION].

CHANGE FROM STATUS QUO: One minus [IN MOTION] has been changed to a plus; all double pluses have been weakened to a single plus.

THE ENGINE-POWERED SHIP'S CREW: [+ SMALL], [+ CLOSE-KNIT], [- TRADITIONAL], [+ FOCUSED INWARD], [+ IN MOTION].

CHANGE FROM WOODEN SHIP: One more plus [TRADITIONAL] has been changed to minus.

7. Now compare the semantic feature inventory for the final bridge metaphor with the target. The change needed now is just making the minus on [TRADITIONAL] a double minus, the plus on [IN MOTION] a double plus, and reversing the value for a single feature, as [FOCUSED INWARD] goes from plus to minus. The resulting total change is still a large one, but it has been done gradually.

8. Prepare a campaign for introducing the series of metaphors to your people in meetings, talks, memoranda, or whatever is most suited to your situation.

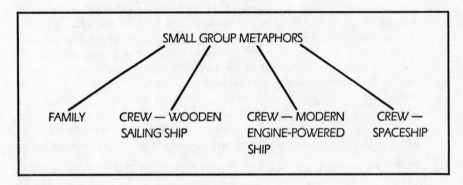

FIGURE 12. SMALL GROUP METAPHORS

Because presuppositions are so powerful, you can often set a metaphor in motion without actually stating it in so many words. In the "Wagons—*HO*!" example, it's because almost everyone can be counted on to associate that phrase with the wagon trains of the Old Western Frontier. At other times it's because of the presuppositions of certain words, even when they are not tied to a large and complex metaphor like the Old West. If you see Mr. Jones arrive and you say to the person next to you, "Guess who just slithered in the door," you don't have to say openly, "Mr. Jones is a snake." The grammar of English takes care of that for you, because only certain creatures can be said to slither and the snake is the default option.

A similar example of a metaphor with a twist appears in Tom Peters' and Robert Waterman's *In Search of Excellence*, where they quote James March explaining that his model assumes organizations should be *sailed* rather than driven. Notice how much work that simple sequence of language does. Notice how many things do *not* have to be explained in explicit detail as a result of using it! You can accomplish the same sort of superconductor semantics in your communication with your executives and secretaries by using that as a pattern and saying, "Now we've got to start *flying* this division, instead of sailing it!"

Two items must be pointed out here. First, in this situation the features specifying that the group is located on land, on the sea, in space, etc., appear to be irrelevant to the change and have not been listed in the analysis. It might well be that in another situation, using the same metaphors, they would have to be stressed.

Second — and much more important — there is one feature critical to the situation that you would certainly have discovered, but that you would deliberately leave out of your metaphor as you proposed the change: a feature we could summarize as plus or minus [WITH HUMAN SERVANTS].

The primary reason executives resist having their private secretaries taken away has nothing to do with efficiency or productivity. It has to do with *convenience*. Traditionally such secretaries have not only done the necessary clerical work but have provided many personal services such as going to the bank, shopping for gifts (and exchanging or returning them), addressing Christmas cards by hand, making coffee, and so on. These are services appropriate for servants, and people who have been enjoying them are predictably reluctant to do without them. However, pointing this out is almost certainly going to cause defensive reactions from both groups. The secretaries will not like being portrayed as domestic help any more than the executives will like being portrayed as masters and mistresses. You may eventually have no choice but to Level and bring this out into the open, but you would not *start* that way. Your people are aware of the circumstances, at some level; rubbing their noses in it may not be necessary. You can always bring it in at a later date.

To make a change of this scope work, you need to provide the necessary *physical* support every inch of the way. There must be people "on board" to ease the mastering of the new equipment. The equipment and the software must be well chosen and properly installed. And there must be tolerance for transition pains. The fewer resources you have available for providing such support, the more skilled you must be at providing *linguistic* support. (Of the "We're all in this together, here on the frontier" variety.)

The best plan, in the sense of removing barriers and letting people move forward uncoerced, is this one:

1. Give the secretaries their computers — without moving them anywhere or changing their status — and give the executives modems.
2. Pause, while everyone adjusts to this stage and learns to use the new equipment and be comfortable with it.
3. Give the executives their own computers.
4. Pause again until the dust settles, repeating Step 2.
5. Now move the secretaries.

In preparing the materials you will use to lay the ground for all this, you first match the existing reality at each stage, and then you make the shifts, one at a time. If your choice were to make brief talks in small meetings, with just you and the secretaries and executives present, you could use the summaries below as springboards.

FIRST STAGE

"Our division is a FAMILY. We matter to one another — and that matters to *me*. But a family has a tendency to stay home, a tendency not to go anywhere, and we have reached a point where we must MOVE ON. It's time to begin thinking of ourselves as the crew of a proud ship, with a brisk wind filling our sails. . .

SECOND STAGE

"There was a time when a small wooden sailing vessel was the best this division could manage — and we were loyal to her, and happy to be aboard. But our voyage has been a *successful* one. And now we can all climb down the ladders and move to a NEW ship — a sleek, modern vessel, with powerful engines. On such a ship, the old sails, on which we once depended, are no longer useful. . .

THIRD STAGE

"We've gone through many storms together, seen many bright dawns after they were over, and have survived — and it's been great. But now it's time to move out to the STARS! And we can't do that from a ship that is tied to water, no matter how modern she may be. Now we need something new — now it's time for us to leave the sleek ship that has served us so well, and go on board a *new* ship — a *space*ship — time to turn our eyes to the promise of the future. . ."

And there you are, safely installed.

Is this "corny"? Certainly. Is that a problem? Absolutely not! When people face changes that they perceive as threatening, they are completely uninterested in novelty and elegance. Ronald Reagan steadily maintained — with overwhelming success — a flood of corny images and symbols and metaphors. Every element of change he proposed was carefully presented as a metaphor for the eyes and for the ears. And those metaphors were chosen from the most comforting and familiar set available to our culture. The Old Western Frontier. The Proud Ship Sailing. Main Street. The Loving Family Gathered Round The Hearth. Reagan has been the beloved Norman Rockwell of politics; he earned the title of "Great Communicator" by being corny. Corny — hokey, even — is precisely what you need to introduce major change.

How to Find a Metaphor

No one argues about the usefulness of metaphors. But it's often hard to think of one when you need it, because we don't store information in our memories in a way that provides us with a handy Metaphor Directory. The following steps will help you in any metaphor search:

1. Write down the semantic features that you know your metaphor must have.
2. Answer the question: WHAT HAS THOSE SEMANTIC FEATURES?

3. Choose the best answer — the closest and most appropriate fit — for your metaphor.

4. Double-check the result for undesirable consequences. For example: "The Vice President is the spare tire of government" might seem like a good metaphor at first. Vice Presidents, like spare tires, can be said to have the features [+ READY IN EMERGENCIES], [+ NECESSARY IN EMERGEN-CIES], [+ IN PERFECT REPAIR], [+ USEFUL], etc. But when you check the metaphor carefully you will find it contaminated — because "spare tire" has already been used as a very familiar metaphor for a roll of superfluous fat around the human middle. You would therefore discard it, and try again.[2]

Another useful technique for finding metaphors is to remember that every metaphor is the starting point for a story and to use that knowledge systematically and creatively. In the same way that you can work back and forth between semantic features and reality statements — using one as a sort of jump-start device for the other — you can work back and forth between metaphors and stories, letting one generate the other.

This process is more easily demonstrated than explained. Let's look at an example (based on a story from Ronald Reagan's inventory) to see how it can be mined for linguistic gold.

Once there was a little boy who went into a room and found a big pile of horse manure on the floor — whereupon he cried out excitedly, "I just *know* there's a *pony* in there somewhere!"

You could word the possible metaphors in a lot of different ways, some of them boring ("Every obstacle is a potential blessing") and some of them too indelicate to be stated here. The four items that can worked into your metaphors are obvious and easy: The Optimistic Little Boy. The Pile Of Manure. The Room. The Pony. Once the story has been told, those metaphors are available to you — you can say all of the following sentences to your audience and be confident that they will understand your meaning:

1. "Well, our widget has turned out to be a pony after all!"
2. "All right, everybody — let's buckle down and find the pony!"
3. "Some of us are Pony Finders — and some of us aren't."
4. "If there's a pony in this room, my friends, I can't find it . . . and heaven knows, I've tried."
   (And so on.)

You can also play a game of substitution. using names that are appropriate to your situation. Like this . . .

1. "Faced with a pile of manure, Reagan would look for the pony. He was a Pony Finder."
2. "Faced with a pile of manure, ... would pave it over. He was a Manure Paver."
3. "Faced with a pile of manure, ... would pretend it wasn't there. He was a . . . ."

(And so on.)

When you come across a suitably brief and powerful story like the Pony Finder Story, take a good look at it, and ask yourself, "Is there a metaphor in there that I might be able to use?" And when a solid metaphor occurs to you, ask yourself, "Can I turn that into a story?" Then work both ways. I know no more effective technique for building a successful "culture" for your group than this one.

TALKING AND WRITING DOWN CHANGE: "WHAT WOULD HAVE TO HAPPEN?"

Often, when I am called in because people feel that they are completely *stuck* in their efforts to solve a problem, the reason for the stall turns out to be a linguistic one. Usually the question being asked is "How can we X?" Usually the answer being given is either "We can't" or "Nobody knows"; and usually the barrier is in the way that X has been worded. To get around this kind of barrier, I use the question "What would have to happen before X could happen?"

For example: at one large hospital I found everyone devoting much time and energy to the question, "How can we have more nurses on duty?" I asked, "What would have to happen before you could have more nurses?" and was told, "We'd have to have more money to pay them with, and there just *isn't* any more money!" I asked again. "Okay, what would have to happen before you could have more money, since there isn't any more to be had?" And I was told, "Somebody else would have to give *up* some money." At which point everyone said, "Oh!", and came *unstuck*. Before the ultimate goal of putting more nurses on the floors could even begin to be achieved, they had a subgoal to get out of the way — they had to decide who it was possible to approach about giving *up* some money.

This seems trivially obvious after the fact — always. But once a a project — like increasing the number of nurses on duty — has been written down and discussed at half a dozen meetings, the language used to talk about it and write about it takes on a life of its own. It begins to look like the only possible language for the purpose. If it is the *wrong* language, you will get stuck — and there will either be no change, or a change that is the *wrong* change. Always, when progress seems impossible, stop and ask yourself: AM I ASKING THE RIGHT QUESTIONS? Because without the right questions you cannot possibly get the right answers.

Get a sheet of paper and write down your ultimate goal, no matter how improbable it seems. And then begin asking the question, like this:

YOUR ULTIMATE GOAL — *X-1*

"Before we can have *X-1*, what would have to happen?"

If three things would have to happen, write them down and number them: *X-2, X-3,* and *X-4.* And ask the question again, for each one. "Before we can have *X-3,* what would have to happen?" There'll be some overlap; you'll find that Subgoal *X-17* is what's holding up *X-5, X-9,* and *X-11,* for example. And eventually you will reach the subgoal that is the real bottleneck — the end of the string that, when found and pulled, makes the entire knot untangle.

If you have trouble as you go along, keep asking the following critical questions:

1. "Who will suffer from *cognitive dissonance* if this goal is proposed?"
2. "What reality statements are threatened by this goal?"
3. "What metaphors are threatened by this goal?"
4. "Who will face real world *losses* if this goal is achieved, and what *are* those losses?"

The more different ways you can find to reformulate your goal — the more different ways you can devise to put the problem into words — the more likely you are to work out a plan that will actually lead to a solution.

NOTES

1. The term "modulation," like the term "syntonic," is originally from music theory. In music, modulation is a method for changing smoothly and harmoniously from one key to another.
2. This metaphor appears as an example in Douglas Hofstadter's fine book, *Goëdel, Escher, Bach: An Eternal Golden Braid* (Random House 1980.)

Workout — Chapter 9

1. For an entire article presenting one careful and detailed metaphor after another, read "The Americans: Why We Baffle the Europeans," by Luigi

Barzini, in *Harper's* for December 1981, pages 29-36 and 84-86. Barzini fills in the blank, over and over, in "America is . . . ." and "The U.S. is . . . ." Very useful for stepping outside the American forest and getting a look at the American trees as others see them.

2. Here's a batch of metaphors that don't work; find the problem(s) in each one. Can you fix them? Try converting them to stories.

   a. "The Liberals are eviscerating that legislation the way a butcher plucks a chicken. By the time it is passed, there will be nothing left but the feathers." (Brian Mulroney, quoted in "Talking Tory," by Mark Abbey, in *Canadian Forum* for March 1984; page 9.)

   b. "The economy is much like a huge thundercloud, which from the air looks like a large, stable, at times beautiful white mass, but which on the inside contains very large up drafts and down drafts." (David Birch, quoted in "The Entrepreneurial Numbers Game," by Jay Finegan, in *Inc.* for May 1986; page 36.)

   c. "They kept this thing so close to the vest it was strangled in its crib." (Senator Orrin Hatch, quoted in "On the Hill: Curtain Call," by Henry Fairlie, in *The New Republic* for September 7, 1987; page 17.)

   d. " . . . portfolio manager Laura Luckyn-Malone of Japan Fund thinks the Japanese market can be beaten; she flourishes in its racetrack environment. Her strategy is to spot major economic trends and get aboard the best-looking stocks in the industries likely to benefit most." (In "Leave it to the Locals," by Richard Phalon, in *Forbes* for September 5, 1988; page 163.)

   e. "What counts in the slaughterhouses is having blood on the floor." (Kenneth Monfort of ConAgra's Red Meat Group, quoted in "Calling All Hogs," by Phyllis Berman and Dana Wechsler, in *Forbes* for September 5, 1988, page 48. Berman and Wechsler tell us that a modern slaughterhouse is "a capital intensive factory that works on a low margin and, like any factory, requires a steady stream of material moving through it." Presumably this is what Monfort was trying to explain.)

3. "Ronald Reagan is two of America's favorite characters, the nice boy next door and the lovable, opinionated uncle . . . " (*Time Magazine* for May 6, 1985, page 31; from "The Enigmatic President," by Hedley Donovan.) How does this triple metaphor work? Can you use it as a pattern and construct another one like it? Does it mean that The Nice Boy Next Door *is* The Lovable, Opinionated Uncle?

4. If you use one metaphor in two very different stories, the result can be astonishing. Here's an example for your analysis. "Mushrooms are grown in cool, dark caves in a rich nitrogenous soil and, when they grow to size, are harvested. Similarly, officials can keep the potential dissident in the dark, embed him in manure, and as soon as he sticks his head up, cut it off." (From "Canning Directions," an article by David W. Ewing about ways to fire federal employees, in *Harper's* for August 1979; page 22. Fill in the blanks:

"The goal of the mushroom farmer with regard to crops is ...."

"The goal of the federal official with regard to troublesome employees is ....."

5. Sometimes a very large metaphor can be packed into a very small space. For example, the "Washington Diarist" column in *The New Republic* for January 25, 1988, page 43, had a sentence saying that — compared to Washington journalists — New York journalists are "running at 78 rpm to our 45." Expand that — what does it mean?

6. *Advertising Age* for February 22, 1988, gave one of its "Global Gallery" spaces for "creative advertising around the world" to a British ad for Perrier water. The ad shows a stream of Perrier being poured into a glass from a bottle — and just one word: "Rainbeau." Is this a metaphor? A multiple metaphor? Can you explain it? We wouldn't accept the word "piedball" (French "foot" plus English "ball"); what makes "rainbeau" acceptable?

7. Here's Charles Krauthammer discussing the power of metaphor: "Some years ago in a moment of near whimsey, America's most intelligent liberal, Rep. Barney Frank of Massachusetts, proposed the abolition of all political metaphors. Would we have gotten mired in Korea, he wondered, if we had not been convinced it was 'a dagger pointed at the heart of Japan'? How might history have been different if Korea had the shape of a plum?" ("What Are We Hiding Under the Bandages of Metaphor?" in the *Los Angeles Times* for May 18, 1986.) Can you answer the congressman's question? Is it a silly question? Would it be *possible* to eliminate all political metaphors? If so, would it be desirable?

SIGHT BITES

1. "Come November, Carol will boast a new darker, more stylish cut, a new collar and shoulders to boot. The transition will be gradual, said Joe Fenton, Carol Wright director of marketing, with three different interim portraits so consumers won't be shocked."

   (From a brief report on page 8 of the August 15, 1988 *Advertising Age*, about a plan to update Donelley Marketing's person-icon, "Carol Wright." (Like Betty Crocker.))

2. Aristotle considered metaphor a sign of genius, believing that the individual who could make unusual connections was a person of special gifts. From that ancient tradition has emerged a working definition of metaphor: the capacity to perceive a resemblance between elements from two separate domains or areas of experience and to link them together in linguistic form."

   (From "The Child is Father to the Metaphor," by Howard Gardner and Ellen Winner, in *Psychology Today* for May 1979; page 85.)

3. "The specific skills required of top dogs these days leave little room for the cur to come out."

(From "Facing Up to Executive Anger," by Walter Kiechel III, in *Fortune* for November 16, 1981; page 205.)

4. "It is their speech that renders politicians implausible, not their actions. . . . They become characters in the soap opera of the television news, their slogans and phrases worn so smooth by repeated use that they resemble ancient coins to which nobody can assign either a value or a city of origin."

(From "Political Discourse," by Lewis H. Lapham, in *Harper's* for August 1980; page 9. Notice that Lapham changes metaphors in midstream; does this work?)

5. "Most of our lives are as soft as souffles. It is hard for the hale to realize that even the strongest body is a twig easily broken by the sharp edges of life."

(From "The Technology That Cares," by George F. Will, in *Newsweek* for November 8. 1982; page 112.)

6. "For Dillard . . . language is the house we build to keep out the cosmic weather."

(A comment on Annie Dillard by Verlyn Klinkenborg, in "Nature Calls," *Village Voice* for September 15, 1987.)

7. "There is no such thing as a pure emotion uncontaminated and undefined by its context; if there were, it would be like an egg without a shell, a gooey mess. Yet empty rules without passion to energize them are, like shells without eggs, fragile and hollow."

(From "Two Acts," by Carol Tavris, in *Harper's* for January 1983; page 73.)

8. "What is 'framing a problem,' and why is it so important? Framing a problem involves selecting the context in which the problem is likely to be solved. . . . This representation has been called the problem space or sometimes the decision frame. One useful working definition of 'problem space' is 'the subject's representation of the task environment that permits the consideration of different problem situations and sets limitations on possible operations that can be applied to a given problem.' Identifying the correct problem space is not always obvious and simple, but it is a critically important beginning."

(From "The Critical Role of Context in the Diagnostic Process," by Jerome P. Karrirer and Richard L. Kopelman, in *Hospital Practice* for August 15,1987; page 75.)

9. "If a city exports more conventioneers than it imports, it develops a convention-spending deficit. Easier than building a convention center, and more immediately profitable, would be to forbid local residents to attend conventions in other cities."

(From "Meet Me In St. Louis," by David Owen, in *Harper's* for September 1983; page 13.)

"He talked about 'corporate Kitty Litter problems' . . . where everything looks okay on the surface, 'but don't dig around.' "

(Same article; Owen is quoting from a speech by John D. "Jack" Jackson, on page 11.)

10

Language and the Personal Domain

SCENARIO THIRTEEN   **J**ack Harrington was thoroughly disgusted, and deeply discouraged; that was more than obvious. They'd gone over the figures three times now, trying to explain why they were so high, but he wasn't buying it.

"There's no excuse for this," he said sadly, staring at the spreadsheets the way he would have stared at a bleeding wound. It's just not acceptable. You're not really TRYing, or you wouldn't be bringing me figures like this."

"Jack," Tony said, "we *are* trying. We're worrying our tails off trying to keep these totals down."

"Talk's cheap, Tony," Jack scoffed. "You can't expect me to believe that THIS is the best you can—"

"Jack, you *always* do this! Any time you don't like what you hear, any time you've got your dung-colored glasses on, you say we're not *try*ing."

"Right!" Tracy agreed. "And it's ridiculous. Of *course* we're trying. Why wouldn't we be trying? We work here, *too*, Jack! The problem isn't that we're goofing off, my friend, it's that you're not seeing *anything* clearly."

"That's not—"

"Jack, it *is* true. And we're fed up. We know it's because of your problems at home, and we try to make allowances, but it's getting to be a real drag. You have GOT to quit bringing your personal problems to the office with you and taking them out on *us*."

Jack's face was grim, and a muscle in his cheek had begun to twitch. "Just leave my personal life *out* of this!" he said. "I'm doing my job; you do yours. My personal life has got *zero* to do with the fact that you two can't keep expenses in line."

Tony sighed. "Okay, Jack," he said. "Sorry — we won't say anything more about it. It's a waste of time, anyway. Now let's try one more time to agree on this budget. We've got other work to do. One more *time*, troops — *from the* top!"

By the time Jack got home his head was pounding, and he recognized the sour taste in his mouth as the introduction of another bout of heartburn. He tried to smile at Nora as he walked out onto the patio — until he saw the look on her face. It was a look he knew well; the last time he'd seen it, it had meant shelling out $750 for a new transmission in the station wagon.

It was just too much. He had put up with garbage all day long at Metamega, nobody would listen to him when he tried to talk to them, the drive home had been bumper to bumper at twenty miles an hour all the way, and he could not face any more incompetence in one day.

"DAMN it, Nora!" he said, "NOW what's the matter? And how much is it going to COST me?"

Nora looked startled, and then she sighed. "Jack," she said slowly, "you're imagining things. Everything's *fine* except that you've obviously had another horrible day, and I'm sorry about that. But you've got to quit bringing your problems home from the office and taking them out on *me*."

Poor Jack Harrington, with the burdens of the world on his shoulders and nobody ever letting him talk. Poor Tony and Tracy. Poor Nora. We have a linguistic waste dump here, fermenting away, percolating in the emotional heat, getting nastier and nastier all the time. And very familiar — we all know this scenario. However, the situation is far from hopeless. What's needed is the recognition that you can't clean up a linguistic mess with money or gadgets . . . you have to clean it up the same way it was created — with LANGUAGE.

The Tangled Loop

Let me begin by stating one hard fact: There *isn't* any way to keep your personal life and your professional life separate. It's not possible. If your personal life is a mess, you'll take that mess to the office with you. If your professional life is a mess, you'll take that mess home. Either way, one tangled loop will feed the other, and eventually — inevitably — both aspects of your life will be damaged and you will lose control over both of the language/power domains involved. YOU CAN'T AFFORD THIS. It will affect your performance in seriously negative ways. Being in control of your language environment must, therefore, include control of your *personal* language environment.

People tell me they're different — that they *can* keep these two parts of their lives totally separate. They say things like this:

> "When I walk through my front door at home, it makes no difference *how* bad things are at work — I turn it off! I don't believe in bringing my professional problems home with me."

> "Wherever I am, whatever I'm doing, I give it my complete attention. That goes for work, family, sports, whatever. I just put everything else in a box, with a tight lid on it."

> "When I walk through the doors at the courthouse, I'm *there* — one hundred percent! My family and the problems I have at home just go on hold — they don't exist until I'm home again."

What these people mean is that they have sufficient self-discipline, sufficient iron control, to sort their WORDS into tight compartments. When they're talking to their spouses about the bills, they don't bring up the struggle they're having with the Henderson case; when they're working on the Henderson case they don't say anything about the struggles they're having with their teenage sons. They pride themselves on this system of self-censorship, and they will insist that it works.

They're wrong — very wrong — in two important ways. First: It doesn't work, because no matter how carefully you choose your words your body language will always betray you. People will *know* that something is wrong and that you're keeping a tight lid on it, even if they can't identify the problem in specific terms. Second: It doesn't work, because it creates intolerable tension and stress, which is a sure and certain road to self-destruction. We're talking asthma and heart attacks and migraine and ulcers and depression and fatigue and burnout and *misery* here!

Don't delude yourself; you are no exception to this rule. It's no accident that men, who until recently had almost the total lock on this practice, are the ones who die first. It's no accident that women professionals are beginning to demonstrate the same patterns as they move into roles formerly reserved for males. But you do *not* have to shrug your shoulders, say, "That's life — that's just the way it *is*," and head on down the road to your early heart attack. There is, fortunately, a better way. Stay with me, please.

There's another group of people who use their personal life as a *dump* for all the problems of their professional life. The moment they go through their front doors they begin a detailed recital of every difficulty — or triumph — they've encountered during their working day, and this continues through the evening meal and right on till bedtime. It makes no difference whether you run into them on the golf course on a Saturday morning or meet them at a restaurant for Sunday dinner, the only topic of conversation they *possess* is their work. No matter what subject you bring up, they say, "That reminds me . . . " and they talk about their work. If you were floating down a river with them on a raft in a hurricane, they'd tell you it reminded them of something at work.

The opposite pattern — the one in which the problems of the home are dropped at the office or clinic or salesroom — is less common, but it exists. When it occurs, it means that for every conversation in the workplace, if it's possible to drag in the individual's personal life it *will* be dragged in. And even in the most sensitive negotiations, it means that you can count on a peppering of remarks such as "You sound just like my wife/husband/kid/mother-in-law/Uncle Arlie!"

None of these patterns, and none of their multitude of combinations, is healthy. They are DYSFUNCTIONAL COMMUNICATION, and they will get you in the end. If they don't destroy both your marriage and your career as well, you can attribute that to blind luck.

What you need is BALANCE. You cannot carry everything that happens in your life — good or bad — on your own shoulders; you have to have a support system of other human beings with whom you can share both your problems and your joys. On the other hand, you cannot treat other people as if they were public utilities — animated dumpsters for the deposit of your semantic waste. Let's talk about how that balance can be achieved.

What's In It for You

The world is full of injustices. One of the most bitter is the fact that what you really *are* does not determine how people behave toward you — that is determined by how they *perceive* you. It shouldn't be that way. In a just world, if you were a good person you would be rewarded with the approval of everyone around you. In this real world that is the only one we have to work with, it's not like that.

You may be a paragon of virtue, with the most admirable of records; it makes no difference. If people perceive you as a turkey — of any variety — they'll treat you like one. And you will tend to react to such treatment by feeding that perception.

Clients come to me and say, "Everybody I have to deal with is *weird.* You can't *talk* to these people! You can't get *along* with them. They don't know how to carry on a conversation, they can't follow instructions properly, they can't take criticism, and they blow up over every little thing. It's driving me *nuts!*" They want me to help them find ways to communicate with the strange people who work for them or with them, as well as the strange people who make up their family and their circle of friends, and I do my best. I teach them the *Gentle Art* system and encourage them to put it to use in their lives. And over and over again, after a few months have gone by, the same fascinating thing happens: THEY CALL ME UP AND TELL ME THAT IT'S AMAZING HOW MUCH ALL THOSE OTHER PEOPLE HAVE IMPROVED.

This isn't mysterious, of course. Toxic language is contagious; people pass it along the way they do viruses and bacteria. John arrives at work in a bad mood and he snaps at Mary; Mary, who has done nothing to deserve that, snaps back — which convinces John he had something to be cross about in the first place. The next person Mary meets gets snapped at, too, because she's bristling over John's unprovoked badmouthing. The sequence then repeats itself. The whole group passes the hostility around all day, with everyone growing more and more frustrated. And they all go home and tell their families that the people they work with are *weird*.

Most people understand this, and will agree that yes, this is what happens, and yes, it's ridiculous, and yes, somebody should break the hostility chain. "But," they ask me, "why should it be *me*? *I* didn't start it!"

I'll *tell* you why it should be you. Forget about being noble and saintly and altruistic. That's not required, and I'm not about to ask it of you. It should be you for the most self-centered of reasons: because your physical and emotional health *depends* on it.

Remember the studies claiming that people with Type A behavior — hardworking, hard-driving, ambitious, competitive people — are twice as likely to have heart attacks? Those studies have been clarified recently, and we now know that the critical factor is not Type A behavior *per se* but Type A behavior *plus exposure to hostility*. You can be as hard-driving and ambitious and competitive as you like, with no more risk of heart disease than the most placid and unambitious person you know — provided you are not involved in hostile interactions. But the *combination* of Type A behavior and hostility is a killer.

Then there's the fact that for both Type A people and other people with high blood pressure, significant evidence exists that the more time you spend saying "I" and "me" and "my," the more you are at risk for coronary catastrophe.

Finally, we can throw in the tight link that is known to exist between depression and heart disease — if you're miserable, you're in danger. Especially if you spend a lot of your time complaining about your problems. *Psychology Today*'s "Minding Your Health" column for September 1988 summed it all up very nicely; here are the relevant brief quotations.

> "Harried and hostile people, the classic Type A's, may not always be heart patients in the making. The real danger may arise only among those who frequently face situations with a lot of interpersonal conflict. . ."

> "Researchers have found that self-involved people, whose favorite topic of conversation is themselves, tend to get more than their share of heart problems. . ."

"Depression turned out to be a better predictor of future heart problems than a number of other coronary risk factors, such as the severity of artery damage, high cholesterol levels and cigarette smoking."

Stress is a hazard to your health — no question about it. And those who are most gravely endangered by stress are people involved in *dysfunctional language behavior,* both their own and that of the people around them.

You think you thrive on stress and do your best work in the linguistic equivalent of a combat zone? And you never feel so much as a twinge? According to the *New England Journal of Medicine* for April 21, 1988, most "ischemic events" produce no symptoms. That is: the fact that you aren't having any chest pain tells you little or nothing about your heart's reaction to stress. And even conditions that are unmistakably painful won't announce themselves until they're significantly far along in their development. IT IS THEREFORE WELL WORTH IT TO YOU, AS A MATTER OF YOUR OWN PERSONAL SELF-INTEREST, TO CLEAN UP YOUR LANGUAGE ENVIRONMENT AND GET THE LINGUISTIC TOXINS *OUT* OF IT. This is more important than *anything* else you can do in the way of preventive health care.

The Perfect Conversation

If you spend as much time listening to people with communication problems as I do, you quickly notice that there are five things they all say, even when their individual situations are very different. Here's the list:

- □ "Nobody listens to me when I talk."
- □ "Nobody wants to talk to me."
- □ "I don't have anybody to talk to."
- □ "Nobody pays any attention to anything I say."
- □ "Nobody pays any attention to me."

These statements turn up in differing Satir Modes, with varying intonations and body language, and in many different communication styles. Some people say them almost immediately; others spend hours intellectualizing — telling you that the problem is their weight, or their income, or their education and background, or the field they're in, or the national economy, or Other People — before finally saying those five dreary sentences. Some of these people are verbal victims; some are verbal abusers; some are merely bystanders. Some are powerful and dominating people, with high rank and status; others are the complete opposite. But all of them, without exception, say those same five things.

A careful look at the five complaints will tell you that they are really a single complaint: IN MY LIFE, these people are saying, LANGUAGE DOESN'T WORK RIGHT. The question is: Why should that be so and what can be done about it?

The pattern for the hypothetical ideal language interaction for speakers of American English, the kind of conversation and communication that people are looking for and complaining that they never get, is set out below. Assume that the speakers are Edith, Barry, and Lou, and that Lou speaks first. The conversation (we'll use that word as a cover term) should go like this:

1. Lou chooses himself as first speaker and introduces a topic, talking about it for two or three sentences.

2. Lou chooses Edith as second speaker and lets her know his choice by providing a clear set of cues.

3. Edith accepts the turn and develops Lou's topic further, with one to three sentences.

4. Edith chooses Barry as next speaker and provides the necessary cues for transfer of the turn.

5. Barry accepts the turn and continues the development of Lou's topic, with one to three sentences.

6. Barry chooses Lou as next speaker, providing the necessary cues for transfer of the turn.

7. This continues until either the topic or the time available have been exhausted, with a roughly equal number of turns to speak and duration of turns going to each speaker. At all times, those who are not speaking are listening.

8. Someone chooses himself or herself to be final speaker and concludes Lou's topic, at which point either the conversation is over or a new topic is introduced.

Three elements go into this hypothetical perfect exchange: topics, turns, and listening.

TOPICS

The speaker who starts a conversation gets to introduce the topic. When the topic succeeds, the speaker is listened to and a conversation happens. When it fails, the results are expressed as "nobody ever listens to me" and "nobody wants to talk to me." If you have enough power over the people you are talking to, they may have to sit there and *hear* you talk — but you can't compel them to listen. They may have no choice but to say things like "Really" and "How interesting" when you pause and wait for a response — but you can't compel them to actually *talk* to you. Let's assume that you have everything else (voice quality and body language and personal distance, for example) under control. How do you make your topics succeed? What can you do that will make people pleased to have you as a linguistic partner?

If you don't find other people willing to listen to you, your topics probably aren't well chosen. Here are the steps you follow to find out what's wrong:

1. For one week, to the extent that your situation allows, make a note of every topic you introduce — just two or three words that will let you identify it later. AND DON'T CHEAT. If your topic was "the dog threw up," writing down "veterinary illnesses" is cheating.

2. At the end of the week, get out all your notes and make a master list. If the same topic comes up more than once, put it down and write the total beside it.

3. Examine the list and ask yourself: if someone else were talking to *me* about these topics, would I want to listen? If not, why not?

It's often a shock to read your list. People who have serious problems with topics rarely are aware of how bad the problem is. The most common "topic disorders" produce master lists like these:

The All-One-Topic List of Topics.

> my wisdom teeth (3)
> Harry's headaches (2)
> Bill's appendicitis (5)
> the baby's colic (14)
> my headaches (22)
> the prescription the doctor gave me (2)
> Mother's heart condition (18)
> the dog's mange (7)
> the cost of health insurance (20)
> . . .

The No-Topic List of Topics.

> we're out of orange juice (5)
> the weather's nice today (25)
> we're out of computer paper (4)
> the weather's nice again (11)
> they say it's going to be windy (2)
> glad to see somebody got some orange juice (2)
> the weather's not as nice today (14)
> . . .

The All-Taboo List of Topics.

bowel movements (2)

what happened when the dog threw up (2)

what I promised Tom I'd never tell anybody (3)

what's wrong with your religion (10)

what's wrong with your sex life (10)

how to do an autopsy (3)

my colon cancer operation (9)

what's wrong with your children (15)

. . .

In the first case — the All-One-Topic list — the speaker will protest that the list includes many different people and animals and situations. But a close look shows that *everything* introduced is on the single topic of ILLNESS. When you have a reputation for having only one topic like this, people will quickly stop listening to you and will try to avoid you — even if they were genuinely interested the first two or three times you talked with them. The worst choice for a single topic is yourself; people simply are not that interested in hearing about you personally. We have a special profession in our society, called therapy, in which people are paid very large sums just to listen to you talk about yourself — this alone will tell you that it's WORK. Next on the Awful Meter is some other person, exclusively, as when you talk only about your spouse or your boss or a parent.

The No-Topic list tends to come from people who are knocking themselves out to be polite, to avoid offending others or distressing them, and to stay out of arguments. The problem is that their topics can't be supported. When you tell someone that all the orange juice is gone, or that the weather's nice, there's nothing much to say back. People will try, if they're polite, and the result will be a dialogue like this one:

X: "There isn't any orange juice."

Y: "I know. It's all gone."

X: "I noticed it when I came in. There was some there yesterday."

Y: "Right. There was a little bit left."

X: "But not today."

Y: "No . . . it's all gone."

X: "There ought to be some orange juice."

Y: "I know."

If this is the sort of conversational company you offer, people will flee at the sight of you.

Finally, there is the All-Taboo list. The items on this list are interesting and varied, to be sure. But the only people who are going to join you for a topic list like this are people who have the *same* list, and their primary goal is likely to be telling you what's wrong with *your* religion and children and so on, or discussing *their* most gruesome brush with major surgery. You will still come out of it frustrated. Other people may listen to you with fascination once or twice. But it won't last, because talking to you makes them think about things they would much rather not think about, and that gets old in a hurry.

If you find that your list for the week is one of these, there are two things you can do. You can make yourself a topic list in advance, every week, with *acceptable* topics on it that have been carefully planned. If you have trouble doing this spontaneously, use someone else's list — the table of contents for that week's issue of *Time* or *Newsweek* will do nicely, and will contain material you can read to prepare yourself. You will feel phony doing this, and very awkward. Chances are good that you will *sound* phony and awkward, at first. But that will wear off, as people take up your topics and actually talk about them with you, introducing new material that was not in the magazine. The time will come when interesting and suitable topics will begin occurring to you without prompting, and then you can discard the props. Just be careful that being well-informed on the topics in advance doesn't cause you to deliver *monologues* instead of conversation.

Alternatively, if you're not willing to do this, you can devote yourself to supporting topics introduced by others. This is always welcome. People will be *eager* to talk to you. All you have to do is make sure that you never choose yourself as first speaker, and that you pay attention to those who *do* offer topics so that you will know what the topics are and be able to contribute a few sentences about them.

TURNS

There have been human societies in which people could demonstrate how powerful they were by going out and lopping off others' heads or having them lopped off by staffers. This caused great physical pain in the victim and was unacceptably permanent; in America today, conspicuous decapitation is not allowed. But we have a contemporary equivalent: the demonstration of one's power by monopolizing the conversational space (which — although it takes up *time* — we call "the floor.") This causes pain in the victims also, and when chronic it may cause permanent damage. Unlike decapitation, it is never *brief*.

In the Perfect Conversation framework on page 210, no one speaks for longer than a few sentences. In the real world, people who are anxious to display their power will do everything they can to hold the floor interminably, while listeners fume in helpless irritation. If a group has the misfortune to include two such chest-thumpers (or their Placating equivalents) they will struggle endlessly to take the turn away from one another and hold on to it, and no one else will get to say a single word.

It's important to understand that such power is *phony* power, which could easily be taken away. It signals not strength but weakness and a feeling of insecurity. The person who does it is tolerated and endured, not respected. And when someone comes along with sufficient clout to make the previous monologuist listen in suffering silence, all the former victims will participate in the takeover with great pleasure and enthusiasm.

This sort of language interaction — verbal bully plus circle of victims — is interesting in only one respect: WHEN YOU SEE IT HAPPEN, ALWAYS BE AWARE THAT YOU ARE OBSERVING WEAKNESS, AND PLAN YOUR STRATEGY ACCORDINGLY.

Now let's consider how linguistic traffic is regulated during the conversation in which everyone present would prefer to approach the "ideal" model and keep the turns moving along in an efficient and productive fashion.

There are five rules to follow. Be warned that they apply in full only for adult mainstream Anglo Americans, particularly males. It is by no means a universal law that only one person may talk at a time, for example. There are many cultures in which overlapping turns are not considered rude or unusual, and there are many cultures in which direct eye contact signals anger or is simply rude. When you are interacting with people from other ethnic groups you will have to be sensitive to their signs of unease and make necessary modifications to avoid problems. This is essentially the same thing as driving your car on what Americans consider to be "the wrong side" of the road in a country that regulates its auto traffic in that way. But linguistic traffic laws are not openly marked in the way the rules of the road are.

Rule One. Turns are passed from one speaker to another after *optional* pauses, or at the end of a sentence. Until this happens, everybody else listens.

If you are trying to capture the turn, wait for one of these pauses; if you are trying to pass the turn on, *produce* such a pause. People who stop to think in mid-sentence confuse others, who may then interrupt because they assume the pause was a turn-passing cue. People who talk on and on without pauses cause equal confusion; eventually they too will be interrupted, as the listeners decide that nothing but brute force will ever get them to stop.

WATCH FOR SIGNS OF DISTRESS in nonstop talkers if you have no reason to think the monologue is a power play — they may just not know how to pass on the turn. In such a situation, *get syntonic.* Match your breathing rate to theirs. Begin nodding politely in rhythm with their words. Say an encouraging "mmhmm" or two in appropriate spots to demonstrate your good will and prove that you're listening. And then take the turn smoothly by benevolent interruption. Never just jump in, and cut these people off, with resulting serious loss of face for them, but don't simply sit and suffer, either. They will appreciate your help.

Rule Two.　The cue for passing on the turn is direct eye contact.

It may or may not include additional supporting body language and words, such as, "Bill, what are your feelings about this?". Speakers who pass on the turn by words only, without eye contact, are engaging in dominance displays and should be ignored. If the speaker looks you directly in the eye at a pause, take the turn; if you are trying to pass the turn on, follow that procedure. With cultures that object to direct eye contact, make it as brief as possible.

NOTE: If you are trying to *get* the turn, avoid giving "go on talking" cues such as smiling, nodding, and "mmmhmmm"-ing. Women in particular, especially when trying to get the turn from men, often make this mistake and then wonder why they never get to talk.

Rule Three.　When speakers give obvious turn-passing cues but make no selection of next speaker, self-selection is allowed.

The best way to accomplish this is by referring directly *to* the previous speaker. "I agree wholeheartedly with what Bill has been saying. And I would like to add . . ." "I think you're absolutely right. And I'd like to just add a few words here . . ." Or, if you outrank Bill markedly, and the occasion is a meeting of some kind, say, "Thank you, Bill, Now . . ." and move on.

Rule Four.　To avoid taking the turn, never look directly at the speaker; when you make eye contact impossible, you are giving a clear signal that you do not wish to talk. (Imposing the turn on someone who is doing this is a power play.)

Rule Five: Help The Helpless.　When it's obvious that Bill wants to talk, and you know no reason why Bill should *not* be allowed to talk — but the speaker appears to be oblivious to it all — take the turn yourself and then pass it on unobtrusively to Bill. (And see the discussion of Rule One above.)

I want to insert one note of clarification here. Certainly there are times when people hold the floor for quite a long time, with the others present willingly listening to them. But this is not conversation.

In the same way that football games are suspended to allow for halftime shows, conversations can be suspended in favor of other language events, such as telling a story, telling a joke, or presenting an extended lecture. Such events are inserted *into* conversations, and the conversation itself, with its associated rules, is put on hold until they are over. Sometimes two or more people will decide to spend an interval of time entirely in this way — as happens when several men get together and exchange war stories — with no conversation except the barest minimum taking place. This is not a suspension of the rules listed, but a suspension of the conversation itself. The verbal bully's contribution is to insist on putting on such events in spite of other people's lack of interest or their actual resistance.

Because the idea of rules in informal language interactions is unfamiliar, you may feel that the rules above apply only to business settings, formal negotiations, meetings, and the like. This is a mistake. The rules apply just as rigorously in your home and with your friends as they do in your professional and public life. If you want your children to grow up to be people who are willingly listened to by others — which is as valuable to them as a college education, and a lot cheaper — you have to provide them with a suitable model. They will not learn successful communication in an environment of linguistic anarchy. The only thing significantly different about Personal Domain interactions is that there are usually fewer people to share turns with, so that you get to talk more often during any single episode.

If you are convinced that your kids don't respect you, that your spouse isn't interested in talking with you, that your relatives try to avoid you, and that none of your friends will willingly listen to anything you say, it is *overwhelmingly* probable that you violate the linguistic traffic rules with all of them.

People in your family and your circle of friends will be extremely tolerant about your topic choices, and may be genuinely interested in such topics as your illnesses and complaints. Topics that would bore strangers and business associates into semicoma often are good topics with those who love you. But if you consistently violate the traffic rules, they *can't* carry on successful conversations with you, no matter how willing they may be. When an honest self-examination reveals to you that this is what is going on in your personal life, you are the only one who can correct the situation, by making a deliberate and strenuous effort to follow the traffic rules in future.

When I explain this to clients, I usually meet resistance. Like professionals who insist that they can't let people talk because they would never shut up, clients will say, "If I followed those rules, I'd never get a word in *edge*wise!" Like the professionals, they are the victims of distorted perceptions of time. But when they make a genuine long-term effort to regulate their personal language interactions by the rules above, they discover to their amazement that they actually get to talk *more often* and *for longer periods* than they did before. When the problem at home has been the other way around — that is, when what they hear at home is a constant complaint of "You never *talk* to me!" — they discover that following the five rules puts an end to that complaint as well, without forcing them to spend large amounts of time in conversations they'd rather not have.

Think how much confusion, how much waste of time and energy, now much hostility and stress and carnage, would result from trying to do without traffic rules on our streets and highways! Unregulated linguistic traffic doesn't produce the kind of spectacular catastrophes that a "do whatever you feel like" system would produce on the road. But it is just as counterproductive and just as dangerous, in a less obvious fashion.

Trust me: You will *never* be able to build a support group, or do any significant networking, in your professional or your personal life, unless you follow the linguistic traffic rules. People simply will not participate. THERE IS NO SUCH THING AS NETWORKING BY FORCE.

More About Listening

We have always known that when people talk about something that distresses them they become upset. We notice their breathing rate increasing or becoming irregular; we notice their skin color changing. We see their muscles stiffen and — if they are like Jack Harrington — we sometimes see a muscle twitch or jerk, out of their control. Systematic scientific observation has proved that these phenomena are evidence of *stress*, and that stress is reflected in physiological changes such as higher blood pressure and faster pulse. And scientific research has proved unambiguously that stress is implicated to some degree in all physical and emotional illnesses.

What we did not know, prior to the invention of the continuous computerized heart monitor, was that the act of talking itself — no matter what about — causes the same physiological effects.

James J. Lynch directs a clinic for patients with high blood pressure at the University of Maryland School of Medicine. He was not looking for language-related phenomena when he prescribed twenty-four-hour heart monitors for these patients; it was simply part of the process of diagnosis and treatment. The discoveries he made — that blood pressure rises when you talk and falls when you listen — were accidental byproducts. But they were then energetically pursued by Lynch and his associates, who were amazed to find that although blood pressure rises much more *steeply* when speakers are emotionally involved, it also rises during the most innocuous speech. In fact, it rises if speakers are doing nothing more than reading a telephone directory aloud. The same effect occurs during signing, for deaf speakers; it is absent in schizophrenics.

The phenomena are so reliable that Lynch has been able to teach people with high blood pressure to moderate it by their language behavior alone — a matter of grave importance for patients who cannot tolerate the usual diets and medicines prescribed for the disease.

It's critical to understand that the beneficial effects of listening — not only a lower blood pressure, but also slower pulse and improved chemical regulation of body processes at every level — occur only during *real* listening. If you are rehearsing in your mind what you are going to say when you get the turn to speak, or talking to yourself silently on some other subject, or sitting on the edge of your chair desperately trying to grab the turn, the benefits do not occur. They are the result of *syntonic* listening, when you give the speaker your full attention.

Listening, therefore, is not only crucial to effective communication, it is a major component in personal stress management — right up there with meditation and biofeedback and massage and many expensive trendy processes. Listening is not something you should consider because it constitutes Being Nice. Listening is in your own self-interest. Listening is good for your physical and your emotional health, and is actively and directly therapeutic.

Listening — which is free! — is therefore a multiple blessing in your life. It causes people who interact with you to perceive you as interested, as considerate, as caring, and as linguistically competent. It enables you to obtain the information you need in order to tailor your own speech for maximum efficiency and effectiveness. And at the same time, it preserves your health and sanity. The time you spend learning to listen properly is one of the most valuable investments you could ever make.

Taking Out the Trash

You don't keep garbage in your house or on your person. The crisis caused by lack of a way to get rid of garbage — at any level — is acute. But the very parents and teachers who train us in the disposal of every other sort of waste leave us to our own devices when it comes to dealing with *linguistic* waste.

Most of this book has dealt with *external* language toxins. But there are also internal ones, personal ones, that are just as nasty to have around. We produce these toxins and dangerous wastes while TALKING TO OURSELVES — something all of us do almost nonstop, usually silently, when we aren't talking to somebody else. We create little tape recordings in our heads with unpleasant happenings preserved on them, and we play them over and over, so that the unpleasantness is perpetuated.

Therapists (Albert Ellis, for example, with his Rational Emotive Therapy) spend lots of time trying to teach people not to produce those tapes. Most people never get such training. But *without* going to a therapist you can do a lot to take out your personal linguistic trash and dispose of it. Here are some suggested techniques that many people have found helpful.

The Letter You Don't Mail. When you would like to tell somebody off, but good reasons exist for refraining from doing so, go home and write a letter in which you say every single thing you want to say — but don't mail it. (*Any* letter written in anger or the heat of emotion should sit unmailed for at least twenty-four hours and be reviewed when you've calmed down — you may then decide not to mail it either.) It may seem to you that this takes a lot of time and energy that could be better spent in other activities. WRONG. What it does is get rid of trash in your head that would otherwise keep rotting away there — leading to the production of tapes that replay the conflict over and over again and seriously interfere with your other activities. Get it out of your system instead. Write it all down. If you don't like to write, put it all on a cassette tape. But get rid of it — by making it external rather than internal, so that you can *dispose* of it.

Now you have this letter or tape that you aren't going to mail or share: what should you do with it? You have two choices, depending on how objective you are capable of being. If you are able to look at yourself in a detached and rational way once a little time has gone by, keeping these items can be very useful. Going back and reviewing them twice a year will let you observe what kinds of things cause you to become upset or angry, how well their importance correlates with the intensity of your response, how much (if at all) this changes over time, and so on. It may let you spot patterns that provide you with valuable information about yourself.

If this is true for you, I suggest that you keep your letters or tapes; they will then function much as a journal does, but in a specialized area of your life. Get a three-ring binder, name it "Hostility Dump," and file the letters or tapes away inside.(You can buy plastic pages for three-ring binders that will hold six cassette tapes at a time.) Put the journal somewhere that ensures its privacy, and use it well.

But suppose you are *not* detached and rational. Suppose that when you re-read one of these letters or listen to one of those tapes six months later you become just as distressed as you were originally. Or suppose you find yourself thinking that it's a terrible waste to hide anything so brilliant and being tempted to send it off to one of the publications in your field.(I see articles in professional journals from time to time that have obviously resulted from just such a judgment.) Suppose that instead of helping you learn about yourself, having the letters or tapes available for review only adds to the stress in your life.

IN THAT CASE, DESTROY THE LETTERS OR TAPES AT ONCE. Create them . . . read them over or listen to them as many times as may be necessary to achieve the feeling that you are *through* with them. . . and then destroy them. For you, keeping them would be a serious mistake.

Talking to the Plastic Head. Another way to get rid of linguistic wastes is by talking to something inanimate that can stand in for the real world counterpart. My favorite choice is one of those plastic (often styrofoam) heads you can buy anywhere that wigs are sold. Set it up at a proper height for the purpose, stand back, and give it hell.

This is especially useful when you know very well that what has upset you is trivial, and you just want to get rid of it quickly — when it's not worth preparing a letter or tape about. And it's useful if you are someone who should not keep the letters or tapes, but you don't trust yourself to destroy them.

Translation Exercises. In addition to the language associated with words, there are other "languages" which can be used to express meanings. There are the languages of art, of sculpture, of crafts, of dance, of music, etc. You may want to translate the stress source in your life into one of these languages instead of (or in addition to) writing it down or recording it.

In my own case, for example, I reach a point where I cannot face even one more word. My professional life consists entirely of reading words, saying words, listening to words, writing words, and analyzing words. Sometimes I grow profoundly sick of words and everything to do with words! At such times, I translate anything that's bothering me into a collage. I can't draw or paint or sculpt, but I can cut and paste, and my mailbox provides me with an endless supply of collage materials. I don't consider any mail except pornographic mail — and the letters that come from genuinely wild-eyed hate groups — to be "junk" mail. It's all collage material.

Choose the medium that is most accessible for you and in which you feel you can best express your meaning.

Listening Again — to Music. Music has come to be recognized as one of the most powerful of all languages. Not just in the esthetic sense. Not just in terms of the well-known motivating effects of marches. Those still remain, of course — but music has now been proved to be actively therapeutic. It reduces the amount of painkilling drugs patients require, even during and after surgery. It shortens the time people must spend in hospitals. It provides an alternative means of communication in speech disorders and deficits — it's often surprising how well people who are unable to speak may be able to sing. It can provide the same relaxation and stress reduction that listening or meditation provide. Music is good for you personally.

Provided you *listen* to it! Just having it playing in the background, as with canned music tapes, is not enough. That may cause people to work faster in an office, or buy more goods in a grocery store; such effects for "background" music are well established. But it won't improve your physical and mental health. To get the full benefit of music, just as is true for the benefit of any other form of listening, you must give it your attention.

Any kind of instrumental music will do for this purpose. Not just classical or New Age. Marches will do. Popular music or rock and roll — as long as it's only melodies, and no words, and you don't know the words so well that you supply them as you listen. Whatever music *you* can listen to with pleasure. If you don't know precisely what you might like, and have no preferences, I have three recommendations:(1) the instrumental music of Bach and Albinoni; (2) any Gregorian chant; and (3) Brahms' compositions for violin. But if you try these, and you find that they upset you in the same way an argument does, try other varieties until you find something that works for *you.*

The Man/Woman Problem

Life is not easy for women at the moment. Today when so many women must work, whether they like it or not — but when our culture continues to assign them the primary responsibility for such things as childcare, the care of elders, and the emotional work of marriage and family — women need all the help they can get. Unfortunately, many things allegedly created for the specific purpose of providing such help turn out to be at best full of potential pitfalls and at worst actively dangerous to women. Assertiveness training, for example.

Certainly there are fine assertiveness trainers out there, with the very best of intentions, who are working hard to make things better for women. Certainly women do need to learn to stand up for their rights and to express themselves without being doormats. But there is a very serious problem when assertiveness training (or anything of the same genre) is provided to women without any accompanying training in basic *political* skills. Let me sum this up, as emphatically as I know how:

IF YOU ALWAYS SAY THE WRONG THING, ASSERTIVENESS TRAIN-ING WILL ONLY TEACH YOU HOW TO SAY THE WRONG THING FAR MORE OPENLY AND ARTICULATELY — THIS IS *NOT* AN IMPROVEMENT.

First, get your communications act together; then you may find assertiveness training very valuable.

Let's take a look at a scenario for an all too common situation in which this problem is clearly demonstrated.

SCENARIO FOURTEEN   **"M**r. Nelson," Janet said, "I don't think you understand the problems that I am facing every single day. I don't think you have any grasp of what they are like, and I don't think Metamega is making any effort to help with them."

Paul Nelson looked at her hard, and his eyebrows rose, but when he answered he didn't seem annoyed. "I see," he said. "Well, why don't you help me out, then, Janet — tell me what it is that we're missing, and perhaps I can do something about it."

"In the first place," she began, "when I get up in the morning I can't just eat breakfast and go to work. I have small children at home that have to be dressed and fed and driven to their sitter's house before I can even BEGIN to think about coming here. I get up at *five*, Mr. Nelson, in order to be here by nine o'clock, and even then it's difficult. If Metamega really CARED about its women employees, it would have childcare available on *site*, so that we wouldn't already be worn out before we even get here — and so we could concentrate on our work instead of worrying about our KIDS all day long."

Nelson shook his head, and she was pleased to see signs of genuine concern on his face. "How many children do you have, Janet?" he asked, and when she told him, he made a careful note and told her courteously to continue.

"I also have an elderly mother-in-law to look after," she said. "My husband means well, but it's hard for him to find time to check on her or to pick up her medicines or anything else she needs — and I'm not willing to neglect her just because his schedule is so complicated."

"Good for you," said Paul. "I'm glad to hear that."

"And that's not *all*."

"There's more?"

"There certainly *is*."

She ran through the list, being very careful not to seem overly dramatic about any of it, presenting the information concisely and logically. Through it all, Paul Nelson listened with scrupulous attention, nodding his head and making sympathetic noises. By the time she got to the end of it, she was feeling confident and hopeful. She knew how good he was at accomplishing the seemingly impossible — his support would be very valuable to her, and to the other women at Metamega who shared her concerns.

"Well, Janet," he said, when she was through, "you've certainly opened *my* eyes!"

"I intended to," she replied. "Something has to be *done*."

He sighed, and leaned back in his chair, looking at her over steepled fingers.

"Janet," he said solemnly, "I have *always* suspected that women — especially women with family obligations — have no business being anywhere except at home *with* those families. That's considered an old-fashioned and outmoded view, I know — but it's one that has seemed compelling to me. And now, you've *convinced* me! No question about it — *nobody* could handle all those problems that you've been trying to deal with."

"But, Mr. Nelson — "

He cut her off. "Don't you worry about a thing," he said. "You don't even have to give notice, Janet. If you can give us a week, and maybe show one of the other secretaries the things that have been your personal responsibility, we'll manage."

This was not what Janet had had in mind, of course. Now she faces a degrading scene in which she must plead with Paul Nelson for her job and convince him that she *can* get her work done in spite of all her personal problems. And she has dug this pit by herself, *for* herself. Nelson is too skilled in the use of language and in gameplaying to say, "You poor little thing!" But that is the standard line in interactions like Scenario Fourteen, with minor variations for Poor Old Things, Poor Dears, and Poor Kids.

When a woman appears before a superior with a list of the standard personal problems, assertiveness only makes things worse. A man who might be sympathetic to a woman in tears will respond as Nelson did when the case is made assertively. A woman is just as likely to be unsympathetic, because she has all the same problems to deal with, and she has managed.

This is all wrong. You bet. Women ask me, "Why is it that when a *man* asks for help because a wife or child or parent is sick, he almost always gets it? And even if he doesn't get the help, he gets sympathy? But when a woman has the same problem she's expected to tough it out?"

The answer lies in the set of reality statements our culture uses to define men and to define women. When a woman complains about problems associated with doing things that are *expected* of women, sympathy is unlikely. Men get very little sympathy for complaints that work is too physically demanding, or that hours are too long, or that they are frightened — because the set of reality statements includes "Men are physically strong," "Men have great physical endurance," and "Men are always brave." The difference is of course that few men are required to wrestle tigers, while a very large percentage of women are obliged to carry a heavy load of family duties in addition to their duties in the workplace.

You can't change this situation; you can't revise our current version of reality to make it more palatable. That task is the task of decades, if not centuries. But you *can* be aware that the Poor Little Thing Ploy is lurking about, and avoid walking headfirst into it. Instead, sit down and work out a careful strategy that doesn't leave you so vulnerable.

One more thing . . . Recently, there's been a flood of books about man/woman relationships. *Newsweek* for June 1, 1987 calls it a "new, multimillion-dollar publishing phenomenon" in which writers are "still mining the apparently inexhaustible plight of being a woman, but they're starting to blame most of women's problems on men." There's *Men Who Hate Women & the Women Who Love Them: When Loving Hurts and You Don't Know Why*, by Susan Forward and Joan Torres; there's *How To Love a Difficult Man*, by Nancy Good; there are a dozen others, all with titles we could summarize like this: *Rotten Men and the Women Who Put Up With Them.*

I understand the comfort women find in reading a skillfully-drawn portrait of a rotten man and thinking. "That's *him*! That's my Significant Other! Thank god — I'm NOT the only one who realizes that his behavior is awful!" Especially when they are likely to have been told over and over again that they're exaggerating, that they should quit making mountains out of molehills, that they should be grateful that good old Significant Other doesn't *really* give them a hard time, that it's time they grew up . . . all the usual victim-blaming. But once these books have transmitted this message — I'VE MET THE MAN, AND YOU'RE RIGHT: HE'S ROTTEN — they offer slim comfort and potentially dangerous advice.

The two concepts I find most unpalatable in these books are the following:

1. Men are the way they are because they are men, and they can't change.
2. Something has to be done to improve the relationship so you won't get hurt so badly — and *you* are going to have to do it. Men can't do it (See 1 above) or they won't do it.

In addition, some of them contain the really cruel claim that men grow up to hate women and treat them badly because of the parenting they get. Since most of that parenting is done by women, this is equivalent to saying that *women teach* men — their sons — to be misogynists. It's a rare family in which the father/son contact is extensive enough to lift that blame off the shoulders of mothers.

This is not the place for me to attempt to refute the *How to Deal With Rotten Men* books, and there is much within them that I would fully support. I do want to say, however, that when you are involved in a long-term relationship with a man whose abusive behavior is *verbal* rather than physical, it simply is not true that he can't change. It's very *convenient* for him to be able to present that claim and point out that even women professionals will back him up in it — but you should not allow him to get away with it. Furthermore, if you use the techniques of *Gentle Art* syntonics, it's not true that he *won't* change. It may take him awhile, but he can change, and he *will*.

Workout — Chapter 10

1. Keep a topics list for yourself for one full week. Then prepare a master list and evaluate it. How good are you at introducing topics? Is your list a surprise to you?

2. "A perfectly tuned conversation is a vision of sanity — a ratification of one's way of being human and one's place in the world. And nothing is more deeply disquieting than a conversation gone awry. To say something and see it taken to mean something else; to try to be helpful and be thought pushy; to try to be considerate and be called cold; to try to establish a rhythm so that talk will glide effortlessly about the room, only to end up feeling like a conversational clod who can't pick up the beat — such failure at talk undermines one's sense of competence and being a right sort of person. If it happens continually, it can undermine one's feeling of psychological wellbeing." (Deborah Tannen, quoted in "Noted With Pleasure," from the New York *Times Book Review* for March 2, 1986.)

   What do you think — does Tannen state the case accurately? Do you agree that "nothing is more deeply disquieting than a conversation gone awry"? Consider her description of how it *feels* to be involved in such a conversation — does it describe your own perceptions when your conversations don't go well? If not, remember it anyway; you are sure to interact with people for whom it *is* an accurate description, and it will provide you with valuable clues to behavior that would otherwise mystify you.

3. Physicians are famous for violating the rules of conversation. In the famous Rosenhan experiment (see page 4), the phony patients kept trying to talk to the doctors in the mental hospitals, but failed 94 percent of the time. Here is a typical attempt considered by the researchers to be a *success*, presumably because the doctor did at least say something: "Pardon me, Dr. X. Could you tell me when I am eligible for ground privileges?" "Good morning, Dave, how are you today?" I myself have heard many doctor/patient exchanges like this one:

PATIENT: "Am I having a heart attack?"

DOCTOR: "When did the pain start?"

PATIENT: "About an hour ago. Am I having a heart attack?"

DOCTOR: "What kind of pain is it — crushing? burning?"

PATIENT: "More like crushing. Do you think it's a heart attack, Doctor?"

DOCTOR: "Have you ever had a pain like this before?"

(And so on.)

Write the rule or rules necessary to account for such conversations. Do these rules apply in professions other than medicine?

4. Japan's Nippon Telegraph & Telephone has 17,000 telephone information services, bringing in more than 150 million dollars a year. You can dial a number and listen to the voice of Ghengis Khan; you can dial sounds of the desert; you can dial a tape of Richard Nixon. According to *Advertising Age* for February 1, 1988 ("In Japan, voice of authority, or flattery, a call away," by David Kilburn): "NTT's own services meet a wide range of unusual needs. The flattery line tells you how marvelous you are, while the apology line gives a series of increasingly groveling apologies, Japanese style. Both the apology line and the stress-reducing line are very popular in the early evening." (On page 46.)

Would you be interested in such a service in the United States? What particular messages would you be most interested in? Assume that you are setting up a business to provide this service — how would you market it? Can you write a brief advertisement that specifies exactly what service is being offered and why people ought to pay for it?

5. In all the other *Workout* sections in this book, the reading I have recommended has been an article. This time, I'm going to suggest an entire book: *Minding the Body, Mending the Mind*, by Joan Borysenko, published by Addison-Wesley in 1987. Few things are as important to your success as your health, and that makes the time spent reading Borysenko's work an excellent investment. For the nonspecialist, I know no better source for information about what is now being called "mind/body medicine."

SIGHT BITES

1. "*Personality Classifications.* Figure 1 shows the results of testing in two type A personalities who could be termed 'carriers.' That is, they not only exhibit the classic characteristics of the type A personality, but also induce type A behavior in others. The men, who did not know each other, are presidents of major banks."

(From "Predicting Workplace Blood Pressure," by Robert S. Eliot, in *Practical Cardiology/Special Supplement* for *1987*; page 5. Do you know any Type A "carriers"?)

2. "Morale comes down from the sky like rain. If you're the boss and you're feeling lousy, watch out — you're like the plague going around. If I wake up in a terrible mood, I don't go near my store — I work at home. I don't want to bring any of my people down."

   (Stew Leonard, Sr., quoted in "Beyond Positive Thinking," a special report by a number of people in the December 1988 issue of *Success*; page 34.)

3. "In less than a half-hour of air-time, Sam Donaldson zapped Ferraro 18 times, George Will 11, and Brinkley himself 3. By contrast, when Jody Powell joined the learned pundits for some ten or twelve minutes of chat, he was interrupted only once."

   (From "Lesser Miscreants," by Geoffrey Stokes, in the *Village Voice* for August 18, 1984.)

4. "Scientists have found a new clue to how the brain may interact with the immune system, possibly helping explain why . . . people under stress may be more likely to get sick, it was reported yesterday. Researchers at the University of Texas in Galveston showed that a key part of the immune system — white blood cells — have receptors for a hormone produced in response to stress."

   (From "Brain-Immunity Link Discovered", in the New York *Times* for November 12, 1987; United Press International.)

5. "Of course, the effect of prolonged stress is not as visible and not as dramatic as the loss of a finger, nor is the cause as simple to isolate. But is stress any less incapacitating or demoralizing? One reason the question has not been raised more often, particularly in cases of psychiatric distress at the executive level, is that most managers recognize that a claim for emotional disability hardly enhances their future prospects at their own or any other company."

   (From "Can Companies Kill?" by Berkeley Rice, in *Psychology Today* for June 1981; page 81.)

6. "Stress-resistant people . . . have a specific set of attitudes toward life — an openness to change, a feeling of involvement in whatever they are doing, and a sense of control over events."

   (From "Psychological Hardiness: The Role of Challenge in Health," by Maya Pines, in *Psychology Today* for December 1980; page 34.)

7. "As we expected, hassles turned out to be much better predictors of psychological and physical health than life events. The more frequent and intense the hassles people reported, the poorer their overall mental and physical health. . . . Our results also suggest that the effect major life events do have may occur through the daily hassles they provoke."

   (From a research report titled "Little Hassles Can Be Hazardous to Health," by Richard S. Lazarus, in *Psychology Today* for July 1981; page

62. The phrase "major life events" is used to refer to such things as marriage, divorce, getting or losing a job, retirement, and the like.)

11 Lying

Introduction

SCENARIO FIFTEEN "**M**orning, Tom," said John Martin. "Make yourself comfortable."

Tom Lee sat down, but he didn't get comfortable and he didn't bother to return the greeting. "Look, John," he said impatiently, "I've got enough work on my desk for six people. What do you want?"

"I want to let you know that I heard your speech for the national association yesterday afternoon. In fact, I *taped* that speech."

"Yeah? What did you do that for?"

"They tell me you give good speeches, Tom. I thought I might learn something."

Tom Lee grinned at the other man. "Well?" he asked. "*Did* you learn something?"

John leaned back in his chair and crossed his arms over his chest. "Yes," he said. "Yes, I did. I learned that you're a LIAR, Tom."

Lee's eyes narrowed, but the expression on his face did not change, and he spoke softly. "Maybe you'd better explain that," he said.

"Happy to!" John sat up and referred to the yellow legal pad in front of him on the desk. "First — you claimed Metamega had profits of over two million dollars on its health care products line last year. That's false — that's at least a hundred thousand worth of false. Second — you claimed we'd have the new line on the shelves in six months . . . and you know as well as I do there's no way we can do it in less than a year. And third — *third*, Tom — you lifted your three closing paragraphs, word for word, from the talk I gave in Atlanta in October. And not one word of credit for me . . . you passed those paragraphs off as your *own*. How's that for an explanation?"

"You *serious?*"

"You bet I am."

"A little bit of hype, Martin? A little bit of friendly borrowing, all in-house? What's the big deal?"

"You're a *liar*, that's the big deal! You'll get away with it, because I'm not about to embarrass the company by calling you on it — you knew that before you *did* it. But I want you to be aware that I *know* what you did."

Thomas Lee shrugged. "You're entitled to your opinion, Goody Two-Shoes," he said. "But I don't call that lying."

"Say what?"

"*You* heard me, Martin! *Lying* — that's heavy stuff. I didn't tell any lies. You want to *preach*, fine! Just don't pick ME for your congregation. I've got better things to do with my time."

"Oh, hell, Tom," said John disgustedly. "Go on, then. Get out of here before I say something I'll regret later."

Tom shrugged again, and stood up. "*You* called *me*, fellah!" he said as he headed for the door. "I didn't volunteer!"

This is an ugly exchange, and unfortunate. From Thomas Lee's point of view, John Martin is a nit-picking moralizer. Lee would say that it's customary to inflate the numbers a little when you're trying to promote your company or your products, and that as long as it isn't carried to extremes everybody *expects* you to have some slack in your figures. He would say that the paragraphs he took from Martin's speech were nothing but general material that represented what he would have said anyway, if Martin hadn't ripped off his ideas. Being called a liar for such items infuriates him. And he'll go out of his way to watch every word Martin says from now on, watching for even the most minute deviation from absolute truth.

Martin, on the other hand, feels entirely justified in his accusations. But what brought them on wasn't Lee's inaccuracies. It was the fact that Tom used the material from his speech without asking for permission and without giving him credit. That made him angry enough to go back and listen to the speech as a prosecutor listens, searching for any other falsehood, large or small, he could add to his list.

The rivalry between these two men, both dominant males with short tempers, is very typical. This time their disagreement revolves around their differing ideas about honesty, and that's also typical. Nobody likes to be lied to; nobody likes to be called a liar. In this chapter we'll take a thorough look at the subject of lying, to determine why something on which there appears to be such strong agreement is such a source of controversy, and to see what can be done to deal with it in our language environment. And then we'll come back again, briefly, to Scenario Fifteen.

The Brain as Mismatch Detector

Two metaprinciples of syntonics have been introduced in earlier chapters of this book: ANYTHING YOU FEED WILL GROW, and ANYTHING YOU STARVE WILL FESTER OR DIE. Now we need to add a third metaprinciple:

ANY MISMATCH IS A WARNING SIGN.

We've discussed a number of different kinds of mismatch already, and have seen this metaprinciple borne out. For example:

☐ When the sensory Modes used by two speakers do not match, distrust is created and rapport is hard to establish.

☐ When the Satir Modes used by two speakers do not match, the feedback loops that would result from such a match are interrupted and slowed down.

☐ When the intonation a speaker uses with a sentence does not match the normal intonation that goes with those words, it signals that something unusual is going on and that the listener may be under verbal attack.

☐ When a speaker's inner feelings do not match the words spoken, that mismatch will be betrayed by the body language.

☐ When the rhetorical structures of public language — for example, the various parts of a metaphor — do not match, that language loses its power to persuade.

George Miller has said that the human brain is a mismatch detector; the examples above demonstrate that mismatch detector in action. The brain has a tendency to run along on automatic in many language situations; but anything unusual, anything that does not *fit*, will bring it back to full alert. Suppose you are listening to a sermon, and suddenly you hear the minister use an obscenity. You are listening to a lecture on physics, and suddenly you hear the professor recite a nursery rhyme. You are ignoring the blur of irrelevant noise all around you at a cocktail party, and suddenly you hear someone across the room mention your name. You will *notice* these phenomena, in a way that you do not notice the ordinary language in which they have turned up. For one thing, you will notice that you *are* noticing — you will become aware of the fact that you are actively paying attention.

Any deviation from normal of this kind — any mismatch in the CONTENT of the language you are processing — will catch your attention, and will do so in a way that you are consciously aware of. But there are many *other* kinds of mismatch detection, just as important to your communication strategies, that ordinarily go on well below the level of your conscious awareness. Bringing those processes to conscious awareness also — so that you can make systematic use of them with regard to the problem of deception — is the subject of this chapter.

A lie is a chunk of language that does not *match* the speaker's (or the writer's) internal knowledge and/or feelings. When all the channels of communication are SYNTONIC — when a speaker's internal knowledge and feelings, body language, and words all *match* and are congruent with one another — lying is impossible. And the cue that tells you to be wary, the cue that tells you someone is trying to deliberately deceive you, will always be MISMATCH. Where lying is concerned, you have three goals:

☐ You need to know what the word "lie" means to you and to the people you are interacting with.
☐ You need to be able to tell when you are being lied to.
☐ You need to know how to be perceived as telling the truth yourself.

Achieving these goals requires you to become accustomed to making full conscious use of the mismatch detection capacity of your brain. As always, the necessary information is part of your internal grammar and is ordinarily reflected in your "gut feelings." What you need is convenient and reliable *access* to that information. Let's begin with the problem of definition.

DEFINING THE WORD "LIE"

The word "lie" is a reality gap word, like "failure." People in our society do not disagree about whether lying is wrong. Everyone — even the criminal — strongly objects to being lied to, criticizes people for being dishonest, and demands honesty from others. But when it comes to a clear statement of what is and what is not a lie — a statement of what the word "lie" *means* — this seeming consensus collapses into chaos. My favorite example of an open statement about this situation came from a department chairman who said to me, with complete seriousness, "Suzette, that wasn't a lie. It wasn't *true* — but it wasn't a lie. Not in *that* situation."

For some people, the following statement holds: A LIE IS ANYTHING YOU SAY OR WRITE WHEN YOU KNOW THAT IT IS NOT TRUE. For these people the word "lie" has attached to it the semantic features [+ MESSAGE], [+ FALSE] and [+ DELIBERATE], and that's the end of the matter. Such people will tell small children that there is no Santa Claus and that they are taking the sick dog to the vet to have it killed.

They will tell a woman that she is too fat and that her dress is ugly; they will tell a disabled man with an obvious deformity that they can't stand to look at him. If they are clergy, they will tell parishioners that their spouses have committed adultery; if they are physicians, they will tell patients that they are going to die; if they are teachers, they will tell students that they are going to fail and might as well give up.

There are obvious disadvantages to this stance. You can't maintain it and be an advertising executive, or a stockbroker, or a politician, or an insurance agent, or a lawyer. You can't maintain it and be a professional athlete. You are going to find it extremely difficult to maintain it and sell ANYthing — unless it is genuinely true that your widget is the best of all possible widgets, offered at the lowest possible price on the best possible terms. You can't maintain it and expect people to enjoy being with you — they will flee you as they flee an oncoming tornado, and for much the same reasons.

There are other people whose internal grammars show "lie" with a semantic feature specification like this one: [+ MESSAGE], [+ FALSE], [+ DELIBERATE], [- GAME]. When you are dealing with *these* people, it is obviously critical for you to know whether they consider what's going on to be a *game* or not. No poker player would call you a liar if you used body language to convince another player that you had three pair when you really didn't — society agrees that poker is a game. In card games, deliberate deception is not only allowed but encouraged, as long as it isn't directed toward your partner. In such cases, "it's not true — but it's not a lie."

The man who reacts to a woman's furious "But you *lied* to her!" with a bewildered "But if I hadn't said *that* she wouldn't have gone to Bermuda with me!" is demonstrating that for him the word "romance" is marked [+GAME]. And that man is genuinely baffled by the charge that his falsehoods are LIES. For him they are not lies — they are *plays* or they are *moves*; whether they are true isn't even relevant. He views the woman's anger as he would view it if she lost her temper when he took $500 away from her in a game of Monopoly — as irrational and childish.

There are people for whom the critical semantic feature is not plus or minus [GAME] but plus or minus [KIND]. For them, a statement that is false — but kinder than the corresponding truth — is not a LIE. A lie is always going to be marked [-KIND]. The falsehoods about how nice you look, and how well-behaved your kids are, and what a pleasure it would be to watch your home movies are due to this [-KIND] rating. And it becomes important, in these cases, to know how many minuses [KIND] *has* for an individual. Professors who let students waste year after year in an unsuitable graduate program, always saying, "Oh, you'll make it — just *hang in* there!" would tell you that of course they are not *lying*. Because lies are *un*kind, and what they said was a kind thing to say. They are people who have half a dozen minuses before [KIND] in their definition of "lie."

This matters. When you must deal with a false utterance, it's *extremely* important to know whether it represents gameplaying behavior or kindness behavior. One way to find out is by initiating a conversation that sets up GAME as the context and noting what the response is. Like this:

> YOU: "Jim, this advertising campaign has put us right out in center field, in plain view of the stands. We're claiming that nobody's speedboats are as safe as ours — but I'm not sure that's true. What do you think our next play ought to be?"
>
> JIM: "That depends on who we've got for quarterback."
>
> or
>
> JIM: "That depends on whether the customers are going to be disappointed in us if the claim doesn't pan out."
>
> or
>
> JIM: "That depends on whether we're going to get caught."

In the first example, Jim is comfortable thinking of a possible falsehood as [+ GAME]. In the second, kindness is more likely to be the relevant feature. In the third example we have something else entirely — this is a man for whom a falsehood is not a lie if you can get away with it.

I'm not sure that English has a word or phrase for the critical semantic feature used in making this distinction. But we all know what its content would be, and we understand how to predict Jim's behavior with regard to lying. (This phenomenon — when you can express an idea in a language, but it has no accepted surface shape, because no word has been chosen to express it — is called a "lexical gap.")

It's a mistake, by the way, to assume that whether someone is religious or not matters here. All religions agree that lies are *wrong*. But for any individual to perceive a given false statement as ruled out by religious convictions, it must first qualify *as* a lie for that individual.

DETECTING LIES

People use a variety of words in an effort to avoid the bald word "lie." They talk of fibbing and hedging and exaggerating and distorting and misleading and embroidering and evading. Nations talk of "covert operations." Scholars substitute the hifalutin term "deception." For convenience, we will continue to simply use "lie" as a cover term for all of these varieties of falseness.

The first principle of lie detection is this:

WHEN SPEAKERS BELIEVE WHAT THEY ARE SAYING — FALSE OR NOT — THERE IS NO LIE TO DETECT.

All the reliable techniques for discovering that people are not being truthful depend crucially on the observable mismatch between their verbal and nonverbal communication. This mismatch is caused by the discomfort they feel when they lie, which "leaks" their intentions to the skilled observer.

If speakers are *not* uncomfortable with a statement they are making, because they don't consider it a lie, there is no discomfort there to be leaked. And no amount of skill will make it possible for you to detect what does not exist.

There are people who betray no discomfort even when they know what they are saying is false and would agree with you that it's a lie, because they simply *aren't* uncomfortable lying — the usual label for such people is "sociopath." What makes the sociopath so dangerous is the seemingly total lack of any consciousness of guilt or responsibility. Sociopaths lie well because they have no conscience, and are highly successful in such endeavors as fraudulent investment schemes. It's fortunate that sociopaths are rare. Because their lies are almost always detected only because of real world *facts* that prove their statements false — usually much too late to help their victims.

The techniques described in this chapter are of little use when — through innocence, ignorance, or sociopathology — the speaker feels no inner uneasiness about a false statement. But such situations are not the usual ones. Most of the time, you will be dealing with the garden variety of falsehood. The usefulness of the ability to detect signals of lying when they *are* present goes without saying.

Your brain's lie detector mechanisms are your primary sensory systems. You can SEE lies, you can HEAR lies, and you can FEEL lies. Sometimes it seems that we can smell or taste lies as well; we recognize the criminal in the line "What a sweet con!" We are all familiar with the "gut feeling" that someone is (or isn't) lying. It's a sensation we can't explain, one that has profound effects on our behavior with regard to the person we're suspicious about. Such feelings are often reliable and should not be ignored, especially when we can find evidence to support them. But it's difficult to make them systematic. It's best to watch and listen for signs of lying, and use the "gut feeling" as a backup system to check the other indications against.

Hearing is the most reliable sense for spotting lies. This comes as a surprise to many people and contradicts popular wisdom. Our mainstream culture devalues hearing, giving far more weight to such visual information sources as the printed word, movies, television, maps, charts, and diagrams. We say "I won't believe it till I see it" and we defend items that we have seen "right there on the page in black and white." We tend to assume, therefore, that we will be better able to tell that people are lying if we can *see* them. That's false. For at least two very good reasons.

First: The face and body are easier to control than the voice is; the face is easiest of all. People are good at putting on false expressions and can become highly skilled at doing so. Learning to assume false intonations, on the other hand, is very difficult indeed. Most people, especially under stress, are hopelessly bad at this.

Second: When you are "face to face" with a speaker, there is a lot of competing data to be processed. You have to observe facial expression, posture, gesture, distance the speaker maintains from you, etc. Factors that have nothing to do with the speaker's honesty — such as physical appearance, clothing, expense of surroundings, and presence or absence of status symbols — can seriously distort your judgment. When you have nothing to attend to but the *voice*, on the other hand, none of those distractions can interfere.

When you have reason to wonder about someone's honesty, then, the best way to proceed is to talk to that person on the telephone. Never go into a face-to-face meeting for delicate negotiations without talking to your negotiating opponents on the phone *first*, if you have any choice in the matter. When you have them on the line, here are the steps you follow:

1. Ask questions, or bring up topics, about which you can be absolutely certain of the facts, and about which the person has no reason to feel anything but casual.

2. Listen carefully to the responses. YOU ARE LISTENING FOR THE SPEAKER'S *BASELINE* VOICE, PARTICULARLY IN TERMS OF ITS PITCH, ITS VOLUME, AND ITS RHYTHM. You want to know how the speaker sounds when telling the *truth* about something that has no particular emotional freight attached.

3. Next, switch to a subject that you suspect *will* be important to the speaker. If you can think of a plausible question about which the speaker might *prefer* to lie to you, ask that question. (It doesn't have to be a question connected with your upcoming negotiation. And it should not be a question that is offensive or confrontational.)

4. Listen carefully to the responses. YOU ARE LISTENING FOR MISMATCH — FOR A DEVIATION FROM WHAT YOU HAVE IDENTIFIED AS THE SPEAKER'S NORMAL VOICE PATTERNS. You want to know how the speaker sounds when telling a lie. With most people, the pitch of the voice will go *up* if they are trying to deceive you, for example. But just hearing a high-pitched voice is not an indication of lying — it may be that the

speaker's voice is always high in pitch. What you are listening for is a *change* in pitch from the baseline that you have established.

5. Repeat Steps 1-4 until you are satisfied that you can tell whether the speaker is or is not truthful. And remember both the normal voice patterns and the ones that you felt exhibited either lying or tension, for use when you are talking to the individual in person.

Recently I've seen advertisements for a machine that you can use to detect signs of this kind in people's voices — I have no idea how well it fulfills its description. However, you cannot always have that machine with you. There will be situations when you'd have no way to conceal it, situations when it would be an inconvenience to lug it about, and so on. I strongly advise you not to become dependent on any such gadget — you need to be able to rely on your own ears, which are always going to be part of your available equipment.

Now, when you must rely on your *eyes*, what do you watch for? Again you watch for mismatch. Again you need a baseline against which to make your comparisons. Cultures that insist on a leisurely period of small talk before negotiations of any kind begin are very wise. Only during that sort of talk can you become familiar with the way an individual's face and body appear in neutral situations. You need that information. Even if you are dealing with a half dozen native–New Yorker Anglo upperclass professional males: insist on a few minutes of conversation on some neutral topic, in order to get as much baseline information as possible.

There are two kinds of facial expressions: planned ones, deliberately put on as a hat would be; and spontaneous ones, which occur without planning. Separate pathways in the brain are responsible for these phenomena. And lengthy research (by Paul Ekman and his associates) has yielded an essential fact to be remembered: SPONTANEOUS EXPRESSIONS ARE MORE SYMMETRICAL THAN PLANNED EXPRESSIONS. That is, the two sides of the face *match* better when the expression is genuine and spontaneous. If you are negotiating with someone whose smile is *always* crooked, perhaps because of the shape of his or her mouth, a crooked smile has no significance. But if the speaker's smile — or any other expression — is symmetrical during neutral conversation, the appearance of its crooked counterpart signals an attempt to deceive.

Warning. Always be careful not to lose track of the fact that your goal is only to determine *whether* people are lying. Finding out *why* they are lying, and deciding whether the reasons justify the lies, are entirely separate matters and require separate skills.

So far as I know, no evidence has yet been found that this correlation between symmetry and truthfulness also holds for body language. But the principle would be exactly the same and is worth applying on an experimental basis. Suppose that you and I were negotiating, and I noted that your gestures were always symmetrical, with both hands involved and matching, during neutral conversation. I would become very alert if I then saw you begin gesturing with only one hand when the chips were down, or if I saw you using both hands but not symmetrically. And vice versa. It is the change from the baseline that matters.

For much more detail about such things as dilation of pupils, eyebrow movements, forehead wrinkling, and the like, I recommend that you go straight to Ekman's writings and his excellent cassette tapes; you'll find references in the bibliography at the end of this book. In most cases, however, you won't need to worry about minute detail; most people are very bad liars, and easily spotted.

Finally, whenever there is mismatch between the words spoken and the speaker's body language, and you have nothing else to go on, ALWAYS BELIEVE THE BODY LANGUAGE. Especially the voice.

How to Be Perceived as Truthful

I will be absolutely truthful with *you* here — in my ideal world, you would never lie. But none of us live in my ideal world or anybody else's. We live in the world of our reality consensus, in which many compromises have to be made. In that world, lying is going to happen, and both you and I are going to tell some of the lies. Our problem is therefore how to function in this world without being perceived as liars.

Almost all lies fall into three basic categories: Polite Lies, Survival Lies, and Incompetent Lies. The first two must be accepted as part of getting along with one another and staying afloat. They aren't going to go away. Whether they *ought* to go away is a subject for philosophers and ethicists and theologians; this book is not the place to discuss such matters. The third category, however, does *not* have to be accepted. Not in competent adults. Not in people who are in positions of power and responsibility, or in those who work for such people and represent them to others. They are yet another form of Malpractice Of The Mouth. There are no excuses for putting up with Incompetent Lies.

Polite lies are dictated by the reality consensus. "Of *course* there is a Santa Claus, Billy!" falls into this slot in the taxonomy of untruths. Telling people who look awful how very nice they look, saying you feel fine when you feel rotten, praising people who don't deserve it — all fall into this slot. Polite lies are as common as weather. Survival Lies are the ones you tell because it is literally a matter of life and death for you to do so; they usually cannot be anticipated. Unless you spend your time in Rambo Mode, you will very rarely need to tell any of these.

All other lies are just incompetence. They don't have to be told. Incompetent Lies are things people say because they can't think of anything to say that would be both appropriate and true. They may not have done their homework; they may be deficient communicators; they may not have engaged their brains before opening their mouths; they may just be too lazy to bother doing better. All of this represents incompetence, and can be avoided 99 percent of the time. Remember the basic principle:

THERE IS ALMOST ALWAYS SOMETHING YOU CAN SAY THAT WILL SERVE YOUR COMMUNICATION NEEDS AND NOT BE FALSE.

The doctor who says "Your appointment is in three weeks" instead of the false "I want to see you in three weeks" — shifting from an utterance about an emotion to the statement of a neutral fact — is not telling a lie. The politician who says "Taxes should be avoided in every way possible" instead of the false "I will never raise taxes" — shifting into Computer Mode — is not telling a lie. The professor who shifts to Computer Mode and says "Passing this test will be difficult for students who have not taken Geometry 101" — instead of the true but callous "You three guys in the back row are going to flunk this test", or the false "I'm sure you three in the back row will do fine" — is not lying. Such choices simply demonstrate competence.

When you know that you're heading into a touchy situation where emotions may run high or where harm can be done, prepare yourself. Be ready for the spots where you might have to lie if the advance work isn't done. Write down — or put on a tape — the questions you expect to be asked, the challenges you expect to face, the utterances that are likely to cause you trouble. Write down or record what you would say in response to them if you were Leveling. And then, if you are convinced that the Leveling response is impossible, take the time to work out some answers that will serve your purpose without obliging you to lie. BEGIN BY TRANSLATING YOUR LEVELING UTTERANCES INTO COMPUTER MODE.

As a safety measure, it's also wise to prepare responses for the exact *opposite* of your expectations. I once went into a meeting of a university curriculum committee to defend my proposal for a new course. I expected to be told that the course was too easy for undergraduates, and I did my homework — I prepared a detailed list of statements demonstrating that it was *not* too easy. I set down all the questions on that topic that I thought were likely, and I worked out responses to each one. I thought I was superbly prepared. But I was *wrong*. What actually happened was something I had not even considered: the challenges, and the questions, all revolved around the committee's conviction that my proposed new course was too *hard* for undergraduates!

I wasn't ready for that, and I had to wing it. I managed to get the course approved, but for only one reason: because I had gone through this process thoroughly so many times before. When the day came that I had to do it without advance warning, I had built up enough skill to carry it off. This is why it's worth doing such preparation when the interaction you're facing is trivial and it won't matter very much if you fail. That way, you build your skill without taking unacceptable risks, and the process will be at least partly on automatic in emergencies.

But suppose you *must* lie. That happens. You may be able to soften it for yourself by deciding that it's not really a LIE, it's just a fib or an exaggeration or an evasion or some such thing. However you label it, you find yourself with no way to avoid saying something that is not true. How can you do that with the least risk of being caught at it? There are four things you can do, as follows:

1. Whatever it is that you must say, try not to say it on the telephone. If that can't be avoided, put a mirror where you can watch yourself as you talk, and monitor the expression on your face. Your smile, your sneer, your anguished frown, can all be "heard" in your voice — if you need to keep a particular expression going, you need the feedback from that mirror. (And I recommend using the mirror for feedback even when you don't need it for this purpose, until you are reasonably certain you have your facial expressions under control. Explain to people that you're training your face, which is the *truth*.)

2. Try very hard to use words that are not contradicted by your body language. If you hate the company you work for and you know that is revealed by your tense muscles and your twitching eyelid, don't SAY "This company is my *life* and I'd *die* for it!" Say "This is the most interesting company I have ever worked for," or something equally innocuous. Remember: body language can always cancel words, but not vice versa.

3. Insert into your utterance, deliberately, the most distracting twirk you dare use. The point of doing this is to divide people's attention so that they will be less likely to notice mismatch as you talk. (This is discussed in detail below.)

4. Use vile rhetoric, so that what you say is difficult to follow and hard to remember. Eliminate all of the devices outlined in Chapter Eight that make your speech memorable and persuasive. OR, use the flip side of this strategy — use all the rhetorical devices you can work in, to outrageous excess. These two strategies are twirks. Their purpose is to concentrate so much attention on the icing that nobody will notice the flaws in the cake.

It will be obvious to you that if you are going to have to lie and be convincing at it, no matter what tactics you select, you should *practice* the lie in advance. You need practice — lots of practice — so that you won't have to be thinking about what you're doing and can put all your energy into doing it *well*.

Lying and Listening

It's hard for a speaker to lie and get away with it. People who know that what they're saying is false — people who are not sociopaths and who have a normal human conscience — are always ill at ease. The signs of that discomfort, leaked by the speaker's nonverbal communication, are almost impossible to hide from a skilled observer. But what about listening? Can you pretend that you are truly listening, when you're really paying little or no attention to what's being said? Can you get away with the message "I'm listening to you" when it's false?

The answer is no, you can't. You can't lie about your listening behavior and get away with it. It is in fact even harder to do that than it is to lie successfully when you are on the speaking end of the interaction.

When you talk, your body language is synchronized with your words in a number of complicated ways. This will come as no surprise to you; it is what you would have expected, based on common sense alone. However, before scientists had modern camera technology available to them — and in particular, the technology that lets them freeze each frame of a movie or videotape for analysis, one microsecond at a time — we did not know that THE BODY LANGUAGE OF THE LISTENER IS ALSO SYNCHRONIZED WITH THE WORDS-AND-BODY-LANGUAGE OF THE SPEAKER. This *was* a surprise, and it is still not as widely known as it ought to be.

This doesn't mean that every time a speaker changes facial expression or body position the listener does exactly the same thing, or that listeners match speakers gesture for gesture as a mimic would. It means that every time there is a *change* in the speaker's body language there is a change in the body language of the listener. The speaker may stand up straighter at the podium; the listener may lean back in the auditorium seat to get more comfortable. But it is the speaker's movements that *evoke* movement in the listener, so that when a film of the interaction is slowed down drastically it looks like a ballet, with the speaker directing. This happens so fast that it is hard to see unless you're watching for it; the delay between speaker movement and listener movement is a tiny fraction of a second. It appears during the first twenty-four hours of life, when the infant has no language of its own but will synchronize its movements to those of the speaker regardless of what language is being spoken. And it is so important that its absence signals that something is wrong and that expert help is needed. This phenomenon is called *interactional synchrony.*

When interactional synchrony is missing, listening is not taking place. No matter how attentive the expression on the listeners' faces, if they are not in sync with the speaker they are faking. They may be hearing, but they aren't listening.

Since you cannot know in advance when the speaker's gestures and facial expressions and postural changes will occur, you cannot practice the "I'm listening to you" lie. If you are not paying close attention to the language of the speaker, both verbal and nonverbal, there will be no interactional synchrony between the two of you. It is in fact physiologically and neurologically impossible for you to fool a speaker who is aware of the existence of interactional synchrony and is watching for its presence or absence. And even the speaker who has never heard of body syncing has a "gut feeling" awareness of what's happening — as evidenced by such remarks as "The minute I started talking his eyes glazed over" or "I could tell she was a million miles away — she didn't hear a single word I said."

Interactional synchrony, when you really are listening, is automatic. You don't have to work at it or think about it; in fact, an effort to be conscious of it will keep you from listening properly and you won't be able to do it. But it can't be faked.

It's a little easier to fake listening on the telephone, where the speaker can't see you. If you intend to lie as a speaker, it's easier to do it face to face; if you intend to lie as a listener, it's easier to do it on the phone. But even on the phone, the lack of any synchronized feedback from you will eventually give you away, and you'll hear a suspicious "Are *you* listening to me?" Because the intonation of your voice — even in such minimal responses as "Mmhmmm" — is part of your body language and active in interactional synchrony. This is one kind of lie it would be wiser never to try.

The Strategic Use of Twirks

Once again, we are about to run head on into the problem of ethics; once again, I will remind you that truly neutral communication does not exist in the real world. However uncomfortable it may make us, language *is* a powerful force, with great potential for both good and harm. We have to eliminate from our minds the idea that it's somehow admirable to use this force in ignorance. Consider how you would react to people who tried to make a case for using a scalpel or a laser in ignorance — you would tell them to learn all there was to know about the operation of those tools, and about their effects, and about their potential dangers, or to STOP USING THEM. Precisely the same attitude should hold for language. I make these preliminary remarks to prepare you for the linguistic phenomenon I call the twirk.

A twirk is an element of language behavior that calls attention to *itself* — attention that has the potential to distract listeners from the rest of your language. The seven-year-old boy of upper-class parents who is asked what six times seven makes and answers with "I ain't got no idea" is using a twirk: his hope is that the "ain't got no" will distract the teacher into forgetting that he doesn't know his sixes and sevens.

Lawyers know all about twirks; Francis L. Wellman's venerable classic, *The Art of Cross-Examination*, advises attorneys to avoid a manner that "divides the attention of your hearers between yourself and your question." It does not tell them to go right ahead and use *exactly* that sort of manner on those occasions when you either have nothing useful to say or prefer for your hearers not to pay close attention to your words — but every competent lawyer knows and uses that technique.

Twirks are a *problem* when they are used without conscious awareness. It's dangerous not to know that the speeches you prepare with such care go largely unheard because something about your language behavior keeps drawing the attention of your audience and interfering with their language processing. It's equally dangerous not to know when the same thing is happening with your written language. Many research studies have proved that most people are rotten judges of what sort of impression they are making on others; it's easy to go through life convinced that you're highly persuasive and believable, basing your actions on that conviction, and to be totally *wrong*. (And to spend many bewildered hours wondering why you are always being passed over for the grant or the job or the promotion.) Much of the time, provided that your nonverbal communication is competent, the source of the error is not in your arguments or your examples but in your twirks.

No twirk is *inherently* either positive or negative — it depends on the situation in which it is used. The incessant use of four-letter words that would be the most negative of twirks in the company of most elderly women may constitute your strongest signal for the metamessage I'M JUST ONE OF THE GUYS when you are in the locker room at the gym.

Here are a few examples of twirks, both positive and negative in effect, to clarify the concept.

□ An unfashionable accent used to speak to a group that does not share it — for example, a Brooklyn or Queens accent used to speak to a group of American Southerners, or an Arkansas accent used to speak to a group of native New Yorkers.

□ Academic terminology such as "albeit, as it were, so to speak" and unfamiliar words from French, Greek, German, and Latin, for a general audience.

□ The use of "like, you know, well, okay" every four or five words — always negative *except* with people who do the same thing.

□ Excessively "correct" linguistic usage — for example, slavish conformity to the pseudo-rule about not splitting English infinitives, or the use of "shall" when common usage would be "will." The flip side of this one, of course, is the "ain't got no" and "didn't do nothin' " twirk.

It would be a twirk to speak to a group while stark naked; no matter how superb your choice of words, nobody would hear them. And there are things that may seem enviable — spectacular physical beauty, for instance — but that so occupy the attention of an audience that they make the speaker's words irrelevant.

In the *New York Times* for August 23, 1987, Maureen Dowd reports of Congresswoman Patricia Schroeder that she "has a tendency to call programs she does not like 'icky,' sign her Congressional mail with a smile face and punctuate thoughts with eye-rolling exclamations like "golly' and 'doggonit' and 'yippy-skippy' — not the perfect candidate that women hoped for, in the view of some." These "tendencies" are of course *twirks*, and they are interfering with Schroeder's effectiveness. That's not logical — but that's the point. Used without awareness, twirks can wreck your plans; used *strategically*, they can be a valuable tool.

A brief piece in *Newsweek* for July 2, 1984 on the Flat Earth Research Society (by David Gates and Jennifer Smith) — commented on the group's written-language twirks, describing a paper as "written in the manner peculiar to neglected polemicists: liberal use of quotation marks, capital letters and boldface type, breathless shortages of verbs and articles and plenty of involuted references and obscure allusions." Anything that shows those twirky characteristics, written by anyone, is likely to be mistaken for the work of a neglected polemicist and to elicit the same reaction that the Flat Earth Research Society elicits. This is a good idea only when you have found yourself obliged to write something that you don't *want* people to find persuasive.

When a twirk has a positive effect, the metamessage it carries is I AM ONE OF YOU or I AM A MEMBER OF A GROUP THAT YOU FEEL ADMIRATION AND AFFECTION FOR. It is noticed, approved, and forgotten, after which the rest of the message can get through. A twirk with negative effects says I AM NOT ONE OF YOU: I AM AN OUTSIDER. Or I AM A MEMBER OF A GROUP THAT YOU DISLIKE AND DISAPPROVE OF. It goes on distracting people and interfering with communication long after it is noticed and disapproved. That's why professional newscasters are trained to use a variety of English called "newscaster English" that is intended to be as close as possible to a genuinely *neutral* accent, offensive to no one. That's why the skilled trial lawyer, addressing a jury in the rural South, is careful to say "I'd rather not keep the jury here past suppertime, your Honor" instead of "I would greatly prefer that the jury be dismissed prior to the dinner hour, your Honor."

Anyone, using audio and video tapes as models, can learn to use twirks strategically in this fashion. (The technique for doing so has been explained in Chapter Eight.) When I discuss this in seminars, people have no difficulty understanding how they would go about it. However, they do raise two objections that require discussion here.

First: People will state that they simply do not believe any of this matters. In some cases, this is arrogance — it applies only to their *own* twirks, which they expect people to "have sense enough" to disregard. They don't mean that they would hire an employee whose every fifth word was an obscenity, or that they would allow their children to say "ain't got no." They *do* mean that if they choose to go on a news program for the general public and say "nephrolithiasis" for "kidney stone" and "myocardial infarction" for "heart attack" they don't believe the public has any right to find that boorish. Nothing can be done about this, and it's a waste of time to try. In other cases, it's ignorance, a genuine lack of information; this can be fixed.

Second: People will state that using twirks deliberately, for strategic purposes, is *lying*. Their position is that using a twirk to transmit the message I AM ONE OF YOU when in fact you *aren't* one of the group addressed is dishonest and unacceptable. When this actually represents a matter of principle — where the individual understands that it may well mean the loss of an election, or a contract, or a sale, and is willing to accept that rather than chance even the smallest deviation from uncompromising honesty — it has my immediate respect. However, such individuals are as rare as vegetarians who refuse to wear leather shoes, and they are going to have extraordinary difficulty functioning in the American professional or business environment, let alone politics or government. They have my respect, and my sympathy.

Assuming that this extreme position is not yours, then, the strategic use of twirks should be looked upon as a metaphor. When politicians who could not sail a raft across a pond say they are setting a course for the nation's future and steering toward the stars of freedom and prosperity, we do not call that lying. When the rural Southern jury hears the lawyer talk of suppertime — despite a degree from Harvard Law — it does not call that lying, either; it calls it courtesy and linguistic competence.

You need to find out what your own twirks are, and get them under conscious control. This isn't easy, and it's likely to take a lot of time, but it's well worth doing. It requires an objectivity about your own language that is hard to come by, and you may find it helpful to ask other people whose judgment you respect to help you. What you're looking for is elements in your speech (or in your written language) that have either a positive or a negative effect that is *independent of* content. Do you throw obscenities in, every half dozen words or so? Do you have an unusual and distinctive accent? Do you keep saying "like" and "okay" and "well" — using what are called "boundary words" in Valley Girl style? Do you talk in jargon incomprehensible to anyone but a specialist in your field? Do you use Latinisms and pepper your speech or writing with foreign words? These are all twirks. There is nothing wrong with using them — but they should be used consciously and strategically.[1]

Finally — The Case of Oliver North

Lieutenant Colonel Oliver North, testifying before Congress and (by radio and television) before the American people, had a difficult task. He had to sit there and say "Yes, I lied, many many times. Yes, what I was involved in — covert operations — are *by definition* lies. But although my professional career has been based upon my ability to lie well and convincingly and without flinching, I am not lying *now* and you must believe me." Many people would have thought this was not just difficult, but impossible; I suspect that for most of us it would in fact have *been* impossible. But North managed it.

For one unforgettable week in July 1987, the American public had an opportunity to observe Oliver North as he showed us what a "great communicator" *really* is. The American people are known around the world for their brief and fickle attention spans and their reluctance to attend to anything verbal for more than five minutes; consider the boom in sales of rental videotapes when the television networks are airing the Republican and Democratic political conventions. But they were absolutely riveted to their television sets by Oliver North. They listened without benefit of musical score or special effects; they listened, seemingly enchanted, to speeches and to lectures and to sermons, for six full days. There has not been, within this generation's memory, any comparable demonstration of the power of what was, after all, only TALK. I am sure that if Lt. Col. North had been trying to hold his audience at gunpoint it would not have worked nearly as well.

What convinced the public that this man — a self-confessed liar and proud of it — should be believed was not his words. It was his *nonverbal* communication, and a set of irresistibly appealing deliberate twirks, that drew the flood of telegrams demanding that Congress stop picking on him. And caused people to suggest, with considerable passion, that he run for President.

North's testimony was set up in such a way that it offered people seriously interested in the power of language an opportunity for real research — a sort of laboratory experiment. In my own case, because I knew that the detection of lies is easiest when you hear only the voice, I listened to his testimony on National Public Radio before watching tapes of the televised version. And when it was all over, of course, I read the transcript.

The result was astonishing. Long sequences that had sounded dubious at best on the radio, and that were very weak in print, were transformed by television into completely convincing language. The Marine uniform was part of it. So was the open Tom Sawyer face, with the light falling on it at just the right angle — a face upturned, as if toward a bank of enthroned inquisitors. The lovely young wife sitting demurely with folded hands and serene face was a part of it. And the lawyer — the abrasive, rude, argumentative, *professionally* obnoxious lawyer — was there as a Living Twirk, to provide strategic distraction whenever it might be useful. The United States Congress never had a chance.

The amount to be learned from doing what I did — reading North's testimony in print, listening to the audio cassettes, watching the videotapes, and comparing the three versions section by section — is worth the modest investment many many times over. I strongly recommend it.

NOTES

1. You will find much detailed information, and a long checklist of typical twirks, in the third book in this series, *The Last Word on the Gentle Art of Verbal Self-Defense*, also published by Prentice Hall. (You are quite right — it was *not* the last word — and I apologize for the confusion. The title was not selected by me.)

Workout — Chapter 11

1. Here are three quotations about non-truths. Are any of them about *lying*, as you define it? Why or why not?

   a. "In the 1987 budget, the deficit was 'cut' $2 billion by delaying the mailing of monthly military paychecks until after the start of fiscal 1988 . . ."

   (From "The Politics of Obscurity," by Robert J. Samuelson, in *Newsweek* for November 30, 1987; page 56.)

   b. "Born Faith Plotkin on New York's Lower East Side, she adopted the catchy surname in the 1960s. To explain its origin, she created a story that included an immigrant Italian grandfather named Corne, a misunderstanding at Ellis Island ('My name-is-a-Papa Corne,' he supposedly told the authorities) and a subsequent Anglicization." . . . Popcorn, who knows a good marketing tool when she sees one, is unembarrassed by the fabrication. 'Some people say it was my best piece of work'."

   (From "Putting Faith in Trends," by Annetta Miller, in *Newsweek* for June 15, 1987; page 46.)

c. About PERT, a computer program designed especially for the Polaris missile project: "PERT supposedly tracked such things as contractor scheduling. Yet later analysis revealed that PERT was not, in fact, used to manage Polaris missile-project schedules and costs. 'The admiral in charge of Polaris development,' says [Rob] Kling, 'was not concerned how PERT was used, only that its presence be visible.' PERT served to sufficiently enhance the image of the Navy teams managing Polaris development so that they were relatively unburdened by the scrutiny and intrusive demands of external review boards."

(From "The Electronic Rorschach," by Daniel Goleman, in *Psychology Today* for February 1983; page 39.)

2. For a detailed analysis of falsehood — especially in recent U.S. politics — read "The Culture of Lying," by Mark Hosenball, in *The New Republic* for July 13 and 20, 1987, pages 16-18. This article presents a taxonomy of lies, with a broad range of examples.

3. Many people have seriously speculated that Coke only *pretended* to be pulling its product off the market, to create publicity for the "returned" Classic Coke. Apply Miller's Law — assume that what they are saying is true. In that case, was the company lying?

4. From "The Culture of Plagiarism," by Ari Posner (*The New Republic* for April 18, 1988; page 19): "Washington is a ghost town. Practically everybody here who's somebody hired somebody else who's a ghostwriter to craft the words that get spoken or published. . . . Hubert Humphrey elicited little more than amusement when he finished a campaign speech in 1972 by crisply folding his address into his pocket, then adding, 'And now for a few words of my own.' "

Why was it dishonest for Senator Joseph Biden to use words from speeches by Robert Kennedy and Neil Kinnock in his own speeches without crediting them, but okay to use a speechwriter's words that way? The words that Biden "borrowed" from RFK were in fact written by Adam Walinsky, but nobody criticized the Senator for failing to credit *him* — does that make sense to you? Can you define "plagiarism" so that it's different in meaning from "using a ghostwriter"?

5. In *Physician's Management's* "Office Tips" feature for May 1988, S. Clarke Smith MD recommends that when you mention needles in front of patients you call them "the short . . . shorter . . . shortest" needles. That way, the patient doesn't have to hear the actual lengths (5/8", 1", 1 1/2") or the words "long, longer, longest." This is a good example of finding a way to say something that conveys the message, is not false, and avoids a potential problem. In your own experience, is there something perceived as unpleasant that you could launder linguistically in a similar way?

6. From "Pee-Wee's Big Adventure," an article about Senator Paul Simon in *The New Republic* for October 5, 1987; page 25: "Simon has turned his appearance into an asset. He has skillfully exploited his looks to drive home

two overarching points about himself: he is trustworthy and he is authentic (an authentic liberal Democrat, in this case.) His looks — he wears drab blue suits, bow ties, and horn-rimmed glasses — are a metaphor, one he invokes relentlessly. . . . In speech after speech, he mentions the bow tie and glasses. This tactic is gimmicky, but it works." Here we have an example of a politician using a twirk deliberately and strategically. Can you think of other such examples?

SIGHT BITES

1. "Among all the professions, only two or three others can compare with political leadership in its demands that the individual be able to think one thing and yet, *within certain ethical and practical boundaries,* say something quite different."

   (From "The Enigmatic President." by Hedley Donovan, in *Time Magazine* for May 6, 1985; page 29. The other professions Donovan was thinking of were physicians, lawyers, and diplomats.)

2. "Regular listeners to Reagan speeches notice how he can make his voice catch, as if at some sudden emotion, at exactly the same poignant phrase in his repeated tales."

   (From "The Reagan Play-by-Play Still Plays," by Francis X. Clines, in the New York *Times* for March 31, 1985. Would you consider this technique of Reagan's to be an attempt at deception?)

3. "For six days in July, Lt. Col. Oliver North played so sweetly on the panpipes of the American dream that he allowed the television public to believe in any and all of its best-beloved fairy tales. The truth of what he was saying didn't matter as much as the timbre of his voice or the tears in his eyes. The audience could choose to see in his performance what it wished to see. . . . "

   (From "Notebook: Landscape with trolls," by Lewis H. Lapham, in *Harper's* for September 1987; page 6.)

12

Conclusion
The Reality Bridge

What Is Reality?

You could fill a very large library with works written by philosophers and scholars trying to answer the question: What is reality? Their work, in the western tradition, can be summarized by the following four positions on the matter:

1. There is a concrete reality composed of things that are "out there" and that will still be "out there" whether anything exists to perceive them or not. There is a "real tree" that falls in the "real woods" and makes a "real noise," even if no living creature exists to hear it and no machine exists to detect it. This reality is stable, and independent of human perceptions; our role is simply to "discover" the facts and laws that pertain to it.

2. It may be that reality is composed of things that are in fact "out there"; but they are grossly distorted by our human perceptions and therefore subject to constant revision. It's unlikely that "real" things are anything like our perception of them.

3. There's nothing "out there" at all; reality is nothing *but* the sum of a human being's perceptions.

4. There may or may not be something really "out there," but in practical terms it makes no difference —the only reality to which we have *access* is the reality we construct with our human perceptions.

For a discussion of this issue, I refer you to the literature. For our purposes, the question is irrelevant. The reality upon which we base our language behavior is the reality .we store in our memory. And no matter *what* may be "out there" when we deal with the reality of a tree or a cow or an office building, we know that the item itself is not stored inside our skulls. We can therefore discuss our model of reality without trying to settle the weighty question of what, *exactly*, it may be based upon.

The model presented below is neither physiological nor neurological; it is METAPHORICAL. The terms used are common ones — although, as you would expect, the definitions given to them vary from person to person. Linguistically speaking, we set up our model of reality in our memory, and we anchor it with three components:

1. PROTOTYPES. A prototype is the representation in our memory, in terms of semantic features and reality statements, of the most typical item of its particular kind. The bird prototype for speakers of American English — the "birdiest" of birds — is much like a robin and very little like an ostrich. The prototype represents the set of specifications against we judge all creatures we encounter in order to decide whether they *are* birds or not.

2. SCHEMAS. A schema is the representation in our memory of a *context*; often it is a location in space, a *place*. It will include prototypes and information about prototypes. Typical schemas include: The Bank; The Classroom; The Restaurant; The Bedroom; The Beach; The Emerald City of Oz.

3. SCRIPTS. A script is the representation in our memory of a *situation* or *event*. For example: Buying A Car; Applying For A Job; Eating Breakfast.

For each of these components there is a continuum from least to most metaphorical, and the items we see fit to store are stored along that continuum. At one end of the WOMAN PROTOTYPE continuum would be your summary representation of the typical average "real world" woman. Somewhere farther along would be the Dance Hall Girl With Heart Of Gold — because such women have actually lived "out there." And at the farthest and most metaphorical point would be women of total fantasy . . . Wonder Woman, for example. This continuum is illustrated in Figure Thirteen.

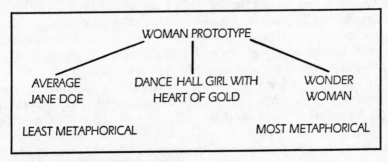

FIGURE 13. WOMAN PROTOTYPE

In order to use the system that we have established, we have to carry out three tasks:

1. We assign things we encounter to already-existing slots; seeing an ostrich, we decide that although it's not very prototypical, it *is* a bird.

2. We create new categories and assign to them things that we cannot fit into an existing slot.

3. We assign things by metaphor, by deciding that *X* is LIKE some established prototype, schema, or script.

Some of the assignments we make in this way are essentially permanent. Barring some remarkable scientific reversal, when we sort a creature into the slot labeled BIRD we leave it there. Others are temporary, as when we assign our corporation to the stored category PROUD SHIP SAILING, way over at the fantasy end of that continuum. It's as if each category had both drawers that you can put things into and close for long-term storage, and hooks that you can hang things on for the short term. What makes anything "nameless" so disturbing to us is that this system won't *work* without names.

My Reality or Yours?

We don't know exactly what the incoming data of reality are like; that's why there is a controversy. Our senses tell us that the railroad tracks come together in a point in the distance, but our experience when we try to walk to that point tells us the perception is false. Our scientific instruments tell us that this world we live on is traveling around the sun at a speed of 66,700 miles an hour — but our senses tell us that's nonsense. The panther I see in my bedroom because of a high fever is just as "real" to my senses as any other panther — my body reacts to them both in exactly the same way. The table that I trust to hold my book because I "know" it to be a solid is actually composed mostly of empty space; this body of mine, that I perceive as equally solid and stable, is the site of wars and massacres on an enormous scale as its cells go about their extraordinary business. If you have any difficulty accepting the dubiousness of our ordinary perceptions, please read *The Secret House* by David Bodanis immediately; that will fix it.

But although we know very little about the data itself, we do know — metaphorically — what we do with it. Assume that we are talking of two human beings, John and Jane. Both — so far as can be known — are facing the *same* external reality, whatever it may be. The data are perceived by their human sensory systems — sight, hearing, touch, taste, smell, and so on. Then, using the reality model in their memories, they process the data, storing some information for retrieval, letting other information pass by without indexing. We can illustrate the results as in Figures Fourteen and Fifteen.

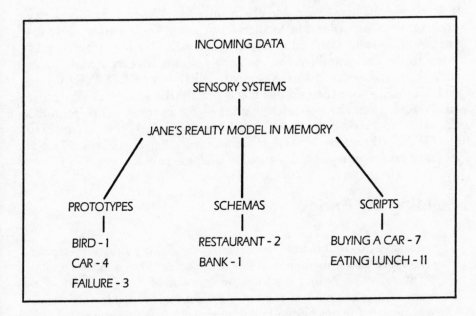

FIGURE 14. JANE'S REALITY

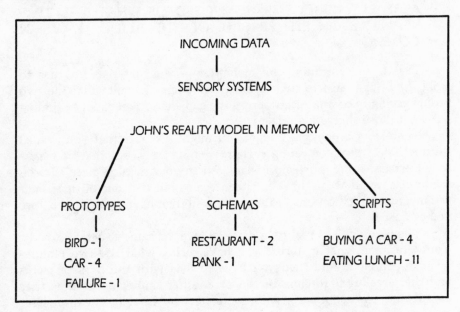

FIGURE 15. JOHN'S REALITY

That is, John and Jane are processing the same incoming stream of data, so far as it's possible to determine. But they are not processing it in exactly the same *way*, and the results are not identical. They may not choose to pay attention to the same things. Their sensory systems are not likely to be identical in strength and skill. The backgrounds they bring to the data are different. And the result is that they both notice something and assign it to the category BIRD — or RESTAURANT — or FAILURE — but they do not mean exactly the same thing by those labels. And when the mismatch matters — for example, when John has FAILURE-1, marked [-FINAL], and Jane has FAILURE-3, marked [++ FINAL], the scene is set for a communication breakdown. This is a reality gap; what is needed is a reality bridge across it.

Building the Bridge

You will have no trouble now constructing the Reality Bridge metaphor. Like the Pony Finder metaphor, it has four parts. There will be a Reality Gap. There will be Reality A's team on one side of the gap and Reality B's team on the other. And then you need a Reality Bridge. The most crucial principle for this bridge-building project is the following:

> A REALITY BRIDGE IS COMPOSED OF WHAT THE TWO REALITIES ON EITHER SIDE OF THE BRIDGE HAVE IN *COMMON*.

That is — continuing the metaphor — the materials you use to build the bridge have to come from those parts of reality that the two groups trying to communicate across the gap *share*. You begin by finding out what those shared materials are.

In building a physical bridge, you might discover that you needed fourteen steel beams meeting certain specifications, but that you have only thirteen — the fourteenth beam is then your missing piece. Or you might discover that you have fourteen beams but that one of them does not meet the specifications — that beam will then have to be fixed before you can use it.

When you build a reality bridge you face the same situation exactly. You determine what materials you have, using what the two realities have in common. And then you have to deal with the missing pieces and the pieces that for one reason or another cannot be used as they are. If you are negotiating with someone who literally does not have any representation in memory for some item in yours, that is a missing piece. It usually indicates only a lack of information or experience. More common is the situation in which the problem lies in semantic features that are different from the ones you need in order to proceed — either because one group has a plus value where the other has a minus, or because the strength of the plus or minus values differs for the two groups.

The tools and the processes that you use to build your bridge are these three:

- □ The grammar of your native language
- □ Your skill in using that language
- □ The principles of *Gentle Art* syntonics

Before the bridge is built, Team A is on one side of the gap and Team B is on the other, and nothing can be done because of the distance that separates them. After the bridge is built, something *can* be done, and the only question is how far each team should have to move to do it.

For Team A to cross the bridge and join Team B on the other side (or vice versa) is a kind of *conversion*, after which you could tear down the bridge because nobody needs it any longer. This is ordinarily appropriate only in very simple situations with trivial consequences. Most of the time nothing so dramatic is either necessary or desirable — conversion is rarely worth the trouble you'd have to go through to achieve it. Instead, your goal is to set up a bridge sturdy enough to allow both teams to go out in the middle and interact successfully.

There is a single set of bridge-building metarules that is part of every technique in the GENTLE ART syntonics system. Here they are:

METARULE ONE. *Identify* the other person's reality.

METARULE TWO. *Match* the other person's reality, temporarily.

METARULE THREE. Introduce change — slowly, always tying the new to the old — to bring the two realities closer together.

Let's take a very basic example. Suppose you must talk to someone who is out of control. Suppose that one of your colleagues (let's call him Tom) has lost his temper in a meeting and is carrying on to such an extent that not only is the negotiation in jeopardy but there is a substantial risk to both his reputation and the reputation of your group. Clearly, the tantrum has to be stopped, and it appears to you that you are the person who has to stop it. You could always knock Tom down or carry him bodily from the room (and I have read materials advising you to shout "Tom — STOP IT!") But there's a better way, and one that doesn't carry the risk of a major loss of face for Tom or for anyone else involved. You use the metarules and proceed as follows:

USING RULE ONE:

You identify Tom's reality by observation, using your sensory systems and the data in your memory. You identify details — he is breathing very fast, he is blinking his eyes rapidly, he is standing up, he is talking fast and high and loud and frantic.

USING RULE TWO:

You match Tom's reality. You begin breathing at the same rate and speed as his breathing; you begin blinking your eyes in synchrony with him. You begin nodding your head in the same rhythm as his speech, and making reassuring sounds in that same rhythm. Then, when the two of you are as syntonic as you can manage, you're ready to lead him out of the situation.

USING RULE THREE:

You introduce change. You begin breathing more slowly, blinking more slowly, nodding more slowly, a little at a time, always waiting for him to adjust before you add more change — until he has followed you as far as is necessary into *your* reality, where things are calm and under control.

If you do this right, it won't take very long and it will work exceedingly well. The real danger is not that the other person will refuse to follow your lead. That happens, and it means only that you have to try again, or try something else. The real danger is that instead of leading Tom toward your reality you will go the *other* direction, with the result being a tantrum for two instead of just for Tom. (I see this happen from time to time when healthcare staff are faced with hysterical or panicked patients, and it's not pretty.) That shouldn't happen if you understand what you're doing and are paying attention every step of the way. Use the techniques you have learned in this book.

FOR RULE ONE:

Apply Miller's Law. Listen syntonically, so that you can achieve interactional synchrony. *Ask* for information when you need it: use your language skills as a way to find out what reality is being perceived by those you are interacting with. Use techniques like semantic feature analysis to help you identify your *own* reality with clarity — if you don't know where you are, you're not likely to be able to lead somebody else there.

FOR RULE TWO:

Match Sensory Modes. Choose your Satir Modes by the metaprinciples. Ask yourself: DO I WANT THIS TO GROW OR NOT? If you must complain, structure your complaint as a three-part message. Find the presuppositions in the other person's verbal attacks and respond to them, ignoring the bait. Express yourself in terms of the metaphor from within which the other person is functioning. If you can use a twirk that will make the other person feel reassured, do so.

FOR RULE THREE:

Use semantic modulation and bridge metaphors to move from the other person's metaphor toward the one you have chosen as target — the one that represents *your* reality. Select topics that can succeed, and introduce them by the rules. Give clear turn-taking cues and follow up on those that are given to you. Make sure you don't use words that are contradicted by your body language. Don't lie if you can help it; if you *must* lie, do it well. Keep the linguistic toxins out of your own language. When you can, Level.

The process is exactly the same, whether the goal is calming down an over-excited colleague, or convincing a supplier to revise a contract, or bringing an end to a strike, or healing a conflict in the personal domain . . . or any one of the myriad other situations, from the simplest to the most complex, in which a communication breakdown stands squarely in the way of a successful resolution. And it is *always* your best choice.

Nothing can be achieved if Team A and Team B insist on sitting on opposite sides of the reality gap with their backs turned and their minds firmly shut, resenting one another and growing ever farther apart.

Nothing of lasting value can be achieved by force — by the linguistic equivalent of throwing one team across the gap into a reality they do not understand and will not accept. That may improve matters for a while, but in the long run it will only lead to new reality gaps and worse problems than the ones you started with.

The only valid way to repair a communication breakdown is by building a reality bridge on which both sides can meet safely and comfortably. YOU CAN DO THAT NOW. You have the necessary information. You have the necessary skills. And you have the power — *real* and lasting and abundant power — that goes with them.

Workout — Chapter 12

1. We used to believe that the way people learned information was by *rehearsing* it over and over and over again. But it has been proved beyond all question that what matters most to learning is not rehearsal but *transformation*. That is, the more different ways a given body of information is presented

to you, the more likely you are to learn and remember it. Using the model of memory presented in this chapter, can you explain why this is true?

2. One of the most astonishing events for Western culture in recent years was the discovery that *visualization* of an event — playing a composition on the piano, playing a particular golf course or skiing down a particular slope, dancing a ballet role — not only leads to as much improvement in performance as "really" carrying out the activity does, but often leads to *more*. The more detailed the visualization is, the more vivid it is, the more effective the technique. What does this tell you about the reality that you construct in your memory? How can you use this new information in your professional or business life? Do you think it would apply to operations performed by surgeons? To summations of court cases by lawyers? To presentations of new advertising campaigns to clients?

   What do you suppose would happen if people tried to "really" do things for the first time without ever having had any experience *except* visualization? If that worked, what would be the impact on the American economy — which industries and professions would be most drastically affected?

3. Choose one prototype, one script, and one scenario, and try making a list of all the elements each would have to contain in your own memory in order to be useful. A good way to do this is to set down everything you would have to program into a computer in order for *it* to deal satisfactorily with the item. This is so difficult a task that it's probably impossible to do it with even rough adequacy. But the attempt is extremely useful as a method for gaining an understanding of the way your memory stores and structures information.

4. When you've gone as far as you can with #3, choose the simplest of your lists and have someone in your circle prepare his or her own version. Then compare the two to see how well the two realities match.

5. George B. Leonard says that "Any serious attempt at including unfamiliar phenomena in a certain verbal realm may change reality as perceived in that realm." ("Language and Reality," *Harper's* for November 1974, page 46.) Do you agree? Why or why not? Can you think of an example that supports your position?

SIGHT BITES

1. "A script is a set of expectations, a codified set of information that seems to be associated in the mind with a particular event . . . "

   (From "A Conversation with Roger Schrank," an interview by Frank Kendig, in *Psychology Today* for April 1983; page 32.)

2. "What Americans carry in their minds is not the historical reality of the cowboy but the myth as it came to them in books and movies, the cowboy according to Zane Grey and John Wayne. Americans, tutored in the lore from childhood, almost unconsciously see cowboy stories as morality plays."

(From "Smile When You Say That," by Lance Morrow, in *Time* for October 28, 1985; page 114.)

3. "Can the human mind grasp anything at all without altering it in the act of grasping it? Have we any notion, then, of what things are like before we make contact with them? These questions were originally asked about the use of our senses to perceive the world around us, but they are easily transferred to our use of language to describe that world. Perhaps the divisions that our vocabulary makes between one kind of thing and another are really alien to the true natures of those things. Maybe the general forms in which we cast our descriptions of the world are really a kind of distorting lens."

(From "The Mysteries of Meaning," by David Pears, in *The New Republic* for May 19, 1986; page 38.)

4. " . . . the process of coming to regard a new opinion as true is one in which we seek to find an opinion that will mediate between the old stock and the new experience; and in this process *any* belief in the old stock, even one in mathematics, logic, or metaphysics, is at the mercy of experience."

(Gerald E. Myers, discussing the philosophy of William James, in "Good In The Way Of Belief," in *The New Republic* for December 29, 1986; page 27.)

5. "There are several billion actual minds. They can imagine ever so many possibilities, each of which can, by a flight of metaphor, be called a possible world."

(From a review of Jerome Bruner's *Actual Minds, Possible Worlds*, titled "The Other Side Of The Mind," by Ian Hacking, in *The New Republic* for June 9, 1986; page 32.)

6. "There are certain words that English ought to have but does not. One is a word for the opposite of memory. *Oblivion* is not quite it. *Forgettery?* That swampy region in the southland of the brain where everything we have forgotten now lies, overgrown with kudzu, something like an enormous automobile graveyard."

(From "Poof! The Phenomenon of Public Vanishing," by Lance Morrow, in *Time* for May 15, 1985; page 86. What is your reaction to the metaphor used by Morrow? Would a Southerner have the same reaction as a Yankee?)

Appendixes

The *Gentle Art* Syntonics System of Verbal Self-Defense — An Overview

Just as there is a grammar of English for such things as the tenses of verbs and the order of words in sentences, there is a grammar of English for verbal violence and verbal self-defense. All native speakers of English know this grammar flawlessly, although many factors — such as stress, nervousness, illness, lack of time, and the like — can interfere with their demonstration of that flawless knowledge. The problem is that the information is not available at a level of conscious awareness, and people cannot therefore conveniently make use of it. The syntonics system of verbal self-defense is designed to correct this problem.

When you use this system, you will not be restricted to sarcastic comebacks and counterattacks for use in verbal confrontations. Instead, you will be able to create for yourself a language environment in which such confrontations will be very *rare*. Furthermore, when they do occur you will be able to deal with them quickly and competently, with no sacrifice of your own self-respect, and no loss of face on either side of the interaction.

This section contains a brief overview of the basic principles of the system, together with three examples of techniques for putting it to use. You will find many more detailed examples of these and other techniques throughout the book; this section is for your reference and review.

REFERENCE ITEMS:

THE FOUR BASIC PRINCIPLES

260

ONE: KNOW THAT YOU ARE UNDER ATTACK.

TWO: KNOW WHAT KIND OF ATTACK YOU ARE FACING.

THREE: KNOW HOW TO MAKE YOUR DEFENSE FIT THE ATTACK.

FOUR: KNOW HOW TO FOLLOW THROUGH.

The first principle is important — most verbal victims are unaware that they are victims. Typically, they feel miserable but they don't know why, and they tend to blame not those who abuse them but themselves.

The second and third principles work together, to help you tailor your responses. When you learn to recognize language modes (like the Sensory and Satir Modes described below) and to construct responses based on rules for their use, you are applying these two principles.

The fourth principle is often the hardest. There are two barriers to its implementation: (1) the idea that if you don't participate in the power game of verbal abuse you are letting the abuser "get away with it"; and (2) the problem of feeling guilty about defending yourself (especially common among women).

MILLER'S LAW:

"In order to understand what another person is saying, you must assume that it is true and try to imagine what it could be true *of*." (George Miller, 1980)

ELGIN'S COROLLARY:

In order for other people to understand what you are saying, you must make it possible for them to apply Miller's Law to your language.

SYNTONICS

Syntonics, in the *Gentle Art* system, is the science of language harmony. The name is taken from the term "syntonic," used in radio telegraphy to describe two radio sets sufficiently well tuned to one another to allow the efficient and effective transmission of information. When people attempt to communicate with each other, they need to try for a similar syntonic state.

PRESUPPOSITION

A presupposition is anything that a native speaker of a language knows is part of the meaning of a sequence of that language — even if it does not appear on the surface of the sequence. For example, every native speaker of English knows that the meaning of the sentence "EVen JOHN could pass THAT course!" includes two more propositions: that the class is somehow second-rate, and so is John. The sentence means: "Even John (who, as everybody knows, is no great shakes as a student) could pass that course (which, as everybody knows, is a really trivial class.") But the negative comments about John and the course are not there in the surface structure of the sentence; they are presupposed.

Most verbal attacks, with the exception of the very crudest ones, are at least partly hidden away in presuppositions.

First Technique — Using the Sensory Modes

Human beings can't survive without information. We need data from the outside environment and from our bodies; we need data from other human beings and living creatures. And we need a system for *managing* all this data, or it would be impossible to deal with. Information that's coming in has to be processed: it must be selected, and understood, and then either discarded or indexed for storage in memory. Information going out has to be processed also, so that it can be expressed for other people to understand. Our primary mechanism for this processing is the set of sensory systems — sight and hearing and touch, taste and smell, etc.

Each of us has a preferred sensory system that we find easiest to use, and that helps us the most in understanding and remembering. And when we express ourselves, we often demonstrate that preference by using one of the language behavior modes called Sensory Modes. Like this —

SIGHT: "I really like the way this looks."

HEARING: "This just sounds great to me."

TOUCH: "I don't feel right about this."

SMELL: "This whole plan smells fishy to me."

TASTE: "This leaves an awful taste in my mouth."

People who hear you matching their preferred Sensory Modes are more likely to trust you and to listen to what you say. They think of you as someone who speaks their language and shares their perceptions. This is the easiest of all the *Gentle Art* techniques, and is one that you can put to use immediately.

Under normal circumstances, people can switch from one Sensory Mode to another without any difficulty. But when they're under stress they tend to get locked in to their preferred Mode. The more upset they are, the more trouble they will have understanding communication in other Sensory Modes, and the more trouble they will have using other Sensory Modes to express themselves. In such situations, you will improve communication drastically if you *match* the Sensory Mode they are using.

You'll have no trouble identifying the Sensory Mode coming at you. Because you are a fluent speaker of English, you will do this automatically. You can then tailor your own response for maximum efficiency and effectiveness by following these two simple rules.

RULE ONE: MATCH THE SENSORY MODE COMING AT YOU.

RULE TWO: IF YOU CAN'T FOLLOW RULE ONE, USE NO SENSORY MODE LANGUAGE AT ALL.

Second Technique — Using the Satir Modes

Dr. Virginia Satir was a world-famous family therapist. As she worked with clients, she noticed that the language behavior of people under stress tends to fall into one of the following five categories: the Satir Modes.

BLAMING:

"WHY don't you ever think about anybody ELSE's feelings? Don't you even CARE ABOUT OTHERS?"

PLACATING:

"Oh, YOU know how I am! Shoot — whatever YOU want to do is okay with ME!"

COMPUTING:

"There is undoubtedly a good reason for this delay. No sensible person would be upset about it."

DISTRACTING:

"WHat IS the MATTER with you, ANYway? Not that *I* care! YOU know me — I can put up with ANYthing! However, common sense would indicate that the original rules should be followed."

LEVELING:

"I like you. But I don't like your methods."

Each of the Satir Modes has a characteristic style of body language. Blamers shake their fists or their index fingers; they scowl and frown and loom over people. Placaters cling and fidget and lean on others. Computers are stiff and rigid, moving as little as possible. Distracters cycle through the other Modes with their bodies just as they do with their words. The body language of Levelers is distinguished by the absence of these other patterns, and by the fact that it is not in conflict with their words.

The first four Satir Modes are examples of the lack of a *personal* syntonic state. People use Blamer Mode because they are insecure and afraid that nobody will respect or obey them. They use Placater Mode — saying that they don't care because they care so very much. They use Computer Mode — saying "I have no emotions" — because they are afraid of the emotions they actually feel and afraid to let them show. Distracter Mode cycles through all of these states of mismatch and expresses panic.

Only with Leveler Mode do you have a syntonic state. To the extent that they are capable of accurately judging their own feelings, people using Leveler Mode use words and body language that match those feelings.

As with the Sensory Modes, people can ordinarily switch from one Satir Mode to the other, but tend to become locked in to a preferred Satir Mode in situations of tension and stress.

The rules for using the Satir Modes are based on the same metaprinciple as those for using Sensory Modes: ANYTHING YOU FEED WILL GROW. When you match a language pattern coming at you, you feed it and it escalates. The difference between the two techniques is that it's always a good thing to match another person's Sensory Mode — because increasing the level of trust and rapport is always a good thing — but you should only match a Satir Mode if you want to feed that pattern.

Here are the results you can count on. BLAMING AT A BLAMER causes fights and scenes. PLACATING AT A PLACATER causes undignified delay. COMPUTING AT A COMPUTER causes dignified delay. DISTRACTING AT A DISTRACTER is panic feeding panic. And LEVELING AT A LEVELER means an exchange of the simple truth, going both ways.

In any language interaction, once you've recognized the Satir Mode coming at you, you have to choose your response. You make your choice based on the situation, on what you know about the other person, and on your own communication goals. Here are the two rules you need:

RULE ONE: IF YOU DON'T KNOW WHAT TO DO, USE COMPUTER MODE.

RULE TWO: IF IT WOULD BE DESIRABLE TO HAVE THE SATIR MODE COMING AT YOU ESCALATE, MATCH THAT MODE.

Third Technique: Recognizing and Responding to the Verbal Attack Patterns of English

Many people don't realize that they are verbal victims because the verbal abuse they are subjected to is not *openly* abusive. Most verbal abusers don't just spit out curses and insults. Instead, they use verbal attack patterns (VAPS) that are part of the grammar of English verbal violence. These patterns are just as dangerous as shouted obscenities, but much more subtle.

The attack patterns discussed below have two parts. There is the BAIT, which the attacker expects you to respond to. It's easy to recognize, because it's the part that *hurts*. And then there is the attack that matters, which is usually hidden away in the form of one or more presuppositions. Here's an example.

"If you REALLY loved me, YOU wouldn't waste MONEY the way you do!"

The bait is the part about wasting money; that is what the attacker expects you to respond to. You are expected to take the bait and say, "What do you MEAN, I waste money! I DO NOT!" And then you are off to a flaming row — not a good way to handle the situation.

The important part of the attack is not the bait, but the presupposition at the beginning — "YOU DON'T REALLY LOVE ME." Instead of taking the bait, respond directly to that presupposed attack.

Say "When did you start thinking that I don't really love you?" or "Of *course* I love you!" This is not what the attacker expects, and it will short-circuit the confrontation.

Here are some other examples of English VAPS. You will find more information about them throughout the book, together with suggested responses.

"If you REALLY wanted me to get good grades, YOU'D buy me a comPUTer like all the OTHER kids have got!"

"A person who REALLY cared about his health wouldn't WANT to smoke!"

"DON'T you even CARE if the neighbors are all LAUGHING AT US?"

"EVen a woman YOUR age should be able to cook a decent LUNCH!"

"EVerybody underSTANDS why you're so TOUCHy, you know!"

"WHY don't you ever LISTEN to me when I talk to you?"

"SOME people would be FURIous if they had to put up with an employee who never did her share of the work!"

"You KNOW I'd never tell you how to run your LIFE — but DON'T MARRY that woman!"

"YOU'RE not the ONly person around here who has PROBlems, you know."

"EVen if you DO forget my birthday again, I'LL still love you."

"You could at LEAST get to WORK on time!"

It's important to realize that what makes these examples attacks is not the words they contain. For English, more than half of the information is not in the words but in the body language, including the intonation of the voice. To recognize a verbal attack, you have to pay attention to the intonation — the melody of the voice — that goes *with* the words. Any time you hear a lot of extra stresses and emphasis on words or parts of words, you should be on the alert.

THERE IS NO MORE IMPORTANT CUE TO RECOGNIZING VERBAL ATTACKS THAN ABNORMAL STRESS PATTERNS. The sentence, "Why do you eat so much junk food?" may be very rude and unkind, but it's not a verbal attack. The attack that goes with those words sounds like this: "WHY do you eat SO MUCH JUNK food?"

In dealing with verbal attack patterns, you have three rules to follow. Here they are.

RULE ONE: IGNORE THE BAIT.

RULE TWO: RESPOND DIRECTLY TO THE ATTACK HIDDEN IN THE PRESUPPOSITION(S).

RULE THREE: NO MATTER WHAT ELSE YOU DO, SAY SOMETHING THAT TRANSMITS THIS MESSAGE: "DON'T TRY THAT WITH ME — I WON'T PLAY THAT GAME."

Nobody can carry on a verbal attack alone. It takes two people — one to be the attacker, and one to be the victim. People who use verbal abuse do so because they want the fight or the scene and they value the havoc they create. When you take the bait in their attacks and go along with their plans, you aren't showing them how strong and assertive you are — you are giving them exactly what they want, and the more you do that, the worse the situation will get.

EVERY TIME YOU TAKE THE BAIT IN A VERBAL ATTACK, YOU ARE PARTICIPATING IN A SELF-REINFORCING FEEDBACK LOOP. Instead of doing that, use this technique and break out of the loop.

References
And
Bibliography

Articles

Abbey, M. "Talking Tory." *Canadian Forum*, March 1984, pp. 7-13.

Addington, D.W. "The Relationship of Selected Vocal Characteristics to Personality Perception." *Speech Monographs* 35 (1968), pp. 492-503.

Adessa, M. "Sad Hearts." *Psychology Today*, September 1988, p. 24.

Ailes, R. "Scoring on Defense: Tactics to Defeat the Hostile Questioner." *Success*, December 1988, p. 14.

Ajemian, R. and D. Beck. "I've Been Underestimated." (Interview with George Bush.) *Time*, August 22, 1988, pp. 20-21.

Allman, W.F. "Mindworks." *Science 86*, May 1986, pp. 23-31.

————. "Staying Alive in the 20th Century." *Science 85*, October 1985, pp. 31-37.

Alper, J. "The Roots of Morality." *Science 85*, March 1985, pp. 70-76.

Apple, R. W., Jr. "The Presidency. . .The News Conference: A Comparison." The New York *Times*, January 9, 1986.

Arnott, N. "Trouble Spots." *Executive Female*, May/June 1988, pp. 45-48.

Aronovitch, C.D. "The Voice of Personality: Stereotyped Judgments of Their Relation to Voice Quality and Sex of Speaker." *Journal of Social Psychology* 99 (1976), pp. 207-220.

Atkinson, R., and R. Schiffrin. "The Control of Short-term Memory." *Scientific American* 225 (1971), pp. 82-90.

Bailey, R. "Not power but empower." *Forbes*, May 30, 1988, pp. 122-123.

Barber, H. R. K. "The Professional Future of the Ob/Gyn Clinician." *The Female Patient*, September 1986, pp. 9-16.

Barnes, F. "Pee-Wee's Big Adventure." *The New Republic*, October 5, 1987, pp. 25-27.

Barrett, L. I. "A Quick Lesson in Major-League Politics." *Time*, September 5, 1988, pp. 16-17.

————— and B. Seaman. "Yankee Doodle Magic." *Time*, July 7, 1986, pp. 12-16.

Barzini, L. "The Americans: Why we baffle the Europeans." *Harper's*, December 1981, pp. 29-36 and 83-85.

Beattie, G.W. "Planning Units in Spontaneous Speech: Some Evidence from Hesitation in Speech and Speaker Gaze Direction in Conversation." *Linguistics 17* (1969), pp. 61-78.

—————. "The Regulation of Speaker-Turns in Face-to-Face Conversation: Some Implications for Conversation in Sound-Only Communication Channels." *Semiotica* 34 (1981), pp. 55-70.

—————, et al. "Why Is Mrs. Thatcher Interrupted So Often?" *Nature 300* (1982), pp. 744-47.

Bell, C. "Family Violence." *Journal of the American Medical Association*, September 19, 1986, pp. 1501-1502.

Berman, P., with D. Wechsler. "Calling all hogs." *Forbes*, September 5, 1988, pp. 42-52.

Blendon, R. J., et al. "Uncompensated Care by Hospitals or Public Insurance For the Poor: Does It Make a Difference?" *New England Journal of Medicine*, May 1, 1986, pp. 1160-1163.

Bohannon, L. "Shakespeare in the Bush." *Natural History*, August-September 1966, pp. 28-33.

Bolinger, D. "Accent is Predictable (If You're A Mind-Reader)." *Language 48* (1972), pp. 633-44.

—————. "Contrastive Accent and Contrastive Stress." *Language 37* (1961), pp. 83-96.

Brand, S. "Apocalypse Juggernaut, Hello!" *Co-Evolution Quarterly*, Summer 1976, pp. 4-6.

Brown, D. L. "What Goes Up. . . " *Inc.*, July 1988, pp. 25-26.

Bruneau, T. J. "Chronemics and Verbal-Nonverbal Interface." In M. R. Key, ed., *The Relationship of Verbal and Nonverbal Communication*, The Hague: Mouton, 1980, pp. 101-117.

Carpenter, R. H. "The Problem of Style in Presidential Discourse." In J. D. Trent et al., eds., *Concepts in Communication*, Boston: Allyn and Bacon 1973, pp. 110-126.

Carson, T. "The Prime Time of Ronald Reagan." *Village Voice,* September 4, 1984.

Charrow, V. R. "Linguistic theory and the Study of Legal and Bureaucratic Language." In L. K. Obler and L. Nenn, *Exceptional Language and Linguistics* (New York: Academic Press, 1982). pp. 81–101.

Clines, F. X. "The Reagan Play-by-Play Still Plays." New York *Times,* March 31, 1985.

Cohn, C. "Slick'ems, Glick'ems, Christmas Trees, and Cookie Cutters: Nuclear Language and How We Learned to Pat the Bomb." *Bulletin of the Atomic Scientists,* June 1987, pp. 17–24.

Condon, W. S. and L. W. Sander. "Neonate Movement Is Synchronized with Adult Speech: Interactional Participation and Language Acquisition." *Science 183* (1974), pp. 99–101.

————. "The Relation of Interactional Synchrony to Cognitive and Emotional Processes." In M. R. Key, ed., *The Relationship of Verbal and Nonverbal Communication* (The Hague: Mouton, 1980), pp. 49–65.

Conely, J. M., W. M. O'Barr, and A. E. Lind. "The Power of Language: Presentation Style in the Courtroom." *Duke University Law Journal* 6 (1978), pp. 1375–99.

Conway, F. and J. Siegelman. "The Awesome Power of the Mind-Probers." *Science Digest,* September 1983, pp. 72–75, and p. 91.

Cosmides, L. "Invariance in the acoustic expression of emotion during speech." *Journal of Experimental Psychology,* December 1983, pp. 864–881.

Craik, F. I. M., and R. S. Lockhart. "Levels of Processing: A Framework for Memory Research." *Journal of Verbal Learning and Verbal Behavior* 11 (1972): 671-84.

Cousins, N. "Taking Charge of Your Health." *Science 85,* October 1985, pp. 77–85.

Dennett, D. "The Imagination Extenders." *Psychology Today,* December 1982, pp. 30–39.

Dimsdale, J.E. "A Perspective on Type A Behavior and Coronary Disease." *New England Journal of Medicine,* January 14, 1988, pp. 110–112.

Donovan, H. "The Enigmatic President." *Time,* May 6, 1985, pp. 24–33.

Douglis, C. "The Beat Goes On." *Psychology Today,* November 1987, pp. 38–42.

Dowd, M. "Schroeder: At Ease with Femininity and Issues." *New York Times,* August 23, 1987.

Edelman, M. "Language, Myths and Rhetoric." *Society,* July-August 1976, pp. 14–21.

Edelsky, C. "Who's Got the Floor?" *Language in Society 10* (1981), pp. 383–421.

Ekman, P. "Discover the Secrets of Facial Language." *Psychology Today* Tape #20335; 1988.

Ekman, P., et al. "Body movement and voice pitch in deceptive interactions." *Semiotica 16* (1976), pp. 23–27.

—————., and W. V. Friesen. "Nonverbal Leakage and Clues to Deception." *Psychiatry 32* (1969), pp. 88–106.

—————. "The Repertoire of Nonverbal Behavior: Categories, Origins, Usage, and Coding." *Semiotica 1*(1969), pp. 49–68.

Elgin, S. H. "Verbal Self-Defense in Emergency Medicine." *Emergency Medical Services*, September 1987, pp. 49–52.

Ellot, R. S. "Predicting Workplace Blood Pressure." *Practical Cardiology/ Special Supplement 1987*, pp. 3–7.

Epstein, S. E., et al. "Current Concepts: Myocardial Ischemia Silent or Symptomatic." *New England Journal of Medicine*, April 21, 1988, pp. 1038–1043.

Ervin-Tripp, S. M., M. C. O'Connor, and J. Rosenberg. "Language and Power in the Family." In C. Kramarae et al., eds., *Language and Power* (Beverly Hills: Sage Publications, 1984), pp. 116–35.

Ewing, D. W. "Canning Directions." *Harper's*, August 1979, pp. 16–22.

Fairlie, H. "On The Hill: Curtain Call." *The New Republic*, September 7, 1987, pp. 16–19.

Fellman, B. "Talk: the not-so-silent killer." *Science 85*, December 1985, pp. 70–71.

Finegan, J. "The Entrepreneurial Numbers Game." *Inc.*, May 1986, pp. 31–36.

Fischman, J. "Type A Situations." *Psychology Today*, September 1988, pp. 22–4. (In "Minding Your Health.")

—————. "Blood Pressure Woes: The I's Have It." *Psychology Today*, September 1988, pp. 22–4. (In "Minding Your Health.")

Fisher, A. "Science Newsfront." *Popular Science*, January 1988, pp. 8–14.

Forbes, M. F. "Other Comments." *Forbes*, August 22, 1988, page 24.

Frankel, R. M. "The Laying On of Hands: Aspects of the Organization of Gaze, Touch and Talk in a Medical Encounter." In S. Fisher and A. D. Todd, *The Social Organization of Doctor-Patient Communication* (Washington, D.C. : Center for Applied Linguistics, 1983), pp. 19–54.

Fromkin, V. "Slips of the Tongue." *Scientific American 229* (1973), pp. 110–17.

Gantt, W. H., et al. "Effect of Person." *Conditional Reflex 1* (1966), pp. 18–35.

Gardner, H. and E. Winnes. "The Child Is Father To The Metaphor." *Psychology Today*, May 1979, pp. 81–91.

Gates, D., with J. Smith. "Keeping the Flat-Earth Faith." *Newsweek*, July 2, 1984, page 12.

Geller, E. S. "States of Mind: Seat Belt Psychology." *Psychology Today*, May 1985, pp. 12–13.

Goldhaber, G. M. "The Charisma Factor: Why Dan Rather May Be In Trouble." *TV Guide*, May 2, 1981, pp. 4–10.

Goleman, D. "Physicians May Bungle Key Part of Treatment: The Medical Interview." New York *Times*, January 21, 1988.

––––––. "The Electronic Rorschach." *Psychology Today*, February 1983, pp. 36–43.

––––––. "Can You Tell When Someone Is Lying To You?" *Psychology Today*, August 1982, pp. 14–23.

––––––. "People Who Read People." *Psychology Today*, February 1981, pp. 66–78.

––––––. "The 7,000 Faces of Dr. Ekman." *Psychology Today*, February 1981, pp. 43–49.

Graham, J. "The New Wright Stuff." *Advertising Age*, August 15, 1988, page 8.

Greydanus, D.E. "Risk-Taking Behaviors in Adolescence." *Journal of the American Medical Association*, October 16, 1987, p. 2110.

Hacking, I. "The Other Side of the Mind." *The New Republic*, June 9, 1986, pp. 30–31.

Haden, R. "A Comparative Exploration of the Expression of Anger in Fourteen Languages, and Some Implications." *Arktesol Post*, Summer/Fall 1987, pp. 7–10.

Hakuta, K. "Seize The Moment." *Success*, December 1988, pp. 50–51.

Hall, E. "Schooling Children In a Nasty Climate." (Interview with Jerome Bruner.) *Psychology Today*, January 1982, pp. 57–64.

––––––. "Giving Away Psychology in the 80's: George Miller Interviewed by Elizabeth Hall." *Psychology Today*, January 1980, pp. 38–50, and 97–98.

Hall, E. T. "Proxemics." *Current Anthropology 9* (1968), pp. 83–104.

Harbrecht, D. et al. "Can Bush Bounce Back?" *Business Week*, August 22, 1988, pp. 26–29.

Harragan B. L. "Why Corporations Are Teaching Men To Think Like Women . . . And Other Secret Game Plans That You May Not Have Been Briefed On." *Ms.*, JUNE 1977, pp. 62–62 and 87–88.

Hartman, C., "Redesigning America." *Inc.*, June 1988, pp. 58–74.

Harvey, J. B. "The Abilene Paradox: The Management of Agreement." *Organizational Dynamics*, Summer 1974, pp. 1–18.

Hawken, P. "Surviving in Small Business." *Coevolution Quarterly*, Spring 1984, pp. 14–17.

Heller, L. "The Last Angry Men? What Men Really Feel About Working With Women." *Executive Female*, September/October 1988, pp. 33–38.

Henry, G. L., ed. "Legal Rounds." *Emergency Medicine*, July 15, 1986, pp. 53–59.

Hollien, M. "Vocal Indicators of Psychological Stress." *Annals of the New York Academy of Science 347* (1980), pp. 47–72.

Hosenball M. "The Culture of Lying." *The New Republic*, July 13 and 20/ 1987, pp. 16–18.

Hyatt, J., "Ghost Story." *Inc.*, July 1988, pp. 78–88.

Jacobs, N. and S. Hardesty. "Corporate Brides, Is It Worth It?" *Management Digest*, November 1988, pp. S–1 to S–12.

Jones, E. E. "Interpreting Interpersonal Behavior: The Effects of Expectancies." *Science*, October 3, 1986, pp. 41–46.

Karp, W. "Republican Virtue." *Harper's*, July 1979, pp. 27–34.

Kartunnen, L. "Implicative Verbs." *Language 47* (1971), pp. 350–58.

—————. "Presupposition and Linguistic Context." *Theroretical Linguistics 1* (1974). pp. 181–94.

Kassirer, J. P. and R. L. Kopelman. "The Critical Role of Context in the Diagnostic Process." *Hospital Practice*, August 15, 1987, pp. 67–76.

Katz, J. "The Doctor-Patient Conversation." *Hastings Center Report*, June 1986, pp. 41–42.

Katz, J. J., and D. T. Langendoen. "Pragmatics and Presupposition." *Language 52* (1976), pp. 1–17.

Kempton, W. "The Rhythmic Basis of Interactional Micro-Synchrony." In M. R. Key, ed., *The Relationship of Verbal and Nonverbal Communication: Student Edition* (The Hague: Mouton, 1980), pp. 65–75.

Kendig, F. "A Conversation with Roger Schrank." *Psychology Today*, April 1983, pp. 28–36.

Kiechel, W., III. "Facing Up to Executive Anger." *Fortune*, November 16, 1981, pp. 205–10.

Kilburn, D. "In Japan, voice of authority, or flattering, a call away." *Advertising Age*, February 1, 1988, page 46.

Kiparsky, C., and P. Kiparsky. "Fact." In M. Bierwisch and K. E. Heidolph, eds., *Progress in Linguistics* (The Hague: Mouton, 1970), pp. 143–73.

Klinkenborg, V. "Nature Calls." *Village Voice*, September 15, 1987.

Korsch, B. M. and V. F. Negrete. "Doctor-Patient Communication." *Scientific American 227* (1972), pp. 66–73.

Kotker, Z. "The 'Feminine' Behavior of Powerless People." *Savvy*, March 1980, pp. 36–42.

Kotkin, J., and Y. Kishimoto. "Theory F." *Inc.*, April 1986, pp. 63–60.

Krauthammer, C. "What Are We Hiding Under the Bandages of Metaphor?" *Los Angeles Times*, May 18, 1986.

Krier, B. A. "Conversation Interruptus: Critical Social Skill or Just Plain Rudeness?" *Los Angeles Times*, December 14, 1986.

Krippner, S., and R. Davidson. "Parapsychology In the U.S.S.R." *Saturday Review*, March 18, 1972, pp. 56–60.

Kuroda, I., et al. "Method for determining pilot stress through analysis of voice communication." *Aviation, Space & Environmental Medicine*, May 1976, pp. 528–533.

Langer, E. J., and R. A. Abelson. "A Patient by Any Other Name: Clinician Group Differences in Labeling Bias." *Journal of Consulting and Clinical Psychology 42* (1974): 4–9.

Lapham, L. H. "Notebook: Landscape with trolls." *Harper's*, September 1987, pp. 6–8.

—————. "Political Discourse." *Harper's*, August 1980, pp. 8–9.

Lazarus, R. S. "Little Hassles Can Be Hazardous To Health." *Psychology Today*, July 1981, pp. 68–62.

Leonard, G. B. "Language and Reality." *Harper's*, November 1974, pp. 46–52.

Lewis, M. M. "Japanese Takeout." *The New Republic*, October 3, 1988, pp. 18–20.

Lu, C. "Fax Finding." *Inc.*, November 1988, pp. 155–159.

Lynch, J. J. "Interpersonal Aspects of Blood pressure Control." *Journal of Nervous and Mental Diseases 170* (1982), pp. 143–53.

—————. "Listen and Live." *American Health*, April 1985, pp. 39–44.

McCawley, J. D. "Conversational Implicature and the Lexicon." In M. Shibatani, ed., *Syntax and Semantics*, Vol. 9 (New York: Academic Press, 1978), pp. 245–259.

McConnell-Ginet, S. "Intonation in a Man's World." In B. Thorne et al., eds., *Language, Gender and Society* (Rowley, Mass.: Newbury House, 1983), pp. 69–88.

McGowan, M. J. "Communication Is Key To Keeping Patients Pleased." *Private Practice*, April 1987, pp. 15–16.

Marcus, M.G. "The Power of a Name." *Psychology Today*, October 1976, pp. 75–78.

Marty, M. E. "Advice From a Scheduled Man." *The Christian Century*, December 7, 1988, page 1135.

Mehrabian, A. "Nonverbal Betrayal of Feeling." *Journal of Experimental Research in Personality 5* (1971), pp. 64–73.

Middleton, T. H. "The Great Muddling Metaphor." *Saturday Review*, June 14, 1975, page 59.

Miller, A. "Putting Faith in Trends." *Newsweek*, June 15, 1987, pp. 46–47.

Miller, G. A. "The Magical Number Seven, plus or minus Two: Some Limits on Our Capacity for Processing Information." *Psychology Review 63* (1956), pp. 81–97.

Milstead, J. "Verbal Battering." *BBW*, August 1985, pp. 34–35, 61, 68.

Miron, M. S., and T. A. Pasquale. "Psycholinguistic Analyses of Coercive Communications." *Journal of Psycholinguistic Research 7* (1978), pp. 95–120.

Morrow, L. "Poof! The Phenomenon of Public Vanishing." *Time*, May 13, 1985, page 86.

—————. "Smile When You Say that." *Time*, October 28, 2985, p. 114.

Moskowitz, H. J. "Litigation Sickness." *Americans for Legal Reform Newsletter*, April/June 1987.

O'Barr, W. M. "Speech Styles in the Courtroom." In W. M. O'Barr, *Linguistic Evidence: Language, Power, and Strategy in the Courtroom* (New York: Academic Press, 1982), pp. 61–91.

Olsen, E. et al. "Beyond Positive Thinking." *Success*, December 1988, pp. 32–38.

Owen, D. "Meet Me In St. Louis." *Harper's*, September 1983, pp. 8–16.

Parlee, M. B. "Conversational Politics." *Psychology Today*, May 1979, pp. 48–56.

Pears, D. "The Mysteries of Meaning." *The New Republic*, May 19, 1986, pp. 37–41.

Perot, R. "H. Ross Perot on Restoring Nation's Edge." *Los Angeles Times*, December 14, 1986.

Pfeiffer, J. "Science of Business: Democracy by Design." *Science 86*, March 1986, pp. 18–19.

─────. "Science of Business: Different breeds." *Science 86*, January/February 1986, pp. 22–24.

─────. "Science of Business: Striking the right trade posture." *Science 85*, September 1985, pp. 81–83.

Phalon, R. "Leave it to the locals." *Forbes*, September 5, 1988, p. 163.

Pines, M. "Psychological Hardiness: The Role of Challenge in Health." *Psychology Today*, December 1980, pp. 34–44, and 98.

Porter, R. "Big C and ballyhoo." *Times Literary Supplement*, December 11–17, 1987, p. 1370.

Posner, A. "The Culture of Plagiarism." *The New Republic*, April 18, 1988, pp. 19–24.

Rice, B. "Speaking in Public." *Venture*, February 1985, pp. 35–36.

─────. "Newrosis." *Psychology Today*, July 1982, pp. 25–26.

─────. "Between the Lines of Threatening Messages." *Psychology Today*, September 1981, pp. 52–64.

─────. "Can Companies Kill?" *Psychology Today*, June 1981, pp. 78–85.

Richman, T. "Leadership Expert Ronald Heifetz." *Inc.*, October 1988, pp. 37–8.

Rosenhan, R., and L. Jacobson. "Teacher Expectations and the Disadvantaged." *Scientific American 218* (1968), pp. 19–23.

Rosenthal, J. "On Language: Gender Benders." *New York Times Magazine*, August 10, 1986.

─────. "On Language: Filler Fad." *New York Times Magazine*, July 15, 1984.

Rozanski, A., et al. "Mental Stress and the Induction of Silent Myocardial Ischemia in Patients with Coronary Artery Disease." *New England Journal of Medicine*, April 21, 1988, pp. 1005–1012.

Sach, A. "Swinging — and Ducking — Singles." *Time*, September 5, 2988, p. 54.

Sacks, H., et al. "A Simplest Systematics for the Organization of Turn-Taking for Conversation." *Language 50* (1974), pp. 696–735.

Samuelson, R. J. "The Politics of Obscurity." *Newsweek*, November 30, 1987, p. 56.

Schaeffer, D. L. "The Presidential Name Game." *Psychology Today*, October 1984, p. 12.

Schanback, M. "Big Girls Don't Cry." *Executive Female*, May/June 1988, pp. 50–53.

Selwyn, A. P., and P. Ganz. "Myocardial Ischemia in Coronary Disease." *New England Journal of Medicine*, April 21, 1988, pp. 1058–1060.

Sharp, D. "Aristotle's Garage: A Mechanic's Metaphysics." *Harper's*, March 1981, pp. 91–93.

Shapiro, L. "Advice Givers Strike Gold." *Newsweek*, June 1, 1987, pp. 64–65.

Simonov, P. V., et al. "Use of the Invariant Method of Speech Analysis to Discern the Emotional State of Announcers." *Aviation, Space, and Environmental Medicine*, August 1975, pp. 1014–1016.

Solomon, S. D., ed. "Introducing the 1986 *Inc. 100*." *Inc.*, May 1986, pp. 41–62.

Stokes, G. "Lesser Miscreants." *Village Voice*, August 18, 1984.

Streeter, L. A., et al. "Acoustics and perceptual indicators of emotional stress." *Journal of the Acoustic Society of America*, April 1983, pp. 1354–1360.

Suggs, D., and B. D. Sales. "Using Communication Cues to Evaluate Prospective Jurors During the Voir Dire." *Arizona Law Review 20* (1978), pp. 630–642.

Tavris, C. "Two Acts." *Harper's*, January 1983, pp. 71–73.

Wallace, D. "Blueprints for a Better Business." *Success*, November 1988, p. 73.

Wein, B. "Body and Soul Music." *American Health*, April 1987, pp. 66–76.

Weinraub, B. "Presidential Politics: Are Female Tears Saltier Than Male Tears?" *New York Times*, September 30, 1987.

White, W. "Good In The Way of Belief." *The New Republic*, December 29, 1986, pp. 25–30.

Will, G. F. "Technology That Cares." *Newsweek*, November 8, 1982, p. 112.

Williams, C E., and K. N. Stevens. "Emotions and speech: Some acoustical correlates." *Journal of the Acoustical Society of America 52* (1972), pp. 1238–1250.

Wills, G. "The Ultimate Loyalist." *Time*, August 22, 1988, pp. 22–27.

————. "Hurray for Politicians." *Harper's*, September 1975, pp. 45–54.

Wolcott, J. "TRB from Washington: Blow Your House Down." *The New Republic*, October 10, 1988, pp. 4 and 41.

Items Without Byline

—————. "What They're Saying." MD, March 1986, page 25. (In "Vital Signs."

—————. "Tips on Speaking — Lincoln Didn't End At Gettysburg by Saying 'Thank You!'" Physicians Financial News, April 30, 1988, p. PB8.

—————. "The Male Stress Syndrome." Pest Control Technology, July 1987, p. 44.

—————. "The Art of Negotiation." The Royal Bank Letter, July/August 1986, not paginated.

—————. "Global Gallery." Advertising Age, February 22, 1988, p. 20.

—————. "Noted With Pleasure: Talk Is Dear." New York Times, March 2, 1986.

—————. "Office Tips." Physician's Management, May 1988, p. 24.

—————. ."Washington Diarist: Underwear Update." The New Republic, January 25, 1988, p. 43. (By M.B.C.)

Books

NOTE: Books by other authors which I strongly recommend adding to your bookshelf are marked here with two asterisks.

Beattie, G. Talk: An Analysis of Speech and Non-verbal Behaviour in Conversation. Milton Keynes, England: Open University Press, 1983.

** Borysenko, J., with L. Rothstein. Minding the Body, Mending the Mind. Reading, MA.: Addison-Wesley, 1987.

Bierwisch, M., and K. E. Heidolph, eds. Progress in Linguistics. The Hague: Mouton, 1970.

Birdwhistell, R L. Kinesics and Context: Essays on Body Motion Communication. Philadelphia: University of Pennsylvania Press, 1970.

Bolinger, D. Intonation. Harmondsworth, Middlesex, England: Penguin Books, 1972.

** Bolton, R. People Skills: How to Assert Yourself, Listen to Others and Resolve Conflicts. Englewood Cliffs, N.J.: Prentice Hall, 1979.

Carnegie, D. How to Win Friends and Influence People. New York: Pocket Books, 1972.

Cole, P. and J. L. Morgan, eds. Syntax and Semantics, Vol 3: Speech Acts. New York: Academic Press, 1975.

Denes, P., and E. Pinson. *The Speech Chain*. New York: Anchor Books, 1973. (The best nontechnical source on acoustics and physiology of speech.)

Ekman, P. *Telling Lies*. New York: W. W. Norton, 1985.

—————, and W. V. Friesen. *Unmasking the Face*. Englewood Cliffs, N.J.: Prentice Hall, 1975.

—————, et al. *Emotion in the Human Face*. New York: Pergamon Press, 1972.

Elgin, S. H. *The Gentle Art of Verbal Self-Defense*. New York: Dorset Press, 1985. Originally published by Prentice Hall, 1980.

—————. *The Gentle Art of Verbal Self-Defense Workbook*. New York: Dorset Press, 1987.

—————. *Manual for Syntonics Trainers: Level One*. Huntsville, Arkansas: Ozark Center for Language Studies, 1986.

—————. *Language in Emergency Medicine: A Verbal Self-Defense/—Syntonics Handbook*. Huntsville, Arkansas: Ozark Center for Language Studies, 1987.

—————. *More on the Gentle Art of Verbal Self-Defense*. New York: Prentice Hall Press, 1983.

—————. *The Last Word on the Gentle Art of Verbal Self-Defense*. New York: Prentice Hall Press, 1987.

—————. *What is Linguistics?* 2nd Edition. Englewood Cliffs, N.J.: Prentice Hall, 1979.

—————. *Mastering the Gentle Art of Verbal Self-Defense*. (Audio cassette program, with workbook.) Englewood Cliffs, N.J.: Prentice Hall, 1989.

** Everstine, D. S., and L. Everstine. *People in Crisis: Strategic Therapeutic Interventions*. New York: Brunner/Magel, 1983.

Fabun, D. *The Dynamics of Change*. Englewood Cliffs., N.J.: Prentice Hall, 1967.

Festinger, L. *A Theory of Cognitive Dissonance*. Evanston, Ill., Row, Peterson & Company, 1957.

Fisher, S., and A. D. Todd. *The Social Organization of Doctor-Patient Communication*. Washington, D.C.: Center for Applied Linguistics, 1983.

Friedman, M., and R. Rosenman. *Type A Behavior and Your Heart*. New York: Alfred A. Knopf, 1974.

Goodman, G. S. *Winning by Telephone: Telephone Effectiveness for Business Professionals and Customers.*. Englewood Cliffs, N.J.: Prentice Hall 1982.

Gordon, T. *Leader Effectiveness Training: L.E.T*..................: Wyden Books, 1977.

Grinder, J., and R. Bandler. *The Structure of Magic: I.* Palo Alto: Science and Behavior Books, 1975.

—————. *The Structure of Magic: II.* Palo Alto: Science and Behavior Books, 1976.

—————, and S. H. Elgin. *Guide to Transformational Grammar.* New York: Holt, Rinehart and Winston, 1973.

Hall, E. T. *Beyond Culture.* New York: Anchor Books, 1977.

—————. *The Dance of Life: The Other Dimension of Time.* New York: Anchor Press/Doubleday, 1983.

Henley, N. *Body Politics: Power, Sex, and Nonverbal Communication.* Englewood Cliffs, N.J.: Prentice Hall, 1977.

Hofstadter, D. *Goedel, Escher, Bach: An Eternal Golden Braid.* New York: Random House, 1980.

** Hunt, M. *The Universe Within: A New Science Explores the Human Mind.* New York: Simon and Schuster, 1982.

Key, M. R., ed. *The Relationship of Verbal and Nonverbal Communication.* The Hague: Mouton, 1980.

Kleinke, C. L. *First Impressions: The Psychology of Encountering Others.* Englewood Cliffs, N.J.: Prentice-Hall, 1975.

Kramarae, C. et al., eds. *Language and Power.* Beverly Hills: Sage Publications, 1984.

Ladefoged, P. *Elements of Acoustic Phonetics.* Chicago: University of Chicago Press, 1962.

Lakoff, G., and M. Johnson. *Metaphors We Live By.* Chicago: University of Chicago Press, 1980.

Lewis, G. *On The Art of Writing Copy.* Englewood Cliffs, N.J.: Prentice Hall 1988.

Lynch, J. J. *The Broken Heart: The Medical Consequences of Loneliness.* New York: Basic Books, 1977.

**—————. *The Language of the Heart: The Body's Response to Human Dialogue.* New York: Basic Books, 1985.

Miller, G. A. et al. *Plans and the Structure of Behavior.* New York: Henry Holt, 1960.

O'Barr, W. M. *Linguistic Evidence: Language, Power, and Strategy in the Courtroom.* New York: Academic Press, 1982.

—————. and J. F. O'Barr, eds. *Language and Politics*. The Hague: Mouton, 1976.

Obler, L. K., and L. Menn, eds. *Exceptional Language and Linguistics*. New York: Academic Press, 1982.

Odiorne, G. S. *The Change Resisters: How They Prevent Progress and What Managers Can Do About Them*. Englewood Cliffs, N.J.: Prentice Hall, 1981.

Peters, T., and R. Waterman. *In Search of Excellence*. New York: Warner, 1984.

Rosenthal, R., and L. Jacobsen. *Pygmalion in the Classroom: Teacher Expectations and Pupils' Intellectual Development*. New York: Holt, Rinehart and Winston, 1968.

** Rothwell, J.D. *Telling It Like It Isn't*. Englewood Cliffs, N.J.: Prentice Hall, 1982.

** Samovar, L. A., and R. E. Porter, eds. *Intercultural Communication: A Reader. 4th Edition*. Belmont, Calif. : Wadsworth Publishing, 1985.

Trent, J. D., J. S. Trent, and D. J. O'Neill, eds. *Concepts in Communication*. Boston: Allyn and Bacon, 1973.

Wellman, F. L. *The Art of Cross-Examination*. New York: Dorset Press, 1986.

Index